Eat Right

for Your

Metabolism

How the Right Foods for Your Type Can Help You Lose Weight

FELICIA DRURY KLIMENT

McGraw·Hill

New York   Chicago   San Francisco   Lisbon   London   Madrid   Mexico City
Milan   New Delhi   San Juan   Seoul   Singapore   Sydney   Toronto

Library of Congress Cataloging-in-Publication Data

Kliment, Felicia Drury.
        Eat right for your metabolism / Felicia Drury Kliment.
                p.   cm.
        Includes bibliographical references and index.
        ISBN 0-07-146015-2 (book : alk. paper)
        1. Nutrition—Popular works.   2. Digestion—Popular works.   3. Metabolism—
Popular works.   I. Title.

    RA784.K53   2006
    613.2   2005031137

To my daughters, Pamela Kliment Lackman and Jennifer Wellander, for their superb advice and help with the menu plans and recipes. They came through when I needed them, as always.

1 2 3 4 5 6 7 8 9 0   DOC/DOC   0 9 8 7 6

ISBN 0-07-146015-2

McGraw-Hill books are available at special quantity discounts to use as premiums and sales promotions, or for use in corporate training programs. For more information, please write to the Director of Special Sales, Professional Publishing, McGraw-Hill, Two Penn Plaza, New York, NY 10121-2298. Or contact your local bookstore.

Acknowledgments

I was very lucky to have Michelle Mastrisciani as my editor. She worked hard and with great skill to forge the manuscript into its final form. Thanks also to Jenn Tust for the excellent job she did in shepherding the book through production.

This book is printed on acid-free paper.

Contents

Introduction

There were only two hours in the day when Carol, age fifty-two, wasn't hungry. During those two hours she felt content, relaxed, and full of energy. The rest of the day her hunger was out of control and she was restless and filled with anxiety. It was as much the feeling of being out of balance as it was her ravenous hunger that drove her to binging. But going on an eating spree is always a two-edged sword. While it took away Carol's nervousness and obsessive hunger for a time, it left her feeling stuffed and drowsy. It was because of these swings in moods and levels of energy, not her weight problem, that Carol sought out a consultation with me.

Considering the amount of food she put away each day, the fact that her thyroid function was slow, and that she rarely exercised, it's hard to understand why Carol never became morbidly obese. Her favorite binging food was pasta made with white flour. During an eating spree, she'd gobble up one large plateful of spaghetti, go for seconds, and wind up consuming the entire sixteen-ounce box of pasta. Carol could never figure out where she got her ungovernable appetite because other members of her family were small to moderate eaters.

Ann was about one hundred pounds overweight when she came in for a consultation. She blamed her weight on the fact that she craved meat well-marbled with fat and ate enormous amounts of it. She had also had a life-threatening illness that contributed to her excessive weight. Mysteriously enough, these two problems disappeared when she moved from the United States, where she had eaten beef from hormone-fed steers, to Mexico, where all the beef comes from

grass-fed, hormone-free animals. She lost her insatiable appetite for
meat and switched to a vegetarian diet. She said the switch wasn't a
conscious decision, but one that was driven by instinct.

In my private practice as a natural health consultant, I've met people like Carol and Ann who couldn't figure out their appetite problems. In addition, I've treated people like Kathy, an immigrant from the Dominican Republic, who had an onset of rheumatoid arthritis after she moved to the States; Narain, who came to me for help with his alcoholism; and Albert, who after a heart attack became a diabetic, even without a history of diabetes in his family.

Why am I telling you this? All of the people mentioned had unique symptoms and problems, but the root cause was always the same: they weren't eating right for their metabolic type, which means the food they were eating wasn't being properly broken down by their digestive systems. It was their faulty digestion that led to their appetite and health problems.

The best example is Ann, who biologically has a grain-eating metabolism. We can see that this is true because of the change in her cravings and her ability to satiate her appetite only when she switched to meat from hormone-fed animals to grass-fed animals and then to a total vegetarian diet. Her "need" for meat was gone. She had been eating all of her life as if she had a meat-eating metabolism, and only when she met her true biological metabolic needs was she able to gain control of her weight and her health.

This is why I am writing this book. *Eat Right for Your Metabolism* will teach you the three types of metabolisms—the grain eater, the meat eater, and the omnivore (meat and grain) eater—and help you identify which one you are in order to balance your body, lose weight, and prevent disease. The system is easy. First, you'll take the niacin test to discover your true metabolic type, and then you'll find menu plans in Part II that suit your individual needs, whether they are to lose weight, heal your health problem(s), and/or prevent disease. Delicious and easy-to-follow recipes for both meat eaters and grain eaters are also provided by renowned chef Julie Tripp.

Which of the three metabolic categories you fall into depends on whether your ancestors ate meat, grain, or both. Those who give up the nutritional eating habits of their forebears lose some of their natural immunity, so when the individual with a grain-eating metabolism eats more meat than grain or the meat eater becomes a vegetarian, digestive disorders develop. This leads to more serious health problems, including heart disease, diabetes, inflammation problems, autoimmune diseases, breathing disorders, cancer, and obesity.

But people with digestive problems seldom see the road ahead and realize the need to change their diets. People with weight problems are the ones who are most likely to change their diets. The diet or menu plan that presents a single solution, implying there is only one way to take off pounds, appeals to those who crave food so badly that they need a diet they can believe in, like a religious creed, to give them the discipline to stay the course. For that reason, a standardized diet plan is the easiest weight loss plan to stick to.

The trouble with standardized diet plans, which you will read more about in Chapter 1, is not only that they don't suit everyone's digestive metabolism, but also they go against certain dietary rules that apply to everyone. Popular diet plans treat people as if they are all the same, when we know everyone's makeup is unique. Unless the kinds and quantities of foods the individual eats match the kinds and quantities of his or her digestive acids and enzymes, digestion is incomplete. The undigested food turns into highly toxic acid waste, whose inflammatory effects bring on health problems and weight issues.

What you will also learn in this book is that neither the meat eater nor the grain eater is restricted to eating only the foods in their respective categories, so you don't have to worry about giving up your favorite foods. If you are a meat eater, you can eat some grain products, and if you are a grain eater you can eat meat on occasion. *It's a question of proportion.* The menu plans provided will offer guidelines for how to balance your servings. If you are a meat eater, you should eat more of the foods that meat eaters digest well and smaller amounts of the foods in the grain-eating category, and vice versa.

The beauty of eating according to your metabolic type is not only that are you eating foods that your digestive system can break down, but you're also supplying your body with the nutrients you are short in, while eating less of those nutrients that you have in excess. Just as the meat eater and the grain eater can eat the same foods but in different proportions, so their nutritional supplement requirements differ. Nutritional supplements for the meat eater and grain eater are listed in my book *The Acid-Alkaline Balance Diet.*

The primary aim of *Eat Right for Your Metabolism* is to help you find the foods that you can digest easily rather than merely the foods that take off the most weight, because foods that aren't broken down properly ultimately put on weight. Only foods that are digested well—broken down into components that can be utilized by the cells—will, in the long run, keep weight off and maintain the body in a state of health.

PART I

Shedding New Light on Your Metabolism

Why Nutritious Foods Are Not Always

Healthy for You

There's No Such Thing as a Standardized Diet

Why We Should Eat According

to Our Metabolic Types

The biggest problem with diet "experts"—nutritionists who dictate government policy on nutrition; diet gurus who write bestselling books; and nutritionists who plan menus for schools, hospitals, prisons, and other institutions—is their assumption that the same dietary rules apply to everyone. The mistake in recommending a standardized diet is that it doesn't take into consideration the multiethnic society in the United States. Each ethnic group that immigrates to this country brings with it its own culinary tradition—and a digestive apparatus attuned to it. So when immigrants switch to the foods most commonly eaten in this country—red meat, deep-fried foods, soft drinks—they are apt to develop digestive problems, a sign of more serious health problems to come. This scenario has been substantiated by innumerable studies (see "Abandoning the Ancestral Diet Causes Health Problems" later in this chapter) showing that immigrant populations suffer from more degenerative disease in the United States than they did in their countries of origin. The problem boils down to this: when food isn't digested—split up into units that are small enough to be absorbed into the cells and reconstituted into substances that the cells can utilize—the body, though having enough calories for energy, goes into a state of starvation. Without enough nutrients, the cells can't be repaired and regenerated, so they malfunction or die out.

The Myth of the Standardized Diet

Even if your ancestors have lived in the United States for hundreds of years, the typical American diet may not be suitable for you. You know you're not eating foods your digestive system can break down if a half hour to two hours after a snack or a meal you begin to feel unwell or suffer indigestion—although occasionally symptoms of indigestion don't occur until twenty-four hours after eating. People typically associate only digestive tract symptoms such as nausea, acid reflux, ulcers, diarrhea, and colitis with the wrong diet. But in fact all pain, discomfort, and unnatural changes in appearance—red cheeks, chipping and peeling fingernails, hair fall-out, coughing after swallowing food, headaches, restlessness, dizziness, irritability, bursitis and joint pain, insomnia, depression, dry eyes or mouth, cracked lips, chronic colds and/or infections, even floaters in the eyes—are caused by eating the wrong foods.

A sign that what you ate the night before is not right for you is waking up in the morning with a stuffy nose and watery eyes. Dr. Jonathan V. Wright, director of the Tahoma Clinic and editor of the newsletter *Nutrition and Healing*, writes, "If a woman tells me her fingernails crack, split, peel, break easily, or 'layer back' . . . or that her hair is thinning or falling out, I know that her stomach is not functioning properly." In fact, there isn't a single symptom or full-blown illness, gastric or otherwise, that can't be caused by the toxic by-products of an inappropriate diet. This includes bacterial and viral infections. If you are not convinced that your aches and pains are caused by what you eat, go on a one-day water fast. The chances are one hundred to one you'll feel better the next day.

> 66 Pain, discomfort, and unnatural changes in appearance are caused by eating the wrong foods. 99

Most people in their youth and young adulthood can get away with eating just about anything and not experience any adverse symptoms because their digestive enzyme glands can produce all the enzymes necessary for digestion. But enzyme glands that are chronically forced to overproduce are usually worn out by middle age. Without enough enzymes, the food you eat doesn't get digested.

To get the nutritional value you need, follow a diet that fits your particular digestive requirements. No food item, no matter how nutritious, is suitable for everyone. This truth was brought home to me at a dinner party at which the food was unusually rich. I noticed, after the dinner was over, how differently people reacted to the same foods. Some guests remained cheerful and alert, while others complained of feeling stuffed or looked uncomfortable and were no longer socializing. This made clear that quantities of enzymes, acids, bile, and flora involved in breaking down different kinds of protein, fats, and carbohydrates differ from one individual to the next, and that, as a result, diet should be customized to each person's particular digestive needs.

Most people are either red meat eaters or grain eaters, that is, they either have more enzymes for digesting red meat or more enzymes for digesting grains, chicken, and fish. But in terms of the proportions of carbohydrates, fats, and proteins in the diet, humans everywhere have pretty much the same needs. Still, even here there are exceptions.

Stacy, a successful publicist in her early twenties, doesn't fit the stereotype. Although human energy needs require that around 60 percent of the diet should consist of carbohydrates, Stacy can digest only a fraction of that amount. She feels bloated on even small portions of potatoes, pasta, rice, or bread. The meal she digests best is steak or lamb chops along with asparagus, string beans, green peas, or cauliflower. She has enough starch-digesting enzymes to handle the small amounts of starch in these vegetables but not enough to break down the large amounts of starch in potatoes, rice, pasta, and grain products.

A small percentage of people have a problem digesting foods that fit their metabolic type. I'm an example. As a red meat eater I have no problem with beef—a legacy of my English genes—but get nauseated if I eat even a small amount of lamb. Lamb is also a red meat, so as a meat eater, I should have no trouble digesting it.

There are also grain eaters who have a problem digesting foods appropriate to their metabolism. I have one client with a grain-eating metabolism who feels bloated whenever she eats wheat. And then there are people who don't like certain foods in their metabolic category. My grandson Matthew is one such person. He commented, at the age of 6, "I'm a strange man; I don't like butter." He didn't realize how prescient this remark was because he is, constitutionally, a meat eater and meat eaters usually love butter because they have a biological need for it. These are examples of the small number of people who, for one reason or another, can't follow the rules of nutrition that are appropriate for others in their category.

The problem that overrides all others, however, is the attitude of medical scientists and nutritionists who don't recognize that diet should be custom fitted to the individual's biological requirements. Perhaps these scientists' views of diet have been influenced by the ideal of democracy, namely, that all humans, given the same opportunities, can achieve the same goals. Governed by this populist way of thinking, they assume that if people raised under the same circumstances are potentially capable of behaving alike, they also have similar biological requirements and therefore the same dietary needs. So food scientists, instead of seeing the solution to health problems to be one of fitting the diet to the individual, recommend a single diet that they believe will take care of the nutrient requirements of everyone.

> ❝ We are not all created equal: we each have our own dietary needs for our unique bodies. ❞

Dr. Marion Nestle, head of the Department of Nutrition and Food Studies at New York University, illustrates this way of thinking. While her studies on how the food industry contributes to obesity by making food items oversized are on target, her notion of what constitutes a good diet is open to question. She says that everyone should "eat more fruits and vegetables and not eat too much."[1] This implies that neither the kind nor quality of foods, nor matching foods to individual digestive requirements, make any difference to health—as long as people eat plenty of fruit and vegetables and don't eat too much.

That the nutritional requirements of individuals are all the same is also the official position taken by the United States government. In an article in the Health and Fitness section of the *New York Times*, the surgeon general is quoted as stating that "the goal of the government is for all Americans to consume at least three servings of whole grains a day."[2] This recommendation is not based on individual needs but on the fact that the fiber in grains provides excellent roughage and is also a rich source of nutrients. For this reason everyone, except those with allergies to the gluten and gliadin protein in wheat and/or other grains, should eat some grains—but not everyone should or can eat three or more helpings of grain a day. Those individuals who digest grains better than meat can in most cases easily digest that much grain, while individuals with meat-eating metabolisms can rarely do so.

The standardization of the American diet is given further impetus by the dietary guidelines issued every five years by the Department of Health and Human Services and the Department of Agriculture. One important way in which the guidelines for 2005 differ from those of 2000 is in suggesting larger amounts of fruit and vegetables. But like the 2000 guidelines, those of 2005 ignore the fact that people of different ages have different nutritional requirements. For example, the recommendation to drink an 8-ounce glass of milk three times a day to satisfy calcium requirements doesn't take into consideration the findings of research studies that reveal drinking large amounts of milk is unhealthy for teenagers and adults. (See the section, "Milk Can Sabotage Your Diet" in Chapter 3.) As for the recommendation to eat low-fat cheese to keep the amount of saturated fat in the diet small, it's ill advised on two counts. First, it ignores the fact that separating some of the fat from the cheese involves the use of toxic chemicals. Second, it doesn't take into consideration the fact that everyone needs some saturated fat in his or her diet.

Heredity and Protein Choice

Most diet plans, with the exception of the Atkins diet and other high-protein, high-fat, low-carbohydrate diets, treat red meat and butter as though they were poison because of their saturated fat content. Yet red meat and butter contain more minerals and vitamins than any other food. The unfounded advice of so many diets, namely, that red meat and butter should be eaten sparingly, or not at all, doesn't take into consideration either their high nutrient value or the fact that the meat of four-legged animals, particularly beef, is the traditional fare of the many people in this country who are descended from the early colonists—many of whom were from the British Isles.

The British people's taste for red meat goes back at least eight thousand years. The meat-eating proclivity of the ancient Britons was a surprise to archaeologists. They assumed that because the oldest settlements in Great Britain had been founded primarily along coastlines and the banks of rivers, the principal dietary staples at that time would have been fish and plant foods. This theory has been discounted as a result of an analysis of an eight thousand-year-old female thighbone conducted by the archaeologist Glyn Davies of the University of Sheffield in England. Found in a river bank in the central part of England, the patterns of nitrogen and carbon isotopes in the thighbone show that the woman's diet was almost exclusively carnivorous, having only occasionally been supplemented with berries or roots, and showing no evidence at all that the woman had eaten fish! Marks found on the bones of wild cattle nearby are further evidence that eight thousand years ago the English people, even those living beside rivers and other bodies of water, ate meat to the exclusion of fish.[3]

The genes of these meat-eating ancient Britons were transmitted through successive generations and, beginning in the seventeenth century, were brought to the New World. The descendents of these English colonists living in the United States today are still, constitutionally, meat eaters, so that a diet of grains, chicken, and fish is not suitable for them.

The ancient Britons were not the only people who turned their backs on fish as a dietary staple despite having built their settlements alongside rivers that teemed with fish. Paul Theroux in his book *Dark Star Safari*[4] remarks that while walking along the Nile River in Dongola, Sudan, he was surprised at how few fishermen he saw. He was told that the Sudanese in the north were not great fish eaters, because "fish didn't keep in the heat and . . . lamb and camel and goat were tastier."

The Norse people who established a colony in Greenland in A.D. 984—that by 1400 had disappeared—are another example of a people who didn't include fish in their diet despite the abundance of fish in nearby coastal waters. And even during the potato famine when they had hardly anything to eat, the Irish living along the coast shunned fish. They would wade into the water searching for clams washed in by the tide, but they never ventured farther into the water in boats for the purpose of catching fish. Thus even in cases in which a people's favored food staple is scarce, they will often avoid another food that is nutritious and easy to obtain because it is not part of their dietary tradition.

Yet many diet experts ignore the fact that food is an expression of culture. As a result, they don't take into consideration, when formulating diet plans, the melting pot of nationalities in the United States, each requiring a different diet to satisfy their nutritional needs. Nutritionists also have a tendency to base their diets on the research studies that support their preconceived contentions, while ignoring the studies whose conclusions point in the opposite direction.

Making Sense of Ancestral Dietary Traditions

What accounts for a culture's choice of its dietary protein staple? Soil and climate are the principal influences, but religion is also a factor. For example, the ancient Chinese clans chose millet as their protein staple because they believed this grain was the offspring of the Earth God. This is just one example of a culture that cultivated grains despite tremendous obstacles such as unpredictable floods and droughts when they have close at hand equally nutritious and more easily obtainable sources of protein in the form of meat and/or seafood. After a protein staple has been eaten by a cultural group for a long time, the need for it becomes biologically ingrained.[5] Genetically imposed nutritional requirements have evolved from the long-term eating habits of people who live within the same geographical area. This evolution is confirmed by a research study in which scientists examined short segments of DNA of people around the world. The DNA samples revealed that those people living in the same region—and who are therefore highly likely to eat the same kinds of foods—have similarities in their genetic makeup.[6] Thus the structure of the digestive enzymes is determined by the genetic code, whose instructions were inscribed by the foods consumed by a particular cultural group living in the same area for many hundreds or more likely thousands of years.

The genetic determination of our digestive chemicals is getting further recognition as a result of the mapping of the entire genetic code of human DNA. This research has given birth to a new branch of science called *genomics*, whose objective is to discover by way of genetic analysis what foods are best suited to the individual.[7] Although the relevant data on genomic profiles of ethnically diverse individuals have yet to be assembled, several companies are already offering nutritional supplement plans that genomic scientists have worked out on the basis of individual DNA profiles.

> " The structure of the digestive enzymes is determined by the genetic code, whose instructions were inscribed by the foods consumed by a particular cultural group living in the same area for many hundreds or more likely thousands of years. "

An unintended double-blind study in which the "subjects," starving children in Africa, were first fed a European-type food and later a traditional food staple is further evidence that the long-term food habits of an ethnic group are hardwired into their genes. When the usual enriched biscuits and powdered milk fed to the starving children in Ethiopia, Zaire, and Malawi were replaced by a paste made of peanuts, the recovery rate rose from 25 percent to 95 percent. This startling turnaround occurred because throughout Africa peanuts have been a food staple for generations, so the peanuts caused no digestive problems that would have prevented the children's recovery. The compatibility of peanuts to the African digestive metabolism was confirmed by allergy tests given by Nutriset SAS, a French company that manufactures food for humanitarian purposes. *Not one child in any of these African countries had an allergic reaction to peanuts.*[8]

Abandoning the Ancestral Diet Causes Health Problems

That the genes that determine the makeup of individuals' digestive metabolism evolved from the dietary habits of their antecedents is also evident from the health problems of people who give up their ancestral diets. The Masai tribes in East Africa who have replaced their traditional diet of cow's milk and blood with corn and beans are experiencing health problems, such as heart disease and diabetes, that were previously nonexistent in their society.[9]

The East Indians and Pakistanis who replaced their grain-based diet and traditional spices with the typical meat-based American diet when they immigrated to the United States are also plagued with health problems, especially heart disease—unlike those Indian and Pakistani immigrants in this country who continue to eat traditional foods. In a paper published in the *Quarterly Review of Biology*, Jennifer Billing and Dr. Paul Sherman conclude that a diet of highly spiced foods, such as that of India, requires different kinds of digestive enzymes than the traditionally bland diet of northern European countries.[10] Thus people whose ancestors ate spicy foods probably digest food more efficiently when it is seasoned, particularly with the spices indigenous to their country of origin. Such spices may help supplement nutrients that are in short supply in the culture's traditional dietary staples.

The evidence that a radical change in diet causes health problems goes back thousands of years. George J. Armelagos, an anthropologist at the University of Florida in Gainesville, studied the skeletons of Native Americans who lived from A.D. 950 to 1300 in what is now Illinois. He found a sudden increase in the incidence of iron-deficiency anemia from 16 percent to 64 percent and a sudden drop in life expectancy from twenty-six years to nineteen years.[11]

This deterioration in health and longevity coincided with the period during which the Native Americans in Illinois had given up hunting and gathering for intensive farming. The analysis of more than 12,500 skeletons of Native Americans from sites in North and South America shows a far greater incidence of infections, joint disease, dental decay, and anemia from sites where agriculture had replaced hunting and foraging.[12] Jared Diamond, author of *Guns, Germs, and Steel*, writes, "The first farmers in many areas were smaller and less well nourished, suffered more serious disease, and died on the average at a younger age than the hunter-gatherers they replaced."[13] Diamond believes the reason the upsurge in farming triggered infectious disease is because this lifestyle supported a much denser population than that of the hunter-forager. As a result, communicable diseases spread faster. He writes that with a nonmigratory lifestyle the same source of water is often used as a latrine as well as for drinking and cooking, "thus providing microbes with a short path from one person's body into another's drinking water."[14]

It's true that disease travels faster when people live close to each other and use the same water supply for all their needs. But if this was the only reason for the outbreak of epidemics, it would mean that communicable diseases existed in Stone Age cultures and all it took for them to become epidemic was more densely populated communities and the resulting pollution of water sources. In fact, the Stone Age hunter didn't suffer from contagious or degenerative disease, but from snake and spider bites, rashes, upset stomachs, and diarrhea caused by minor parasites and worm infestations. Infection by parasites is thought to have originated from the unintentional eating of insects.[15] But infection would also have been caused by malnutrition because malnourished people are more vulnerable to infection. And malnutrition occurred in Stone Age cultures that lived in areas where the soil was mineral deficient or the rainfall was sparse.

Communicable disease first made its appearance in the Neolithic era, nine thousand to twelve thousand years ago. Researchers measuring the differing proportions of carbon in the collagen (connective tissue) in human bones dating from that time found that the abrupt shift in diet, from the Stone Age fare of wild animals, seeds, nuts, roots, and berries to cultivated plants and domesticated animals, had a harmful effect on health. (See the sidebar "The Beginning of Agriculture.")

Once a seasonal weather cycle developed after the end of the Ice Age, it was possible to grow crops. The majority of hunting-based cultures responded to this ordering of the climate. They

The Beginning of Agriculture

What sparked the beginning of an agricultural economy? In the time preceding and including the last ice age, each climatic period—the warmth and rain, alternating with cold, snow, and ice—lasted thousands of years. But with the end of the Pleistocene Ice Age approximately fourteen thousand years ago, periods of rotating warmth and cold became shorter and shorter until they were compressed into the twelve-month seasonal cycle that exists in temperate regions of the world today. It was this time frame that triggered the emergence, between nine thousand and eleven thousand years ago, of farming cultures in Europe and Asia. The warm season was long enough for crops that were planted in the spring to mature by the end of the summer, and the winter was short enough that, barring droughts, stored grains and root vegetables were sufficient to feed the populace until the next season's crops were harvested.

gave up a life in which they met their nutritional needs by hunting animals that ran free and gathering roots, nuts, seeds, and berries for a sedentary one spent sowing seeds and cultivating crops. The seasonal cycle also lured most of the grassland cultures that had periodically picked up their goods and chattels to go in search of water and grazing for their cattle or sheep to attach themselves to one locale to cultivate or barter for grains to feed their animals during the winter. When this changeover in occupation took place and those who had settled in one place to raise crops had, by force of arms, taken away the hunters' domain of woodland and forest, the defeated hunting bands retreated into the mountains and agriculture became the prevailing way of life on the plains.

While cultivating cereals gave Neolithic cultures more control over their food supply, it had a negative affect on the health of the newly domesticated livestock, and ultimately on that of humans. As long as cattle, hogs, and fowl had lived off wild grasses, they were free of disease, but when they began to feed on cultivated grains, infectious disease broke out. By cultivating the seeds from wild rye, barley, and wheat plants, the agriculturalists converted wild cereal grains into new varieties that animals used to eating wild grasses weren't able to digest. The undigested domesticated grains fermented in the animals' digestive tracts, and the resulting acid waste became a source of nourishment for unfriendly bacteria. (See the sidebar "Standard Versus Natural Diet for Zoo Animals" for more information on the effect of dietary change on wild animals.)

It was at the point when the disease-causing germs in the bodies of domesticated animals became numerous enough to establish colonies and began multiplying too fast for the animals' immune systems to keep them in check that infectious disease in animals made its appearance. This fits in with zoologist Graham Twigg's contention that the Black Death was not transmitted by rats on merchant ships carrying goods from Asia to Europe but rather by European cattle herds that had become infected with anthrax.[16]

Sometime after domesticated animals became prone to infectious disease, the phenomenon of host jumping occurred—the crossover of disease-carrying viruses and bacteria from domesticated animals to man. (Close proximity, however, sometimes conferred immunity. Young women who milked cows seldom caught smallpox.)

Eating infected animal meat wasn't the only reason humans began developing contagious diseases in the Neolithic age. The changeover from a diet of game, nuts, seeds, wild roots, and berries to one of cultivated grains had the same inflammatory effect in the human body as it had in animals, and for the same

Standard Versus Natural Diet for Zoo Animals

That a radical change in diet is as detrimental to the health of zoo animals as it is to humans has been discovered by zoo nutritionists. Dr. Ellen Dierenfeld of the Bronx Zoo and Dr. Mark Edwards of the San Diego Zoo set themselves the task of finding out what particular diet best suited the metabolisms of the various animals in their zoos. They discovered that animals fed the standard zoo diet instead of a natural one develop fertility and other health problems and don't live out their normal life spans. This inspired Dr. Dierenfeld to work out diets for the animals in the Bronx Zoo based on a comparison of the zoo animals' feces, blood, tissue samples, hair, and feathers with those of the same animals in the wild.

"The key to good nutrition," according to Dr. Dierenfeld, "is to look at the composition of their natural foods and duplicate the nutrients even when you can't duplicate the foods." Wherever this approach to diet has been followed in zoos, it has improved the health and increased the life span of the animals.[17]

reason: the digestive enzymes couldn't break down these new genetically variant grains.

The Challenge of Eating Right for Our Metabolism

Such factors as climate, geography, and an urban landscape can make it difficult for people to follow their ancestral dietary traditions. The tremendous industrial growth in the United States in the early part of the twentieth century attracted massive numbers of immigrants from southern and eastern Europe who in their native countries had, for the most part, worked on farms. In the United States they got jobs in factories and lived in urban areas where they had no access to the homegrown vegetables and fresh meat and eggs that were their daily fare in their native countries. Even immigrants who settled in rural areas couldn't grow their traditional dietary staples if the climate and soil were not comparable to what it was in their native countries. Peruvian Indians, fairly recent immigrants to the United States, can only grow quinoa, their indigenous dietary staple, if they happen to live in the Rocky Mountains of Colorado, where the climate and elevation are similar to those of the Andes Mountains in Peru where quinoa is grown. (See the sidebar "Transplanted Diets" for the contrasting story of Italian immigrants to California.)

❝❝ If the diet doesn't suit their metabolic type, however, any beneficial results will be short-lived. **❞❞**

Most people who immigrate to the United States abandon their traditional eating habits and take up the typical American

Transplanted Diets

The northern Italians who immigrated to California in the early part of the twentieth century were luckier than most immigrants who settled in the United States in that the "fertile soil and mild climate of California. . . . closely resembled that of their native country, Italy."[18] Wherever they settled in California they took up farming and raised the same crops they had in Italy, becoming large-scale wine-growers as well as successful vegetable and fruit farmers.

West Africans taken to the Caribbean islands as slaves were fortunate in that the climate and soil on those islands was comparable to those of West Africa. The Garifuna, a West African ethnic group that escaped slavery when their ship was wrecked off the island Saint Vincent in the Caribbean, provide an example of the lengths to which a people will go to retain their dietary staple when the climate and soil favor its growth. After the Garifuna and the French settlers on Saint Vincent lost a war against the British in 1796, the victorious British shipped the Garifuna to Honduras. The Garifuna took cassava, a root vegetable that was a staple of their diet in Africa, along with them, hidden inside their clothes. According to legend, the cassava, soaked with sweat because the Garifuna were so tightly packed together on the ship, was still fresh and moist when they landed. The Garifuna planted cassava wherever they settled.[19] This starchy vegetable is the mainstay of their diet today.

diet of hamburgers, pizza, muffins, chips, cold cereals, cookies, and frozen foods. These nutrient-deficient, inappropriate foods have created a population that is not only the fattest in the world[20] but also one of the unhealthiest among the industrialized nations. The problem in a nutshell is that most people in this country eat foods they can't digest, so the foods stay in the digestive tract and deteriorate into highly acidic putrid or rancid acidic debris. This explains why it's hard to find anyone who isn't suffering from one symptom or another—arthritis, ulcers, insomnia, menstrual problems, chronic fatigue syndrome, and high blood pressure—all of which can lead to more serious degenerative diseases.

Some people recognize that the foods they're eating aren't right for them and begin following a program of so-called "healthy" foods. If the diet doesn't suit their metabolic type, however, any beneficial results will be short lived. If nutritious foods can't be broken down in the digestive tract into a form the body can use, not only are the nutrients in the food lost, the undigested food mass increases toxicity in the body instead of reducing it.

Is Your Diet Causing Your Illness?

How Undigested Food
Poisons the Body

Because people have different quantities and kinds of digestive juices—stomach acids, enzymes, bile, and intestinal flora—they have unique requirements as to the types of protein, fat, and carbohydrates their digestive systems can handle. When they eat food that doesn't meet these requirements, the food doesn't get digested and turns into acid waste. Because it is in the gut that undigested food debris breaks down into disease-causing acid, it is not an exaggeration to say that disease starts in the stomach.

When the quantity of acid waste generated from undigested food is large enough, it eats away the mucous membranes in the esophagus, stomach, and the small and large intestines, causing such disorders as acid reflux, ulcers, spastic colon, colitis, and nausea. What is left of the acid waste leaves the digestive tract by way of the blood and lymph vessels in the small intestines and flows into the circulatory system.

The blood transports the acid waste to the liver to be detoxified. But if the liver is already overloaded with toxins, the acid waste is carried by the blood first to one and then another of the detoxifying organs—the kidneys, the lymph nodes, and the lungs. When these organs are too overloaded with waste to handle it, the acid waste flows back into the general bloodstream in its original form.

That's when the trouble begins, but not right away because the blood has its own defense system against acid waste. The red blood cells use carbon dioxide to generate bicarbonate, an extremely alkaline compound. It also uses phosphate/ammonia to neutralize acid waste. Even the cells are armed with antacids—simple protein and LDL cholesterol. If the body is deficient in these detoxifying compounds but blood calcium levels are high enough, calcium bonds with the acid waste particles to form small, hard, pea-sized residues known as calcium spurs on the heels and, as calcium deposits on the vertebrae, the beginning of osteoarthritis sets in. While osteoarthritis can be painful, for a time at least it prevents acid waste from causing life-threatening degenerative disease.

When all these protective mechanisms fail to either neutralize acid waste or place it out of harm's way, the body's deterioration begins. As the sharp crystals of acid waste flow through the major arteries, they make pits and tears in the vessel walls. This inflames and weakens the arteries, creating the possibility of a life-threatening leak. To prevent this, an adhesive repair protein called *apo*, along with fibrinogen, a blood coagulator, thickens the walls of the arteries. While this prevents blood from seeping out of tears and holes in vessel walls, the narrowed blood vessels slow the flow of blood, thus causing cholesterol, triglycerides, and hardened calcium to stick to the arteries' thickened walls. The narrowed arteries lead to high blood pressure, and the fatty plaques in the arteries spin off blood clots that can trigger heart attacks and strokes.

Finally, the acid waste flows from the arteries into the capillaries. In these microscopic blood vessels, acid waste disturbs organ function by causing the blood in the capillaries to coagulate. This can have disastrous consequences because it prevents the blood from delivering oxygen and/or nutrients to the cells. For example, when the beta cells in the pancreas are deprived of nutrients they stop producing insulin, giving rise to insulin-dependent diabetes. Or when the cells are deprived of oxygen, they generate energy without oxygen. This anaerobic generation of energy causes cells to become malignant. When the number of cancerous cells reaches a critical point, a malignant tumor forms.

If acid waste levels are high enough, they also destroy cells, which are the basic building blocks of the body. This is what happens: cells, like people, need oxygen and nutrients to live; also like people they need to get rid of their waste. To make this possible, minerals create electrical pathways between cells and the nutrient and oxygen-rich fluids that surround them. Acid waste destroys these pathways, cutting off the cells' food supply and the means by which their wastes are eliminated. When cells die out because they aren't getting nourishment and air and are literally drowning in their own waste, the organs in which these dead cells are located begin to break down.

Acid waste not only stops the free flow of food and waste products in and out of the cells, but also when there are leaks in the cells, it slips inside them. When acid waste infiltrates the nerve cells in the brain, it can kill them by damaging the nucleus that controls cellular growth.[1] This can cause Parkinson's disease, multiple sclerosis, or Lou Gehrig's disease (amyotrophic lateral sclerosis), depending on where in the brain the destroyed nerve cells are located.

A Metabolically Appropriate Diet Can Restore Health

Any major illness, and a degenerative disease in particular, points to a lack of balance in organ function. But so do minor symptoms—headaches, insomnia, frequent colds or viruses, pain, indigestion, dry mouth or dry eyes, feelings of restlessness, anxiety or nervousness, a racing pulse, or the inability to sit still for very long. They are all indications that the sympathetic nerves have become dominant in response to the elevated acidity of the body. But while hyperacidity and the resulting health problems are usually the result of the wrong diet, this is not always the case. According to Kansas City cardiologists Dr. James H. O'Keefe, Jr., and Dr. Brian Curtis, writing in the *Mayo Clinic Proceedings*, the sympathetic nerves can become chronically overactive as a result of emotional stress.[2]

> " High levels of acidity in the body cause lack of balance and function in organs. "

In the urban environment, overcrowding breeds chronic anxiety. For example, waiting in line every day to buy a train ticket or getting stuck in a traffic jam maintain anxiety levels at a high pitch, and, as a result, the sympathetic nerves can become chronically overactive. This puts a strain on the heart and circulatory system, a condition that Drs. O'Keefe and Curtis say can cause heart disease. According to Dr. Bruce S. McEwen, "Prolonged stress has been known to weaken the immune system, cause heart disease, damage memory cells in the brain, and deposit fat at the waist rather than the hips and buttocks where they are less likely to increase the risk factor for heart disease and cancer."[3] A study published in the *Proceedings of the National Academy of Sciences* found that severe emotional stress, for example the loss of a job or caring for a sick child or parent, may speed up the aging of the body's cells by causing destructive changes in the genes.[4]

Even a single event, such as a car accident, a surprise party, or the unexpected death of a family member, can cause such a rapid buildup of the stress-promoting hormones that the heart, circulatory system, and vagus nerve lose touch. This can result in rapid heart failure. Perfectly healthy people, even young adults, have had this happen. This finding is based on a study of patients at Johns Hopkins University between 1999 and 2003.[5] The victims did not have diseased arteries or blood clots, but they did have unusually high levels of stress-related hormones such as adrenaline.

It is possible to alleviate the physical trauma caused by emotional stress—irrespective of whether it's sudden and short lived or experienced over a long period of time—by going on a metabolically appropriate diet, because *the elevation of the stress-promoting hormones is due in part to existing acid waste levels as a result of an unsuitable and nutrient-poor diet.*

The Affect of Acid Waste on the Grain Eater and Meat Eater

When the stress hormones are elevated it's a sign that acid waste, triggered by emotional stress and/or metabolically inappropriate food, has thrown the body out of balance, or destroyed homeostasis. This imbalance means that some organs are functioning more rapidly than others. Imbalanced organ function gives rise either to the grain eater or the meat eater.

When you have a grain-eating metabolism, your heart beats faster than usual, your breath comes more quickly than normal, and you think faster and more clearly than you would if you were a meat eater or an omnivore. The downsides are that your overactive heart, brain, and lungs will take away much of your appetite, give you constipation, prevent you from getting as much sleep as you should, and make you feel jittery. The cause? Emotional stress or poor eating habits have unbalanced the nerves that control your organ function, speeding up your heart, lungs, and brain and at the same time slowing your digestive, excretory, elimination, and sleeping functions. These symptoms of imbalance show that you have a grain eater's metabolism. On the other hand, if you have a good appetite, sleep well, have regular bowel function, and are fairly relaxed, your heartbeat and breathing are likely to be on the slow side, your muscle tone will not be strong, and you will not think fast. These are signs that you have a meat-eating metabolism. (See the sidebar "Diseases and Metabolic Type" for more information.)

> " Your goal, whether you're a meat eater or grain eater, is to eat the foods that will most likely balance your metabolism, thereby eliminating disease and helping you maintain a lower weight for life. "

Differences between the meat eater's and grain eater's digestive metabolism are evident from the different ways they handle foods. Meat eaters digest food too fast. They can eat a piece of fruit or a slice of bread and feel hungry a half hour later. They need animal protein and fat, which digest slowly enough to keep

Diseases and Metabolic Type

Meat eaters are more prone to rheumatoid arthritis, ulcers, colitis, severe headaches, diarrhea, and low blood sugar than grain eaters. On the other hand, grain eaters are more likely to develop diabetes, infections—but rarely colds or flu—osteoarthritis, hardening of the arteries, and cancer than meat eaters. If you are an omnivore, that is, all your organs function at the same pace, you are less likely than either the grain eater or the meat eater to come down with serious degenerative disease.

them going for a while. Grain eaters, on the other hand, have such slow digestive metabolisms that meat makes them feel uncomfortably stuffed, while foods such as grains, fruit, and vegetables that are more easily broken down can satiate their appetites for hours.

A far more serious fallout than hunger or feeling stuffed from eating foods that are not suited to the digestive metabolism is indigestion. Very few people are aware of the fact that undigested food debris is highly toxic.

Nor are they aware that they are probably either grain eaters or meat eaters and that if they are meat eaters their digestive systems can't handle large amounts of grain. Likewise, if they are grain eaters they can't digest meat if they eat it too often. The resulting indigestion drives people to take antacid medication rather than change their diets.

Meat eater → digests too quickly → hungry sooner →
eats meat and saturated fat → slows digestion → satiates hunger

Grain eater → digests too slowly → hungry later →
eats grains, fish, poultry, and unsaturated oils →
speeds up digestion → normalizes appetite

Autonomic Nervous System Balance Depends on the Right Diet

The two parts of the autonomic nervous system, the sympathetic and parasympathetic nervous systems, maintain balance—with some assistance from the endocrine glands—by acting in opposition to each other. Each branch increases the speed of the organ systems under its control and slows the organ systems controlled by the other branch. Thanks to this interchange, the two systems work together, creating a balanced metabolism. Individuals who are balanced are omnivores, able to digest grains and meat equally well.

> ❝ Individuals who are balanced are omnivores, able
> to digest grains and meat equally well. ❞

The cooperation between the organ systems and the sympathetic and parasympathetic nerves that control them comes to an end when indigestion occurs too frequently. Acid waste (from undigested food debris or emotional stress) acidifies the blood. This triggers the rise of the stress-promoting hormones, which divert more energy to one nerve branch than the other. The branch of nerves with more energy becomes overactive; the one with less slows too much. The dominant nerve branch uses its extra energy to speed up the reactions of the organ systems under its control, causing the organ systems under the control of the subservient nerve branch to react too slowly. Like an orchestra in which each of the musicians plays at a different tempo, resulting in dissonant and jarring sounds, when organ systems function at different rates, afflicted individuals experience symptoms such as headaches, colds, joint pain, insomnia, and restlessness. They are also limited in the kinds of protein they can digest. When the imbalance results in the sympathetic nerve branch being stronger, the individual is a grain eater. And when the parasympathetic branch takes control, the individual is a meat eater. (See the sidebar "Homeostatic Imbalance and Survival in a Primitive Environment.")

Toxic Chemicals, Acid Waste, and Disease

While acid waste food debris is behind many malignancies, airborne pollutants are also a factor. An example is mesothelioma, a form of

Homeostatic Imbalance and Survival in a Primitive Environment

While in today's junk food environment, homeostatic imbalance is often permanent due to chronic hyperacidity, in primitive cultures where the nutritional value of the diet was high, excessive acid in the blood was a transient state that made survival possible in times of danger. When a threat to life occurred, blood acid levels rose, alerting the adrenal hormones to the necessity of channeling more energy to the organs instrumental in defending the body. This resulted in an increase in muscle strength, better coordination, a faster heartbeat, more rapid breathing, and the production of additional white blood cells and platelets in case of injury. The other organ systems, deprived of their normal allotment of energy, became sluggish. But once the threat was resolved, blood acid levels fell, and stress hormone levels and sympathetic nerve function returned to normal. The body once again became homeostatic, a process scientists call "equilibrium through change."[6]

lung cancer associated with asbestos particles. When these particles are inhaled, large immune cells in the lungs called macrophages devour them. The macrophage cells are unable to "chew up" the carcinogens, however, so they remain inside the immune cells and inflame them. Eventually, the inflammation causes the macrophage cells to die and deteriorate into acidic debris. The lung tissue exposed to these acidic remains also becomes inflamed, dies, and turns acidic. The acid waste in the lungs becomes a feeding station for cancer cells, and the larger the accumulation of acid waste, the faster the cancer cells grow and multiply.

But elevated acid waste from undigested food and air pollutants is not only a direct cause of cancer and other degenerative diseases. It also gives rise to chronic illness in a more circuitous way—by upsetting the body's homeostasis, or equilibrium. (See the sidebar "The Link Between Diet, Underactive Thyroid, and Hyperacidic Urine.")

Eliminate Food Cravings Caused by Food Allergies

Food allergies were one of the first major health problems to emerge as a result of the domestication of wild grain plants in the Neolithic period, so it is not surprising that grains, particularly

The Link Between Diet, Underactive Thyroid, and Hyperacidic Urine

When the thyroid becomes sluggish with the result that less energy is produced, internal function, including digestion, slows, and as a consequence, not enough of the body's acid waste by-products are eliminated. This causes the acid alkaline pH of the urine to fall into the acidic range.

Upon waking in the morning, when energy levels are depressed (a normal waking temperature is between 97.8 and 98.2 degrees Fahrenheit), the acid/alkaline pH of the urine is acidic. But as the morning unfolds, the body temperature rises and energy levels are normalized. When energy levels in the body are normal, digestion becomes more efficient, less acid waste is produced, and as a result the blood and urine become more alkaline. By 1 p.m., when body temperature—and therefore thyroid function—has been normal for several hours, the urine's pH rises and become slightly alkaline, somewhere between 7 and 7.2. But in the evening, as thyroid function slows and energy levels drop, acid particles in the blood from undigested food and metabolic waste begin to rise. To prevent the blood pH from becoming too acidic, the kidneys filter out the excess acid particles in the blood (along with water, urea, and salt), dumping

> them into the urine. This causes the pH of the urine to fall into the acid range again.
>
> While it's normal for the thyroid to be underactive in the evening, during sleep, and upon waking, it shouldn't be underactive all day long, but that's what often happens to people when they reach middle age. The cause is diet. Anyone with an underactive thyroid, before going on thyroid medication, should take the niacin test first, and then test for food allergies. Food allergies are a major cause of low thyroid function.

the gluten and gliadin proteins in wheat, are two of the most common food allergies today. People afflicted with mental disorders are nearly always allergic to grains and polyunsaturated oils, and as a result, find relief on a diet of meat and saturated fats.

Unusual Allergic Symptoms

A seemingly spontaneous reaction like a single sneeze, when it occurs right after swallowing a bite of food or taking a sip of a liquid, is far more likely to be an allergic reaction than a cold. I know my husband is allergic to Earl Grey tea because right after he takes the first taste, he sneezes. Another symptom of food allergies is coughing caused by constriction of the throat muscles. When at a dinner party a woman seated across from me began coughing, I knew it was an allergic reaction to something she had just eaten because it was a dry, tight little cough. An allergy-induced cough can be life threatening if the throat muscles become so constricted that air cannot pass through the trachea into the lungs.

Food allergies can weaken muscles as well as constrict them. When I used to drink tea nonstop throughout the day, by the fifteenth cup the strength left my arms and hands so that if I was holding something in my hands, it dropped to the floor. Going back almost 150 years in history, a famous general had a similar allergic reaction. Stonewall Jackson, one of the top commanders in the Civil War, stopped eating pepper because he said it weakened his left leg![7]

Allergic reactions can even change our perception of the world. This happens to my granddaughter, Katie, when she eats too much salt. Particularly when she puts salt on garlic bread, she says, she feels as though she is living in a dream world. She puts it this way: "I see things, but I don't see them through my eyes. I see them in my mind."

There is no end to the symptoms caused by food allergens, including food cravings. The histamines, generated by the immune cells' reaction to allergy-causing foods, trigger the production of excessive levels of stress hormones, which in turn elevate the blood acid levels. The acidic blood gives rise to a ravenous appetite, particularly for the foods to which the individual is allergic. The stress hormones also speed up the pulse and raise blood pressure, which results in a feeling of euphoria. The desire to experience this exhilarating sense of well-being turns cravings for allergy-causing foods into addictions.

I'll use myself as an example of what can happen to the body when a food craving takes such hold that, unless the body is alkalinized, its effects may be permanent. My allergy to chocolate drove me to binge on it from time to time. During one binge, I ate five chocolate-covered ice cream bars. The next morning a brown age spot about the size of a quarter appeared on my right cheek. When I pressed the spot with my finger, it left an indentation. It was scary to think that a reaction to chocolate had caused a small section of the skin on my face to age overnight. When I woke up the next day and looked in the mirror, the quarter-sized brown spot had shrunk to the size of a pea, and the following day it was gone. To make sure that the dark chocolate on the ice cream bar caused the age spot, I again ate five chocolate-covered ice-cream bars at one time, and the next day history repeated itself. A quarter-sized brown spot appeared on my right cheek. This time it took twice as long for it to disappear. I have no doubt that if I began eating chocolate-covered ice cream bars regularly, the brown spot on my face would become permanent.

Pulse Test

Of course, the best way to get rid of the symptoms of food allergies is to find out which foods are causing them by testing yourself (see the sidebar "Pulse Test to Uncover Food Allergies"). But once you know what foods you're allergic to, it's not always easy to stay away from them. A great help in this matter is Alkalinizing Potato Water (see the sidebar "Alkalinizing Potato Water" in Chapter 5 for the recipe). Drinking a glass of potato water every day cuts down on food cravings because its extreme alkalinity neutralizes the histamine-triggered acidity that drives people to binge on allergy-causing foods.

Pulse Test to Uncover Food Allergies

The pulse test to uncover food allergies was devised by Dr. Arthur Cocoa. Take the following steps to learn which foods you are allergic to.

- First find out what your normal pulse rate is by taking your pulse five times in one day: upon waking, after each meal, and in the evening before bedtime.
- If possible, use an electrical blood pressure device that also measures the pulse rate. It's far easier and usually more accurate than taking your own pulse.
- To measure your pulse by hand, place the first two fingers (but not the thumb) on the wrist, using a watch or clock with a second hand. Count the pulse beat for one minute.

continued

Pulse Test to Uncover Food Allergies, *continued*

- If your highest pulse rate is not over eighty-four and if it is the same every day, you don't have any food allergies.
- Don't eat anything the night before you begin food allergy testing. If you are a smoker, don't smoke during the time in which you are testing for food allergies.
- Test the foods that you eat most often as these are the foods to which you are most likely allergic. Food testing should be done on an empty stomach. In the morning before breakfast is the best time, but anytime during the day when you haven't eaten for a few hours is alright too. Test one food each day.
- Take your pulse just before eating the single food (for example, an egg, apple, or slice of unbuttered bread). Then take your pulse a half hour after eating and one hour after that.
- If your pulse beat at either time is four or five beats higher than before eating, you are having an allergic reaction.
- For people fifty and over, I've found that blood pressure readings are just as effective in revealing food allergies as the pulse rate. Use an electrical blood pressure device.
- A blood pressure reading that is higher than your normal blood pressure, taken a half hour after eating, and/or then one hour later, indicates that you have a food allergy. The higher the blood pressure reading or the more accelerated the pulse, the more allergic you are to the food being tested.

Grain Eater, Meat Eater, Omnivore

Which Are You, and

Why Does It Matter?

Because the individual's choice of protein should conform to his or her digestive metabolism, the advice of various diets as to which protein is "healthiest" should be ignored. The protein that is good for you is the one *you* digest best.

> ❝ There is no "good" protein or "bad" protein. The protein that is good for you is the one *you* digest best. ❞

Eating the protein staples that are appropriate to your digestive metabolism often has the added advantage of doing away with what seem to be food allergies. When you eat protein that isn't compatible with your digestive type, it decomposes in the gut and produces histamines. By eating protein staples that are efficiently broken down, histamines are no longer generated and "allergic" symptoms go away. Symptoms that are assumed to be caused by food allergens quite often turn out to be the result of eating protein foods that aren't digested well.

How to Determine Your Metabolism

There are two tests that can reveal whether you are a grain eater, a meat eater, or an omnivore. The niacin self-test outlined in the following section reveals whether you are parasympathetic dominant, that is, a meat eater, or sympathetic dominant—a grain, fowl, and fish eater—or an omnivore, in which case you can digest meat, fish, chicken, and whole grains equally well. These tests will help you find the diet that fits your metabolism. A second test for metabolism type, the vitamin C self-test, is outlined later in this section. The vitamin C test can be used if the niacin test is inconclusive.

The Niacin Self-Test

The niacin self-test will show whether you have a meat-eating, grain-eating, or balanced metabolism. Follow these steps to take and interpret the niacin test:

❖ Swallow a 50 mg capsule of niacin on an empty stomach. (Niacin can be bought in health food stores and drugstores.)
❖ If, within a half hour, your skin turns red, particularly on your neck and face, and you feel hot and itchy all over or experience vaginal irritation, you have a meat-eater metabolism.

✤ If you don't feel any change in your body, you have a grain-eater metabolism.

✤ If you are warmer, develop a slight pink color in your face, and feel content, sometimes to the point of being euphoric, you have an omnivore metabolism.[1]

How the Niacin Test Works

Niacin, the form of vitamin B_3 used in the metabolic typing test, works because it is acidic. In affecting the acid levels in the stomach, it reveals whether digestion is too slow, too fast, or proceeds at a normal rate, and therefore whether the individual is a meat eater, a grain eater, or an omnivore. The meat eater has excess stomach acid, so the 50 mg tablet of niacin, in adding to that excess, causes a reaction: flushing, a rash, and in women it sometimes causes vaginal irritation. On the other hand, because grain eaters don't have enough stomach acid, the niacin supplement helps normalize it, so it doesn't cause a reaction. The effect of niacin on people with normal stomach acid levels is to generate a feeling of warmth and a sense of well-being. The niacin, added to normal levels of stomach acid, creates a slight acidic excess that acts as a mild stimulant—like a cup of coffee or an alcoholic beverage.

The niacin test, in revealing the level of hydrochloric acid in the stomach, also indicates the amount of enzymes and bile produced in the digestive system. When stomach acid levels are normal, the gallbladder, pancreas, and small intestine produce the required amount of digestive enzymes and bile. Normal levels of hydrochloric acid in the stomach not only stabilize digestion but also kill off some of the bacteria that cause food poisoning.[2]

When stomach acid levels are too high, it's a sign that pancreatic and gallbladder functions are also overactive. The bile duct delivers too much bile, and the pancreas secretes excessive quantities of protease (protein-digesting) enzymes. These are characteristics of the meat eater.

On the other hand, when there is not enough hydrochloric acid, it means that the gallbladder and pancreas aren't producing enough digestive juices. This is characteristic of the grain eater. And if there is not enough acid in the stomach to begin the initial breakdown of protein, it doesn't get digested. Also, when stomach acid levels fall below normal, calcium and the B vitamins aren't absorbed into the cells. (See the sidebar "Niacin Self-Test as a Measure of Potassium and Calcium Levels.")

The Vitamin C Self-Test

If your reaction to the niacin self-test isn't pronounced enough to indicate unconditionally your metabolic type, take the vitamin C self-test outlined here.

* ✣ Take 8 grams of vitamin C each day for three days running. Take one gram at a time, starting after breakfast.
* ✣ If you feel depressed, lethargic, exhausted, and irritable or experience vaginal irritation, you have a meat-eater metabolism.

Niacin Self-Test as a Measure of Potassium and Calcium Levels

The niacin test is a far more accurate barometer of potassium and calcium levels in the body than either the blood test or hair analysis. You may have elevated calcium and potassium in your blood not because you're getting a lot of minerals in your diet or taking mineral supplements, but because your cells aren't absorbing them. And low mineral levels in your hair aren't necessarily an indication that they are low in other parts of your body.

❖ If you feel no change at all, you have an omnivore metabolism.

❖ If you have more energy, sleep better, and feel more content than usual, you are a grain eater.

The Grain Eater

What happens when body function becomes imbalanced? Does it mean you are a grain eater or a meat eater? That depends upon which organs become overactive and which ones function too slowly. When the heart beats faster, the rate of breathing increases, and the individual becomes more energetic, sometimes to the point of feeling anxious, the sympathetic nerves are stronger. While a rapidly beating heart, very fast breathing, and an increase in muscle strength enable the individual to accomplish more than he or she would if organ function was balanced, there is a downside. Digestion becomes sluggish, and the body's ability to eliminate and excrete poisonous waste is impaired. The individual with this particular imbalance can't digest all kinds of protein. He or she is a grain eater.

The reason grain eaters are more apt to develop major degenerative diseases such as hardening of the arteries, cancer, and diabetes than omnivores or meat eaters is because of the greater accumulation of acid waste in their bodies. The grain eater's digestion is sluggish, so some foods don't get digested and turn into acid waste, most of which the grain eater's detoxifying organs are too lethargic to process and eliminate. That's why it's so important for the grain eater to eat the kinds of foods that will bring his or her underactive digestion up to speed.

The diet recommended for the grain eater accelerates digestion because the foods in this diet are broken down quickly. These fast-digesting foods are grains; fermented soy such as tempeh, tofu, and miso; poultry, including duck and goose; as well as seafood and fish. (Fish should include sardines, wild salmon, and anchovies as often as possible because these fish are relatively low in contaminants and high in the nucleotides in DNA and RNA that studies have shown slow the aging process.[3])

Lots of acid-tasting foods such as lemons, limes, and other fruit, vitamin C, vinegar, and yogurt are also an important part of the diet of people who are grain eaters because sour foods bolster their undersupplied stomach acid levels. The normalization of acid levels in the stomach means there will be enough acid to begin the breakdown of protein. This is important because if there is not enough stomach acid to start the digestion of protein, the pancreatic enzymes can't finish the job.

The grain eater is not only deficient in stomach acids but also in potassium. This problem can be overcome by eating dark green, leafy vegetables such as spinach, chard, and kale, which are high in potassium. The grain eater also needs to cut down on root vegetables like carrots, beets, and parsnips because these vegetables are high in calcium, which the grain eater has too much of. Eating the appropriate vegetables, by balancing potassium and calcium levels in the body, also helps speed up the grain eater's slow-functioning digestive system. Once digestion takes place at a normal rate, the acid waste buildup in the blood—which causes the overstimulation of the sympathetic nerves in the grain eater— is reduced. This slows the rapid heartbeat and breathing and accelerates the underactive digestive process, thereby balancing organ function.

As soon as the organs are balanced, that is, working together, hyperactivity and restlessness, common symptoms in individuals who are grain eaters, disappear. The long-term advantage of the balancing of organ function is the prevention of life-threatening chronic diseases that hit the grain eater harder than they do the meat eater or the omnivore.

The sidebar "Grain Eaters Need More of These Foods" summarizes the dietary requirements of grain eaters. Part II outlines menu plans that can help grain eaters eat right to lose weight or for good health.

Grain Eaters Need More of These Foods

Grain eaters need more of the following foods:

- **Green leafy vegetables:** spinach, kale, chard, collard greens, arugula, dandelion greens
- **Potatoes:** preferably undercooked to preserve the nutrients
- **Beans:** black, lima, and kidney; lentils and fermented soy, such as tempeh, tofu, and miso soup
- **Grains:** brown rice, corn, wheat, rye, quinoa, couscous, spelt, oatmeal, millet, barley, kasha, and wheat berries
- **Poultry:** chicken, turkey, duck, and goose (The French in the Gascony region of France have less heart disease than people in other parts of France. This has been attributed to their daily consumption of duck and goose fat.)
- **Fish:** especially sardines, anchovies, and wild salmon
- **Seafood:** such as clams, oysters, shrimp, lobster, crabmeat, and scallops (These are high in minerals.)
- **Fruit and sour-tasting foods:** yogurt and vinegar (Apple cider vinegar is healthier than other kinds of vinegar because it contains less acetic acid.)
- **Unsaturated fats and oils:** extra virgin olive oil (use pure olive oil for cooking), coconut oil (doesn't need to be refrigerated), oil-rich avocadoes, and sesame seeds and flaxseeds to help satisfy the body's EFA (essential fatty acid) requirements.
- **Eggs:** at least five and no more than ten weekly

The Meat Eater

When the adrenal hormones are depressed, the reverse imbalance occurs: the parasympathetic nerves become dominant over the sympathetic system. The parasympathetic nervous system speeds up digestion and accelerates the elimination of toxic waste from the body. On the other hand, it slows down the heartbeat and breathing and weakens muscle tone and thyroid gland function.

The excessively speedy digestion of the meat eater can be slowed down by eating foods that reduce stomach acid levels. Red meat—beef, lamb, pork, veal, and venison—is broken down so slowly it uses up some of the meat eater's excess stomach acid and by doing so normalizes his or her digestion. Nuts and seeds are also good foods for the meat eater because, like red meat, they are digested slowly. And because the meat eater needs to limit consumption of fish, which is a good source of omega-3 oil, the body's omega-3 fatty acid requirements must be met in other ways, such as eating a few walnuts or a lot of lettuce every day. Meat eaters should limit their intake of fruit and other acid-tasting foods so as not to add to their excessive stomach acid levels.

Meat eaters also need to balance their calcium and potassium levels. They have too much potassium and too little calcium. Eating root vegetables helps bring their deficient calcium levels up to normal, while limiting potassium-rich foods like spinach, chard, kale, and other green leafy vegetables is necessary because of their elevated potassium levels. The diet prescribed for the meat eater also normalizes underactive thyroid function, which lessens the fatigue that is a common complaint of individuals with a meat-eater metabolism.

The sidebar "Meat Eaters Need More of These Foods" summarizes the dietary requirements of meat eaters. Part II outlines menu plans that can help meat eaters eat right to lose weight or for good health.

Maybe you are a vegetarian and have found out using the niacin or vitamin C self-test that you have a meat eater metabo-

Meat Eaters Need More of These Foods

Meat eaters need more of the following foods:

- **Root vegetables:** turnips, parsnips, rutabagas, beets, carrots, potatoes preferably undercooked to preserve nutrients
- **Lighter-colored vegetables:** green peas, string beans, cauliflower, broccoli, corn, asparagus, artichokes, cabbage, and brussels sprouts
- **Lettuce:** all varieties, especially romaine and iceberg (Exception: pregnant women shouldn't eat iceberg lettuce because it has been genetically altered.)
- **Red meat:** veal, beef, lamb, pork, venison
- **Nuts and seeds:** as wide a variety as possible, but especially almonds, hazelnuts, peanuts, chestnuts, pistachios, walnuts, cashews, pecans, and macadamia nuts because they have the most fiber and highest nutrient values
- **Saturated fats and oils:** lots of butter (slows up the meat eater's overly rapid digestion), meat fat, including some duck or goose fat because it prevents heart disease, coconut oil (doesn't need to be refrigerated), and extra-virgin olive oil (use pure olive oil for cooking)
- **Some cheese and a small amount of fermented milk products:** such as kefir and buttermilk (These milk products are easy for adults to digest because the lactose has been broken down by the fermentation process.)
- **Eggs:** five to ten weekly (People in many countries have, throughout history, satisfied most of their protein requirements with eggs because they couldn't afford to eat meat on a regular basis.)

lism. In spite of the designation "meat eater," it is possible for vegetarians who fall into this category to eat right for their metabolism. See the sidebar "Vegetarians with a Meat-Eating Metabolism" for some tips on how to do this.

Vegetarians with a Meat-Eating Metabolism

I know vegetarians who, although testing out as meat eaters, are not willing to forgo rice and beans for meat. Such people can't assume that because they feel well they can continue eating vegetarian without inflicting damage on their health in the long run. However, there are two ways they can compensate. Lacto-vegetarians and lacto-ovo vegetarians who eat butter should eat a lot of it. That way they're satisfying one of the most important fatty acid requirements of the meat eater metabolism. Nuts and seeds are another type of food that meat eaters do very well on and are also part of the traditional vegetarian diet. Eating a large variety of nuts along with a meal of rice and beans provides all the amino acids and essential fatty acids the body needs.

Besides meat eaters who won't give up their vegetarian diet, there are individuals who have such quirky digestive metabolisms that, in order to be able to digest their food, they have to ignore all the dietary guidelines that the rest of us need to follow. An exception to many of these rules is Lara, a Russian immigrant living in New York. Although a meat eater, the kinds and quantities of foods she needs to eat to feel good aren't consistent with the meat eater's diet. For example, she eats four to five apples a day, which for the typical meat eater, already burdened with excess stomach acid, would add up to far too much acid. And she drinks a quart and a half of milk a day—although most adults are better off eliminating milk from their diet. While carbohydrates should make up about 60 percent of total food intake, they comprise only about 5 percent of Lara's diet. She doesn't eat potatoes, and she only eats one slice of bread a day. This is the diet that gives her the most energy and keeps her healthy. If she doesn't feel quite right and her complexion takes on a grayish hue, she knows it's because she hasn't eaten enough apples or drunk a sufficient amount of milk that day. She does eat some meat and also some vegetables, but the foods she eats in the greatest bulk are apples and milk.

The Omnivore

If the niacin test indicates that you are an omnivore, that is, your digestion is neither too fast nor too slow, you are lucky on two counts. First, you are more likely to enjoy good health than either the meat eater or the grain eater. Second, unlike the meat eater and the grain eater, you can eat a wide variety of foods. In fact, the late Dr. William Donald Kelley found from his experience as a nutritionist that omnivores do well on the typical American diet found in textbooks.[4]

You Need to Eat Some Foods That Don't Suit Your Metabolic Type

Having either a meat-eater or grain-eater metabolism does not mean that you are locked into eating only those foods in your category. Some people don't fit entirely into one category or the other. It's just that individuals with unbalanced metabolisms, whether meat eaters or grain eaters, need more of the kinds of foods that fall into their metabolic category and less of the foods in the other metabolic category. Grain eaters do well on generous amounts of grains, fish, and poultry. But they should eat some butter to break up the long chain molecules in vegetable and fish oils. They also need to eat meat once a week because muscle meat is the only food that contains liberal amounts of carnitine, an amino acid that is involved in the use of fat in the production of energy in the heart. Some grain eaters, however, have enough meat-digesting enzymes for two helpings of meat a week. By the same token, while most meat eaters can digest only one serving of fish each week, there are a few meat eaters who have more of the enzymes needed to break down seafood than is ordinarily the case among individuals with a meat-eater metabolism. Those meat eater types can eat fish more than once a week.

How much protein, carbohydrates, and fat you should eat is relative. The amount of one food group you should consume in a meal depends on how much you eat of the other two food groups. You should eat roughly four times as much carbohydrate as protein. If you are having about two ounces of protein in a meal, eat approximately eight ounces of carbohydrates. You don't have to weigh your food. Just be sure that there is a lot more carbohydrates on your plate—brown rice, potatoes, whole-grain pasta, or bread—than protein—meat, fish, seafood, or eggs.

You also need almost twice the amount of fat and oil as protein. Of course, all protein contains some fat, so that helps to satisfy your fatty acid requirements. Make sure that the meat or fish you eat is fatty and that you have put some butter or oil, depending upon whether you're a grain eater or meat eater, on your rice, pasta, or potatoes so that you eat almost twice as much fat or oil as protein at the same meal.

> **❝** Meat eaters still need fish. Grain eaters still need meat. **❞**

You Can Eat Protein Foods Not Prescribed in Your Category

The fact that grain eaters can eat chicken and fish as well as grains indicates that their grain-eating antecedents also ate large amounts of fish and poultry. It seems likely that the habit of eating fish developed because large-scale cultivation of grains requires extensive irrigation systems, so farms were located near rivers. This not only ensured the farmer of enough water to irrigate crops but also supplied fish as a supplementary source of protein. It's difficult to speculate why the grain eater digests poultry so well, except that farmers generally raise chickens for eggs, and once the chickens' egg-laying capabilities come to an end, eat the chickens.

Meat eaters, while favoring beef, lamb, and pork, have always included other kinds of protein in their diet. The Germans are meat eaters, but they also eat rye bread, and although couscous and wheat breads are the principal food staples of the Arabs who live in the Middle East, they eat lamb two or three times a week. While people living in cold climates are primarily meat eaters, there are exceptions to this rule. Those living along the coastal regions of Scandinavia and Russia have traditionally relied on fish as their principal source of protein, and the Germans living in the towns that border the Baltic Sea still eat almost nothing but herring for protein. In Japan, while large helpings of rice are eaten at each meal, they are always accompanied by side dishes of meat or fish: to quote Edwin Reischauer from his book *The Japanese*, "Large mouthfuls of rice are alternated with small bites of fish, meat or vegetables at meals."[5]

These variations in the diets of both grain eaters and meat eaters make clear that good health is not dependent on eating only those foods that belong in either the meat-eater or grain-eater category. Smaller quantities of the foods that aren't in an individual's metabolic category should also be included in the diet. The meat eater has some grain-digesting enzymes because meat-eating cultures, having raised cereal grains as feed for their livestock, used what grains were left over to make bread and cereal. Likewise, the grain eater has a small quantity of meat-digesting enzymes because grain eaters, besides including poultry and fish in their diets, also ate red meat on occasion. Most cultures, then, although favoring one type of protein, included small amounts of other kinds of protein in their diet.

Because of the wide range of protein foods eaten by meat-eating and grain-eating cultures, the enzyme glands adapted to produce enzymes for all the kinds of protein a given population cluster has eaten for an extended period of time. However, because cultures typically depended on a single type of protein, such as rice or millet or red meat to supply most of their protein requirements, the largest segment of their digestive enzymes adapted to the breakdown of the primary protein staple. Only a small portion of enzymes adapted to the digestion of protein foods that were eaten occasionally. Because these enzyme requirements are passed on through the genes to future generations, grain eaters and meat eaters should occasionally eat the kind of protein foods that are not part of their everyday diet.

The meat eater needs to eat the following grain-eater foods in these limited quantities:

* Two slices of whole-grain bread daily
* Seafood once a week
* Chicken or some other poultry once a week
* A green, leafy vegetable such as spinach or kale once a week
* One apple, pear, or other fruit three times a week
* A container of yogurt three times a week
* A serving of rice, millet, or other grain twice a week

The grain eater needs to eat the following meat-eater foods in these limited quantities:

* Red meat such as beef, pork, lamb, or veal once a week
* A root vegetable twice a week
* Mixed lettuce salad three or four times a week
* String beans, peas, broccoli, cabbage, cauliflower, artichokes, or asparagus three or four times a week
* Nuts and seeds, but no more than ten to fifteen mixed nuts and a small handful of seeds daily

The Risks of Caffeine to Your Health

It's been happening more often that medical researchers are discovering health advantages in foods that had previously been considered bad for the health. Take coffee. Its so-called health benefits are now being touted despite the legions of studies that show that drinking more than two cups of coffee a day is harmful to health.

For instance, a research study conducted in 2004 at the Johns Hopkins Medical Institute concluded that individuals who drink five or more cups of coffee a day are two to three times more likely to have coronary heart disease than nondrinkers.[6] This study also found that caffeine raises blood pressure, irritates stomach ulcers, worsens urinary tract infections, and makes insulin less responsive to elevated blood sugar.

Findings that indicate coffee can be healthy are now coming out, despite all the studies showing the negative affect coffee has on health. One of these studies found that during asthmatic attacks, coffee opens up spastic bronchial tubes, making it easier to breathe.[7] This is a good use of coffee because it has an immediate benefit and it need only be drunk when an asthmatic attack occurs. But the study that shows that coffee prevents the formation of gallstones by widening the bile duct, enabling bile to flow freely through it, is liable to do more harm than good because it requires drinking five or more cups of coffee daily on a continuing basis. There are healthier ways of preventing gallstones such as adding more olive oil and saturated fats to your diet and drinking a glass of raw beet juice every day.

A European study found that drinking seven or more cups of coffee daily may cut the risk of type 2 diabetes by 50 percent.[8] By drinking that much coffee daily, however, you may avoid type 2 diabetes but end up with type 1 diabetes instead, because, according to the study cited above, coffee can prevent insulin from lowering blood sugar.

Because these favorable studies about coffee have come out, it was inevitable that researchers would find that large amounts of tea also have a salutary effect on health. A study published in the *Proceedings of the National Academy of Sciences* found that when subjects drank five cups of tea daily, their immune cells responded five times faster to germs.[9] This is due to a substance in tea called L-theanine, which causes the immune system's gamma delta T cells to multiply faster. According to nutritionist Penny Kris-Etherton of Pennsylvania State University, there is a growing body of evidence, revealed by blood tests, that tea is an effective immune enhancer.[10] The assumption is that five-cups-a-day tea drinkers are less likely to suffer health problems, because of the increased activity of their immune system's T cells, than people who drink, say, one or two cups of tea or fewer a day.

Could the increase in the activity of the immune cells in people who drink five or more cups of tea a day be caused by the immune system's interpretation of the overload of caffeine as an unfriendly invasion of alien microbes? In that case, the immune killer cells would become elevated as a protection against these foreign invaders. What about the other effects of caffeine in five cups of tea per day? The researchers who recommend drinking large amounts of tea to strengthen the immune system don't address the possible consequences.

Could drinking five cups of tea a day, like coffee, actually contribute to coronary heart disease? A study such as the one carried out at Johns Hopkins on coffee should be done on tea. The caffeine in much less tea can cause an irregular heartbeat even in people who have no heart problems. Most doctors caution their heart patients to drink no more than one or two cups of coffee or tea a day.

There are other harmful substances in tea besides caffeine, such as tannic acid, which is a known carcinogen. Tea and coffee are also common allergens. Avoiding tea and coffee has been shown to alleviate a wide variety of diseases, including eczema, rheumatoid arthritis, Crohn's disease, migraine, irritable bowel syndrome, and hyperactivity.[11]

Milk Can Sabotage Your Diet

Another food recommended for its nutritional advantages without consideration for the harm it can cause is milk. Dr. Duane Alexander, director of the National Institute of Child Health and

Human Development, is quoted as saying, "Without including milk in the diet, it is nearly impossible to meet calcium needs."[12] Some medical authorities, concerned about the deficiency of calcium in the diets of young people, believe that drinking more milk is the solution. A national survey revealed that only 13.5 percent of girls and 35.3 percent of boys between the ages of twelve and nineteen consume the recommended amount of calcium for teenagers: 1,300 mg of calcium daily.[13]

Teenagers may be short on calcium, but they need to satisfy their calcium requirements by eating calcium-rich foods rather than by drinking milk because milk puts them at risk for developing a serious, sometimes fatal health problem later on in life. Milk causes a spurt in growth by stimulating the release of the human growth hormone somatotropin. This increases the teenager's chance of getting cancer as an adult if his or her milk-drinking habit causes growth above a certain height. A study published in the *Journal of the American Medical Association* and conducted at the Dana-Farber Cancer Institute, Brigham and Women's Hospital, and the Harvard School of Public Health found that taller people in general were more likely to get both pancreatic and colon cancer.[14] Dr. Dominique Michaud, an investigator at the National Cancer Institute, states that this increase in cancer risk is related to exposure to the growth hormone in milk during adolescence.[15] (This is the growth hormone that occurs naturally in milk, not the hormone added by dairy farmers to increase cows' production of milk.)

With each generation in America and elsewhere growing taller than the previous one because of increased milk consumption, and therefore increasingly likely to get cancer—as well as diabetes and calcium-hardened tissues—it's time that the human body's calcium requirements were satisfied by eating foods that are high in calcium, such as yogurt, cheese, and root vegetables, rather than milk. (Yogurt and cheese, although made from milk, have been chemically altered by fermentation, so, unlike milk, they don't stimulate the release of somatotropin, the human growth hormone.) See the sidebar "Good Sources of Calcium for Meat Eaters."

Not only should teenagers avoid drinking milk because of the health risks involved when they become adults but also because the processed milk available in supermarkets today won't satisfy their calcium needs. Standard brands of milk produced by agribusinesses have been heated, for the purposes of extending their shelf life, to a temperature of 212 degrees Fahrenheit. Pasteurization at such high heat destroys the acidity in milk; without it calcium can't be broken down, and undigested calcium can't be absorbed and utilized by the cells.

Drinking commercially pasteurized milk not only fails to satisfy the body's calcium requirements, but because undigested calcium particles are not assimilated, adults who drink as little as two glasses of milk a day risk a buildup of excessive levels of calcium in their bodies. Yet a recent revision in the guidelines of the U.S. government's Food Pyramid, published on April 20, 2005, in the *New York Times*, ignores this information by recommending three cups of milk for adults daily, one more cup than it recommends for children![16] In adults who drink milk every day, the calcium is apt to be deposited in the wrong places,

Good Sources of Calcium for Meat Eaters and Grain Eaters

The meat eater, who is deficient in calcium, can satisfy his or her calcium requirements by eating cheese, butter, yogurt, and root vegetables. The grain eater, who has a surplus of calcium, gets more than enough of it in the green, leafy vegetables grain eaters need to eat three or four times a week.

for example, in the reproductive organs, in the bile duct, or in the ureters, the ducts that convey urine from the kidneys to the bladder.

The well-known downside of drinking milk is that it induces the mucus-secreting glands to overproduce. Excessive amounts of mucus cause unfriendly germs to multiply faster because it's a food they thrive on.

But far more dangerous to health than excess mucus is the elevation of blood insulin that the consumption of milk by adults causes. Excessive insulin in the blood makes glucose levels drop drastically. This gives rise to binge eating, which brings the blood sugar back up; however, because blood sugar goes too high, insulin again rises excessively and once again causes the blood sugar to plummet. These wild swings in blood sugar give rise to hypoglycemia (low blood sugar), and when the overproducing insulin glands stop working, the hypoglycemic individual becomes diabetic.

Elevated insulin levels have also been implicated in the development of cancer. Women with breast cancer who have high insulin levels are six times more likely to have a recurrence.

The deficiency of a nutrient in the body is not always the result of a diet that is lacking in that particular nutrient. Calcium deficiency is a case in point. The body can be deficient in calcium even though the diet meets the calcium requirements if the individual lacks vitamin D or the mineral boron. Both are necessary for the absorption and utilization of calcium.

Vitamin D is found only in the fat in meat, milk products, and seafood. The low-fat diet, by depriving the body of vitamin D, could be responsible for the widespread calcium deficiency in teenagers. In a study published in *The Archives of Pediatrics and Adolescent Medicine*, 24 percent of the 307 teenagers tested had a severe deficiency of vitamin D, and 42 percent were slightly deficient in the vitamin.[17]

The only way to overcome nutrient deficiencies is to eat the foods that are indicated for your metabolic type. The metabolically appropriate diet is geared toward normalizing mineral levels in the body and providing the fats and oils needed to assimilate mincrals. The danger to health caused by consuming large quantities of milk to overcome a calcium shortage make it clear that foods should not be evaluated solely on the basis of their nutrient values but also on what effect they have on long-term health.

Is Your Diet Causing Your Weight Problem?

Why a Standardized Diet Doesn't Work

After you've taken the niacin test and found out whether you're a grain eater or a meat eater, the next step is to find the menu plan for your metabolic type in Part II of this book. There are grain-eater and meat-eater menu plans for those who want to stay healthy and slim, and also grain-eater and meat-eater menu plans for those who want to do away with their health problems, including excess weight and obesity. If, however, you still need to convince yourself of the value of going on a diet that is custom designed for you, as opposed to the "one size fits all" type of diets you've read about everywhere else, read this chapter and find out why those diets don't work.

The Case Against the Low-Fat Diet

One problem with low-fat diet advocates is that although they allow some polyunsaturated oils for salad dressings, sauces, and for sautéing, they typically suggest removing as much saturated fat from foods as possible—for example, taking out the fat under the skin of the chicken before cooking it, cutting all the fat off red meat, and eliminating the yokes from eggs before scrambling them.

It's been established scientifically, and for very good reasons, that the diet should be made up of 25 percent fat and/or oil. Yet some low-fat diets recommend a diet in which there is less than 7 percent fat. Such a diet predisposes to cancer and blindness by preventing the absorption of vitamins A and D. Even low-fat diets that recommend as much as 15 percent fat and/or oils in the diet, only 10 percent below the scientifically determined amount, are depriving the body cells of the two substances that make up the structure of the membranes that surround cells. These two substances are fatty acids and protein. Even if the low-fat diet is high in protein, without an adequate amount of fat in the diet the protein can't be absorbed and utilized. Without adequate fat and protein, cellular membranes deteriorate, causing the structure of organs in which these cells are located to literally fall apart.

I witnessed firsthand the effects of a low-fat diet on Kenneth, a colleague. His doctor put him on an anticholesterol medication and suggested that he eliminate all fat from his diet because he had a cholesterol reading of 250. Kenneth stopped putting butter on his bread and olive oil on his salad, gave up red meat, and removed the fatty skin from chicken before roasting it. After a year on this low-fat diet, his cholesterol dropped to 135. His doctor took him off medication but encouraged him to stay on the low-fat diet.

Metabolically speaking, we all need fat. Kenneth, a meat eater, had given up the fat and oil that meat eaters need, namely generous amounts of butter, some meat fat and a small amount of poultry fat, and olive oil. He admitted that for the twenty-year period in which he had eaten practically no fats and oils, he had felt so "lousy" that "to tell the truth, life wasn't worth living." He was fatigued and depressed. At the age of fifty-four, he was forced to give up his teaching position at a university because he could no longer focus on his work. He had also become fearful of crowds, and in the last two years had become afraid of dying, perhaps with good reason. His chest had caved in, his face was gaunt, and his eyes were bloodshot.

Twenty years on a nearly fat-free diet had made Kenneth feel continually anxious. To relieve his anxieties, he had to raise the fatty acid levels in his blood. For this purpose, he began taking two teaspoons of cod liver oil twice a day and ate red meat three or four times a week, which he cooked rare and left some of the fat on. He also had three tablespoons of butter a day.

The cod liver oil supplied the omega-3 fatty acids—docosahexaenoic acid (DHA), eicosapentaenoic acid (EPA), and alpha linolenic acid (ALA)—and the saturated meat fat provided arachidonic acid (AA) from the omega-6 group. These are the fatty acids most critical to brain function, no matter what metabolic type you are. Adding butter to the diet broke up the long molecular chains of these essential fatty acids into shorter ones that fit into the receptors of the brain cells. Kenneth took vitamin E to prevent the polyunsaturated oil residues inside his body from turning rancid. He made a complete recovery.[1]

Without enough fatty acids in his blood to keep the body alkaline, Kenneth's alkaline reserves had dropped. When that happens, blood acid levels rise. Blood hyperacidity triggers the elevation of cortical hormones that cause stress. Like a seesaw in which the higher in the air one end is, the lower the opposite end, Kenneth's elevated stress hormones caused a corresponding decrease in the health-promoting hormones such as testosterone that stabilize the nerves and stimulate the brain cells.

Grain eaters' fatty acid requirements can be met by:

- ❖ Three or more tablespoons of extra-virgin olive oil daily
- ❖ Three or four avocados weekly
- ❖ One tablespoon of coconut oil daily five times a week
- ❖ Fatty fish to satisfy omega-3 oil requirements three times weekly

❖ One tablespoon ground flaxseed or sesame seeds three or four times weekly
❖ A mix of ten to fifteen oil-rich nuts four or five times weekly

Meat eaters' fatty acid requirements can be met by:

❖ Three to four tablespoons of butter daily
❖ One tablespoon of coconut oil daily five times a week (optional)
❖ Some red meat fat four times weekly
❖ One to two tablespoons of extra-virgin olive oil daily
❖ Goose and/or duck fat once a week
❖ Three or four avocados weekly
❖ A mix of twenty-five to thirty oil-rich nuts and one tablespoon of a mix of seeds five times weekly

The Importance of Fats and Oils

Nuts and seeds were a vital source of fatty acids in Paleolithic cultures. The widely held belief that Stone Age peoples fulfilled the body's fat requirements from the wild animals they subsisted on is a myth. There is much data on aboriginal peoples living in the twenty-first century in remote areas of Russia, Canada, Scandinavia, and Africa that indicates they supplement the sparse fat on game animals with oil- and fat-rich foods such as fish oil and fish eggs, organ meats, shellfish (crabs, shrimp, and lobsters), and seeds and nuts (75 percent of most nuts consists of oil).

There are some experts who insist that seeds are for birds, and nuts for squirrels and other rodents, not people. They hold that it is demeaning for humans to eat the same foods as animals that are lower on the evolutionary scale. For instance, Dr. T. L. Cleave, in his book *The Saccharine Disease*, has this to say about the consumption of seed and nut oils: "Evolutionarily, these oils make us not so much men as the equivalent of a flock of greenfinches."[2] It apparently never occurred to Dr. Cleave that the oil in seeds and nuts satisfied most of the fatty acid requirements of his Stone Age ancestors. In fact, this is why both the meat eater and the grain eater need to make nuts and seeds part of their diets. Nuts and seeds are a dietary legacy from our Paleolithic hunter ancestors, transmitted to us genetically over thousands of generations. It also makes sense that the meat eater needs more nuts and seeds than the grain eater, because the meat-eater diet is carrying on the red meat eating tradition of the Ice Age hunter.

Research studies have found that nuts are an incredibly valuable supplement to the diet. One study, written up in the *Journal of the American Medical Association,* included eighty-three thousand subjects (nurses) whose nut-eating habits were tracked for sixteen years. According to this study, women who consumed about five handfuls of a mix of nuts—including almonds, peanuts, Brazil nuts, cashews, and macadamia nuts— each week were 30 percent less likely to develop diabetes than women who hardly ever ate nuts.[3] Two studies, the Physicians' Health Study, with twenty-two thousand subjects, and the Adventist Health Study, which included forty thousand subjects, have confirmed that eating nuts prevents heart disease.[4] The high levels of fiber and magnesium in nuts, the monounsaturated fats, which nuts have in common with olive oil and avocados, and the folic acid, zinc, and copper all help lower blood pressure and prevent hardening of the arteries. Nuts also contain the mineral boron, necessary for calcium metabolism. Because nuts are digested slowly, they are an ideal food for meat eaters with their too-speedy digestive metabolism. The meat eater usually has no trouble digesting a large handful of nuts four or five days a week. Grain eaters should also include nuts in their diets, but because nuts are digested slowly and grain eaters are slow digesters, so as not to slow down their digestion even more, they should eat only about half the amount meat eaters eat. (See the lists for grain eaters' and meat eaters' fatty acid requirements earlier in this section.)

Because most nuts contain more omega-6 than omega-3 fatty acids, include omega-3–rich flaxseeds and walnuts with the mix of nuts and seeds you eat. A good way to increase your intake of vitamin E is to eat almonds and hazelnuts. Hazelnuts contain the highest amount of the amino acid tryptophan of any nut. They also contain the most folate, a B vitamin. The nuts that are highest in calcium are almonds and Brazil nuts, while almonds, cashews, pine nuts, and Brazil nuts have the most magnesium. The nuts high in potassium are almonds, Brazil nuts, cashews, pine nuts, pistachios, and walnuts. If you have trouble seeing in the dark or are bothered by the glare of light, you should eat pistachios for their high vitamin A content. Because there is more vitamin A in the eyes than in any other organ, normal eye function is dependent upon adequate vitamin A in the diet. The nuts mentioned above, eaten together, supply the body with an incredibly wide range of nutrients.

" Research studies have found that nuts are an incredibly valuable supplement to the diet. "

Although almonds have more nutrients and fiber than any other nut, the Turks claim that the walnut is the healthiest nut. Their evidence is purely anecdotal, but the fact that walnuts are the centerpiece of Turkish folk medicine suggests their claims as to the potent healing power of the walnut contain a good deal of truth. The story of Abdul is one illustration of the healing power of this nut. Abdul had never been sick a day in his life; he said that he didn't know what pain or discomfort felt like. He attributed his perfect health to having followed the advice given him by his great-grandmother the day he boarded a ship, at the age of eighteen, to sail from his native Turkey to the United States. As

he and his great-grandmother were saying their last farewells—
this was the last time they would see each other—she gave him a
piece of advice. She told him to eat four walnuts (eight halves) a
day in the morning before breakfast. He followed her advice.
Eighty years later, the night he celebrated his ninety-eighth birth-
day, having spent the day weeding his lawn, he died in his sleep.
This story alone doesn't prove that walnuts were responsible for
Abdul's long and healthy life, but taken together with similar
anecdotes, it is impressive.

A friend of mine recently spent some time in Turkey, where
she learned of the exalted place walnuts have in the pantheon of
Turkish healing remedies. Eating walnuts daily for the prevention
of illness is still a common practice. A Turkish herbalist gave her
the following recipe to increase the walnuts' nutritional value.
Soak three walnut halves in distilled or spring water for eight
hours at room temperature. Drink the water on an empty stomach, preferably in the morning, then eat the walnuts. The water
predigests the walnuts by absorbing the nutrients from the fiber.
The walnut water removes calcium deposits from the body, reg-
ulates bowel function, alleviates the adverse effects of strokes,
improves brain function—the two halves of the walnut are a
replica of the two hemispheres of the brain—and clears the body
of parasites. (Parasites are known to hate black walnuts—but they
don't like other kinds of walnuts either.)

Like the Turks, we should satisfy our fatty acid needs from
whole nuts rather than the oil extracted from them. Using polyunsaturated oils in salad dressings, sauces, and for cooking overloads
our bodies. The polyunsaturated fatty acids that the body doesn't
need stay inside the body and become rancid, destroying oxygen
and generating free radicals. Instead of making polyunsaturated
oil a part of your diet, snack on nuts and seeds or add them to
stews and salads. Some West Africans living in the United States
have held on to the African tradition of putting ground peanuts
in chicken stew, in spinach, and using roasted peanuts as an

accompaniment to grilled plantain. Whether you are a grain eater or a meat eater, nuts and seeds are a good diet food because they're digested slowly, so they satisfy the appetite for a long time.

> " Eating nuts and seeds can speed up metabolism if you are a meat eater. "

Why Fats and Oils Are Essential to Health

There has been too little recognition in industrialized nations that more fats and oils need to be consumed during pregnancy if the fetal brain is to develop normally.[5] A study completed in 1991 at the University of Minnesota measured the fatty acids of pregnant women, which revealed that the level of omega-3 fatty acids was far lower than that of women who were not pregnant.[6] Nonindustrial cultures knew from experience passed down through families that supplemental fats and oils should be given to pregnant women to assure the normal development of the unborn child. In some regions of the Alps in Switzerland, pregnant women were encouraged to eat extra portions of raw butter and cream. Thousands of miles in an easterly direction, the Masai, a cattle-herding people of East Africa, prepared the bodies of young women for pregnancy six months before marriage by giving them milk from cows that were grazing on the first grass of the season because young grass produced the creamiest milk. (It also contains the most nutrients.) In coastal communities in Africa, extra portions of crabs, lobsters, and fish eggs were allocated to pregnant women. Organ meats with their high fat content were another valued supplement eaten by pregnant women in Africa.

In preliterate cultures where food was sometimes in short supply, the primary purpose of eating was not for pleasure but to boost energy, strength, and good health. These simple-living but wise people knew that the most important foods in this regard were fat and oil. They didn't need to know why fats and oils were so important to health; they had the proof of their importance right before their eyes. When the tribe had plenty of fat and oil to eat, its members were healthy and strong.

The folk wisdom of tribal cultures in regard to the importance of fat and oil is backed up by medical science's findings as to why the human body can't do without these basic foods. Fats and oils are the only foods that supply the oil-based vitamins A and D. These two vitamins make it possible for the body to utilize minerals, protein, carbohydrates, and fat. Vitamins A and D also make the synthesis of hormones possible. The meat eater and the grain eater both need fatty acids, although the meat eater needs more saturated fat (from butter and meat fat) while the grain eater needs more unsaturated oil (from olives, flaxseeds, sesame seeds, and fish). The role the oil-based vitamins play in the absorption of minerals is perhaps their most important function, because the body can't synthesize minerals from simpler substances the way it can amino acids, fat, vitamins, and enzymes. Furthermore, the body can't store minerals.

Dr. Weston Price, in the book *Parental Malnutrition and Physical Degeneration*, wrote of the importance of fats and oils in the indigenous diet.[7] He noted that of all the primitive groups he studied, those who were the strongest, had the healthiest physiques, and had the least decay in their teeth lived on the coast, where they had easy access to seafoods with their high concentrations of the oil-based vitamins A and D.

A group of anthropologists, economists, and paleopathologists who examined the skeletons of Native Americans living in the western hemisphere over the last seven thousand years came to the same conclusion as Price. They found that coastal peoples whose chief food staple was seafood rich in the fat-soluble vitamins A and D were the healthiest.[8]

There is as much need for vitamins A and D in today's industrialized world as there was in indigenous cultures. And because these fat-soluble vitamins are found only in fats ands oils, these foods must be eaten in large amounts. Research studies show that a deficiency of dietary fats and oils contributes to the development of various ailments, including eclampsia during pregnancy, liver disease, and skin problems. Dutch researchers writing in the journal *Thorax* found that two-year-old children who consumed whole milk and butter, both rich in vitamins A and D, were more likely to be free of asthma at the age of three than two-year-olds who drank low-fat milk and ate no butter.[9] Several other research studies show that growing children need more fat than protein in their diets. A diet that is low in fat and high in protein produces tall, skinny, and nearsighted individuals due to vitamin A depletion.[10]

> " Research studies show that a deficiency of dietary fats and oils contributes to the development of various ailments, including eclampsia during pregnancy, liver disease, and skin problems. "

The traditional diet of the Inuit who lived above the Arctic Circle was composed almost entirely of meat and fat. Yet only 35 to 40 percent of their diet was made up of meat; the remaining 60 percent consisted of fat. John Speth, an archaeologist at the University of Michigan's Museum of Anthropology, states, "There is plenty of evidence that the hunter/gatherers in all regions of the world discarded fat depleted animals even when food was scarce."[11]

The Dangers of Eliminating Saturated Fat from the Diet

Until a little over fifty years ago, people ate saturated fat as a matter of course. Red meat well marbled with fat and liberal amounts of gravy poured over the meat, along with mashed potatoes and butter, were the dinner staples in most households. And it was common to have eggs every day for breakfast. The latter practice, it turns out, was good for mental function, according to a study carried out at the University of California, Berkeley. Two groups of men were compared. One group suffered from one form or another of dementia, including Alzheimer's disease, and the other group did not. There was only one significant difference in their diets. The group of eighty-year-olds who were mentally alert ate at least one egg daily; the group with deteriorating mental function did not.[12] (See the sidebar "Why I Recommend Eggs.")

But eggs, dairy products, and red meat, because of their high cholesterol content, came under attack in the 1950s, and as a result, the American diet changed direction. Polyunsaturated oils, fish, chicken, and rice began making inroads on the traditional dinner menu of meat and potatoes, while processed cold cereals and muffins replaced the customary bacon-and-eggs breakfast. Research studies conducted in the 1950s laid the groundwork for this change in eating habits. They purportedly showed that during World War II, when the Europeans were deprived of eggs, butter, and other foods high in saturated fats and cholesterol, they didn't die of heart attacks in such large numbers as they did before the war. These conclusions were erroneous. Fifty thousand autop-

Why I Recommend Eggs

The saturated fat in eggs has a purpose. It breaks down and assimilates the protein in eggs. That's why eggs are easily digested and the reason I recommend them in substantial amounts for both the grain eater and meat eater. They are so thoroughly broken down in the digestive tract that there is no acid waste debris left over to poison the body. Remember, eggs are the sole food source for embryos, so nature created in the egg a food with all the nutrients in perfect balance.

sies of people who died during World War II when saturated fats were scarce showed advanced hardening of the arteries. They just died too young to have heart attacks! (See the section on cholesterol in my book, *The Acid-Alkaline Balance Diet.*)

A long-term research study, published as a book in 1980, strengthened the claims of those who championed a low saturated fat diet.[13] The study, which lasted more than twenty years, tracked the health and eating habits of twelve thousand middle-aged men who came from seven different countries: the Greek islands, Italy, Yugoslavia, the Netherlands, Finland, Japan, and the United States. The objective of the study, referred to as the Seven Countries Study and conducted by Dr. Ancel Keyes, a physiologist from Minnesota, was to find out which country had the healthiest diet. The results indicated that the Mediterranean diet of the Greek islands and Italy produced men in the best physical shape; the runner-up was Japan.

Keyes attributed the superior health of the subjects on the Mediterranean and Japanese diets to their consumption of unsaturated oils, and the poor health of the other subjects to the saturated fat in their diet. Thus Keyes' conclusions lent support to the idea that at the time had captured the attention of the medical profession and public alike: that saturated fat was harmful to the cardiovascular system.

This fixation prevented Keyes from giving enough weight to other food items in the diets as part of the explanation as to why the Mediterranean and Japanese diets were healthier. There were, in fact, additional reasons that could account for the superior health of the subjects on the Mediterranean and Japanese diets. During the time the study was going on, the Italians, Greeks, and Japanese ate a lot of freshly caught fish and fresh, lightly cooked vegetables, whereas the diet of the less healthy men included canned foods, food that was overcooked, and very few fresh vegetables. But Keyes' conclusion that saturated fat in the other subjects' diets accounted for their poorer health confirmed the conviction that was making a lot of waves at the time and still is: that saturated fat, because it raises blood cholesterol levels, is bad for the heart and circulatory system.

In the 1960s, a man named Phil Sokolof did even more to popularize a diet low in saturated fat and high in polyunsaturated oils. At the age of forty-three, Sokolof had a heart attack that came close to killing him. Convinced that his cholesterol level of 300 was the cause, he became a crusader on behalf of a diet that was practically free of saturated fat. To carry out his message, he established a foundation that conducted campaigns educating the public to the dangers of saturated fat and cholesterol. But Sokolof based his conviction on a false premise: that cholesterol readings of 300 and over are directly related to heart attacks and stroke.

Sokolof, who died of heart failure at eighty-three,[14] was apparently never aware of research studies that show no direct link between heart attacks and cholesterol—until cholesterol readings climb into the stratosphere. As for the low saturated fat diet, a study conducted by the International Atherosclerosis Project shows that atherosclerosis is as prevalent among vegetarians as meat eaters.[15] In fact, eating some saturated fat appears to prolong life, according to a study published in the medical journal *Circulation* that shows that the death rate from all causes is higher than the national average in individuals with cholesterol levels lower than 180 mg/dl.[16]

Polyunsaturated oils such as corn oil, safflower oil, and sunflower oil, not saturated fats, are the major culprits in heart disease. In a British study published in *Lancet*, several thousand men were put on a diet in which saturated fats were reduced, unsaturated oils increased, and smoking prohibited. One year later, these subjects had experienced 100 percent more deaths than those on a saturated fat diet that was sparse in polyunsaturated oils and whose subjects continued to smoke![17] That nature recognizes the body's need for saturated fat is indicated by the fact that more than 50 percent of the calories in mother's milk is fat, *almost all of it saturated.*[18]

Which Fats and Oils Should You Eat?

Your choice of fats and oils should depend on which ones you digest best. If you are a grain eater, you can digest a greater quantity of polyunsaturated oils because these come from plants, and grain eaters are essentially plant eaters. These oils have another advantage: they speed up the grain eater's sluggish digestion. The meat eater does well on butter, meat fat, and nuts and seeds because they slow his or her overactive digestion.

Just as our Ice Age ancestors ate nuts and seeds by cracking open the shell rather than extracting the oil, so should we. Extracted oil oxidizes when exposed to heat and light. Another reason to avoid bottled polyunsaturated oil is that it's easy to eat too much of it. When you use polyunsaturated oil for cooking and put it in soups, sauces, salad dressing, and so on, the body receives an overload. The oil not utilized undergoes changes in its chemical structure and becomes rancid. It's hard for the body to eliminate rancid oil so it stays in the body, generating free radicals that destroy oxygen.

> **" "** That nature recognizes the body's need for saturated fat is indicated by the fact that more than 50 percent of the calories in mother's milk is fat, *almost all of it saturated.* **" "**

The Case Against the High-Protein Diets

The renewed popularity of beef, due largely to Robert Atkins' high-protein, low-carbohydrate diet, is the cause of the comeback of a crime that was once rampant in the Old West but died out in the nineteenth century—cattle rustling. The rise in beef prices as a result of the increase in beef sales is responsible. Newborn calves, not yet branded, are being stolen from grazing lands on ranches, loaded into pickup trucks, and sold on the black market for a considerable profit.[19]

But the theft of calves may be much less of a problem than the situation that caused it—the increase in the consumption of beef. Too much of any kind of protein in the diet is dangerous to health. Just as a low-carb diet doesn't supply enough fuel to satisfy the body's energy requirements, Atkins' advice to eat as much red meat as it takes to satisfy the appetite not only goes against the body's fairly modest protein requirements, it also causes health problems. A high-protein diet creates an excessive amount of acid in the body that inflames tissues, provides a favorable environment for yeast and unfriendly bacteria, and increases the risk of kidney stones. Furthermore, a study cited in the *New York Times* found that adults on a low-carbohydrate, high-protein diet experienced a 50 percent loss of calcium in their urine.[20]

Another problem with eating too much protein is that, because the body is unable to store it, the body gets rid of it by using it as a fuel to make energy. Protein is the body's least favorite fuel source because the liver has to convert the protein to glucose before it can be used. This conversion eats up a lot of enzymes and energy, with the result that a given amount of protein generates much less fuel than the same quantity of either carbohydrates or fat. Using protein as fuel has another downside, which makes it easy to understand why the body prefers burning carbohydrates. Carbohydrates are a clean fuel. When burned, they produce carbon dioxide and water, which are effortlessly eliminated by the lungs, whereas the burning of protein gives off acid residues. The other downside to the use of protein as fuel is that the unused carbohydrates are converted to fatty acids and stored in the fat cells.[21]

Using excess protein as fuel is just one piece of evidence that points to the danger in following a low-carb, high-protein diet. Research on protein in the diet found that it should comprise no more than 15 percent of the diet. Dr. Vernon R. Young, a biochemist at the Massachusetts Institute of Technology—confirming the work of scientists who used mice and other rodents as subjects—helped establish the baselines for humans' daily nutritional requirements for protein. Young analyzed the blood and urine of students at MIT to determine the amount of proteins essential for the rebuilding of muscle and the movement of nutrients across the cell membranes. He concluded that protein should comprise just 15 percent of the diet.[22]

The conclusion that carbohydrates should make up 60 percent of the diet is backed up by the body's enormous energy needs, while the recommended 25 percent fat to 15 percent protein in the diet corresponds to the ratio of fat to protein in the body.

The 60-25-15 percent ratio of carbohydrates, fat, and protein in the diet is also consistent with the quantity of starch, fat, and protein enzymes produced by the digestive enzyme glands. Thus a high-protein diet over a long period of time depletes the protein-digesting food enzymes, forcing the body to use the enzymes reserved for breaking down cancer cells for the digestion of protein instead. Overconsumption of protein can also lead to vulnerability to infection. (See the sidebar "Overconsumption of Protein Promotes Low-Grade Infections.")

Overconsumption of Protein Promotes Low-Grade Infections

Charles' PSA (prostate specific antigen) level was around 1 until he reached his early sixties; then it shot up to 4. The doctor explained this rise in his PSA as the result of a low-grade infection in his prostate, possibly linked to a decrease in testosterone that comes with age. When the infection caused his white blood cell count to go above normal, Charles took antibiotics and his PSA dropped from 4 to 2, but the infection always recurred. Because testosterone helps prevent prostate infections, Charles tried to raise his testosterone levels by taking a combination of herbs that are high in this male hormone: saw palmetto, pygeum, red clover, and nettles, as well as zinc and vitamin B_6. The supplements made no difference either in his PSA level or his prostate infection.

Then, out of the blue, it was painful for Charles to urinate. A blood test indicated that he had a low-grade infection in his bladder. Could there be a connection, I wondered, between the chronic low-grade infection in his prostate and his bladder infection? Charles' prostate infection may have actually started in the bladder. The bladder is directly above the prostate, so the circulating blood could have picked up germs in the bladder and deposited them in the prostate. Charles' urologist wasn't interested in this scenario; his concern was Charles' bladder infection because that was his present problem. He cited four possible causes: emotional stress, flying in an airplane, an infection in the lungs, or a head cold—without even considering diet!

Looking at the possibility that the same condition had caused an infection in both the prostate and the bladder, I suggested Charles' diet as the cause. He followed the grain-eater's diet, which was suitable for him, but the amount of protein he was eating, a one-pound serving of fish two or three times a week and most of a whole chicken twice a week, was excessive. What made me suspicious that this overload of protein was the cause of his bladder infection and his high PSA level was the elevated urea level in his urine.

Urea, a by-product of protein digestion, is inflammatory. The urea flows from the liver into the blood, the kidneys separate it out, and it becomes part of the urine. The elevated urea in Charles' urine, if chronic, would inflame the bladder, and an inflamed bladder acidifies the pH balance of the urine. Germs multiply in an acid medium, and when their numbers reach a critical level the immune system fights back by producing a higher than normal number of white blood cells, a sign of infection.

A few weeks after Charles cut down on his servings of fish and chicken and began eating more vegetables, his low-grade bladder infection cleared up and his PSA dropped from 4 to 2. Six months later, Charles hadn't had a recurrence either of the prostatitis or the bladder infection.

The Case Against the Glycemic Index

One or the other of the three basic food groups—meat, fat, or carbohydrates—has variously been held responsible by nutritionists and diet book authors for the rising incidence of obesity and health problems in the United States. In the 1980s many diet plans recommended avoiding or limiting red meat and saturated fat, and a number of diets still do. But the majority of the diet gurus today have focused their ire on carbohydrates. The two leading low-carbohydrate promoters, the late Robert Atkins[23] and Arthur Agatston,[24] argue that because carbohydrates raise blood sugar—the amount of sugar that a given food releases into the blood is measured by the glycemic index—those individuals who wish to lose weight and/or avoid diabetes should make carbohydrate foods the smallest part of their diet.

> ❝ The glycemic index measures how much a particular food causes blood sugar levels to rise. Foods with a glycemic index of 70 or more cause a considerable rise in blood sugar levels, foods that register a glycemic index of 56 to 69 raise blood sugar moderately, while foods whose glycemic index is 55 or less cause a very small rise in blood sugar. ❞

Eating too many refined carbohydrate foods does raise blood sugar, which can be dangerous to health, particularly in people who are overweight, because in the obese, fat molecules prevent insulin from lowering elevated blood sugar levels. When so much sugar remains in the blood that it spills over into the urine, the individual becomes diabetic.

Low-carb diet authors tend to assess carbohydrate-rich foods strictly on the basis of their glycemic index, without taking anything else into consideration. Many complex carbohydrates register high on the glycemic index but aren't particularly fattening and don't lead to diabetes because they don't spark food cravings.

On the other hand, when you eat a large quantity of foods that are high in refined carbohydrates—that is, starch—because these carbohydrates are not locked up in fiber, the foods are converted into sugar too quickly. The sugar enters the bloodstream all at once. This raises the blood sugar excessively, which in turn raises blood insulin levels. The overload of insulin takes so much glucose out of circulation that even if you just finished eating a meal containing large amounts of refined sugar and starch, you feel a craving for more of the same in order to bring blood glucose levels back up to normal. Eating additional portions of sugary or starch-laden foods causes the blood sugar to spike again, and the cycle starts all over.

While food products made with refined flour and sugar should be avoided because they cause blood sugar and insulin to fluctuate wildly, thereby fueling the appetite, there are other carbohydrate foods that, although registering high on the glycemic index, don't have that effect. Carbohydrate-rich foods such as whole grains, as well as vegetables and fruit, while high in sugar and/or starch, seldom trigger food cravings the way refined food products do—and therefore don't cause the blood sugar to oscillate.

Such foods seldom cause too much weight gain or trigger diabetes. For example, whole-wheat bread has a glycemic index of 68 and white bread registers 70, a negligible difference. Yet the individual who eats a slice or two of whole-wheat bread or pasta made with whole-grain flour is not nearly as likely to take additional helpings as someone who eats toast made with white bread or pasta or cake made with refined flour. Two other whole grains that have high glycemic indexes, millet (71) and couscous (65), are unlikely to be overindulged in, despite their high glycemic index, because they don't spark an appetite frenzy. The vegetable that is highest on the glycemic index is the parsnip, yet it is doubtful that very many people who eat parsnips acquire an addiction to them despite the elevation in blood sugar they cause. To complicate matters there are a few foods such as watermelon that contain a lot of sugar but don't register high on the glycemic index!

Another fault in the low-carb diet authors' across-the-board limitation on foods that register high on the glycemic index is that they don't take into consideration that people often eat high-glycemic foods together with foods that have moderate or low glycemic index readings, and as a result, the glycemic index readings average out. For example, a meal consisting of meat, mashed potatoes with butter, salad with olive oil, and a vegetable with fruit for dessert would have a glycemic index that is somewhere in the moderate category because it is made up of both high and low glycemic ranked foods. Such a meal is not especially known to generate a craving for additional helpings.

> " For the most part it is only the high glycemic foods that are made with refined flour and/or white sugar that spark the desire to binge and therefore lead to weight gain. "

Still, Agatston makes short shrift of any foods that contain more than a hint of starch or sugar. Even carrots are forbidden in the Agatston diet, although according to Dr. Marion Nestle it would take more than a pound of carrots to raise the blood sugar as high as the index warns.[25] (See the sidebar "Glycemic Load.")

Agatston's admonitions against any food, no matter how healthy, which contains more than a trace of sugar, is based on the assumption that all sugar causes the blood sugar to rise. That may be so, but there are sugars that stimulate the pancreas to produce more insulin, thereby lowering sugar levels in the blood.

Vegetables that contain many beneficial plant sugars, some of which stimulate the production of insulin, include all the root

Glycemic Load

An effort has recently been made to improve the accuracy of glycemic index readings by measuring the amount of carbohydrates in foods. This is referred to as the *glycemic load*. The glycemic load also measures how fast a carbohydrate-rich food turns into sugar. While foods with a low glycemic index usually have a low glycemic load, there are a few foods with a high glycemic index whose glycemic load measurement brings their glycemic index down somewhat.

vegetables as well as brown seaweed and shitake mushrooms—the latter are particularly high in such sugars.[26]

In most low-carb diet books glucose is the only sugar considered, even though its only use is as a fuel. Of the eight essential sugars, only glucose and two of the three sugars from which it is derived—sucrose and fructose—are linked to diabetes. One of the milk sugars, galactose, actually lowers blood sugar. Another is a plant sugar called *mannose*, which, although like glucose it is used by the cells to make energy, doesn't cause diabetes or the destruction of blood vessels in the eyes. Furthermore, it reduces inflammation caused by allergies. (See the sidebar "Plant Sugars and Glyconutrients.")

Not only do authors of low-carb diets fail to discriminate between healthy and unhealthy sugars, they also consider any food that is low on the glycemic index fit to eat. For example, Agatston includes in his diet such low-glycemic foods as lentils, soy milk, and low-fat, artificially sweetened yogurt. This is an example of how a single objective, in this case reducing weight by eating foods that are low on the glycemic index, prevents an author from recognizing the drawbacks such foods might have in terms of other health concerns.

Plant Sugars and Glyconutrients

Plant sugars in the body don't always exist alone; some of them bond with either protein (glycoprotein) or fat (glycolipid). These glyconutrients are located on the surface of every cell and serve as a communications link between cells. In that role they pass on orders to the immune defense cells to bind with invaders and antibodies; they also help keep the hormones in balance and help the blood to clot.

For one thing, while the individual with a grain-eater metabolism usually does very well on lentils and soy products, meat eaters are apt to have a problem digesting them. For another, artificial sweeteners, which Agatston recommends because they don't raise blood sugar levels like natural sugars do, are toxic. Agatston, however, does not address this issue. Both diet gurus forbid fruit and fruit juices in the early stages of their diets. They are right about fruit juice, given its huge concentrations of fructose. But if you are a grain eater, eating one or two whole fruits a day actually causes weight loss because the acid in fruit normalizes the grain eater's deficient stomach acids, thus improving protein digestion. Moreover, the grain eater digests fruit so slowly that it satisfies the appetite for a long time. Dr. Atkins, in his book *The New Diet Revolution*, forbids bananas altogether because of their high carbohydrate level. Not only does this ban deprive the body of the alkalinizing effect of the raw starch in bananas and the high levels of alkaline-forming potassium and magnesium that bananas contain, but it also deprives the body of a food that is dense enough to satisfy the appetite for a long time.

The conclusions drawn by the authors of a recent statistical research study on the subject of carbohydrates also play into the hands of the low-carbohydrate advocates.[27] They blame the finding that over a thirty-year period, women have increased their consumption of calories by 22 percent and men by 7 percent on the overeating of cookies, pasta, soda, potatoes, and bread—not differentiating between white and whole-grain bread and lumping potatoes and bread together with cookies, pasta made with white flour, and soda. Many mainstream nutritionists advised that the Department of Agriculture should decrease its recommended amounts of grains—without indicating that this decrease should come from a reduction in the consumption of refined, white flour products rather than whole-grain breads and cereals.

This confusion has caused many people to eliminate or cut down on healthy as well as unhealthy carbohydrates. For example, there has been a drop in sales of fruit juices because of the simple sugars they contain. This drop in sales is significant enough that the companies and farmers affected are fighting back. Citrus growers in Florida are spending millions of dollars on a new ad campaign.[28]

The low-carb mystique has also made deep inroads into beer sales because Arthur Agatston, in *The South Beach Diet*, wrote that beer contains maltose, a form of sugar. Annheuser-Busch has spent one million dollars on advertisements in thirty-one newspapers, including the *New York Times*, denying Agatston's claim. An eight-ounce bottle of beer contains ten grams of carbohydrates, but all the maltose in beer is converted, during the process of fermentation, into alcohol and carbon dioxide.[29]

There are signs, however, that the low-carb craze is losing steam. The NPD Group, a research firm that has tracked the popularity of low-carb diets for a number of years, found that the percentage of Americans on low-carb diets fell 4.6 percent in September 2004, from a high of 9 percent the previous January. These figures are given credibility by the disappointing sales of low-carb food products in general during the last few months of

2004.[30] One newly introduced low-carb product, pasta made with soy, despite a huge promotion, has yet to move from the shelves into shopping carts. (Beef sales, however, have increased, despite the fact that beef's popularity was fueled by low-carb diets.)

Like the enthusiasm behind all food crazes, the energy that fueled the fervor for low-carb diets is apparently starting to fizzle. But it's not only the inevitable waning of enthusiasm for what are after all fad diets that has caused a loss in the number of low-carb consumers, but also the death of its most charismatic leader, Dr. Robert Atkins. When it came out, after he died in 2003 as a result of a fall on an icy sidewalk outside his office, that he was grossly overweight and had coronary heart disease, many began to question whether the low-carb, high-protein diet he advocated was healthy after all.

The low-carb diet has been followed by a trend that targets a single carbohydrate: white sugar. One would think that this is a healthy direction for the low-carb craze to take, but only a few manufacturers have lowered the sugar content of their products. The majority of food product manufacturers are replacing natural, refined sugar with artificial sweeteners such as Splenda (sucralose) and Neotame. Artificial sugars are more dangerous to health than refined sugar. One of these artificial sweeteners, sucralose—according to a 1998 report issued by the Food and Drug Administration—was found, in a study of lymphoma in mice, to alter the structure of the genes making the onset of cancer more likely.[31]

Be Aware of Diet Fads

Fad diets and fast foods have found fertile ground in the United States because there is no traditional diet of healthy foods that would alert people to the danger of following trendy diet plans.

Nor would tradition prevent diet authors from picking and choosing from the mass of scientific data the facts that give a scientific underpinning to their diet plan, while ignoring the scientific information that goes against it.

> " Fad diets are fads because they don't last in the long run. Eating right for your metabolism is what makes sense. "

Thus Robert Atkins, while overlooking the scientific studies that might cast doubt on the health benefits of his low-carb, high-protein, high-fat diet—namely that carbohydrates should make up the greatest part of the diet and protein the smallest—drew attention instead to the fact that when carbohydrate consumption is low, the body—deprived of carbohydrates for the production of energy—burns fat instead. Atkins didn't mention that fat is a dirty fuel, giving off residues of ketones as it burns.

Low-fat diet authors take a different tack. They avoid mention of the body's fat requirement (25 percent of the total diet) by emphasizing the data for which the public has a far greater concern, that fats and oils contain more calories than either carbohydrates or protein.

A practice seemingly beneficial to health but impossible to maintain over the long run—to chew each bite of food one hundred times!—was advocated by Dr. Horace Fletcher at the turn of the twentieth century.[32] While based on research studies showing that the thorough mastication of food promotes good digestion, Fletcher's advice is an example of how some diet plans, despite their healthfulness, are humanly impossible to carry out.

The concept of judging foods as either good or bad for health depending on calorie amounts, blood profile readings, and nutritional guidelines issued by the federal government—a Senate committee headed by George McGovern issued a "dietary guideline" in which it suggested that red meat was dangerous to health—has spawned a healthy backlash. Some medical practitioners and nutritionists have taken issue with evaluating the nutritional benefits of food on the basis of what sometimes amounts to scientific sleight of hand. Instead, they see wisdom in folk medicine, which holds that good health can be achieved not by manipulating the ratio of starch, fat, and protein servings at a meal but by eating fresh unprocessed foods and by detoxifying the body. These alternative health advocates brought back the practice of juicing—using a juicer to extract the juice from vegetables or squeezing the juice of a lemon in a glass of water—to eliminate toxic wastes from the body.

Although a fervent believer in the health benefits of a good diet, Dr. John Harvey Kellogg, who in the early part of the twentieth century had a sanitarium in Battle Creek, Michigan, played heroes and villains with the nutritional needs of the body like the diet gurus of today. He excluded meat from his diet plans because he said it encouraged the growth of unfriendly bacteria and used Bulgarian yogurt as a substitute because it was said to cause the long lifespan of Bulgarians. He apparently didn't consider the fact that the long-lived Bulgarians also ate a lot of meat. In his all-grape diet, Kellogg focused on detoxification without a thought about the nutrients the detoxified body would need to rebuild itself.[33]

Vegetables and Fruits: Never a Fad

When choosing vegetables and fruits, select a rainbow of colors to ensure you gain the entire range of benefits they offer. The various pigments in plants confer particular health benefits.

* **Red and purple plants**—grapes, blueberries, strawberries, beets, eggplant, red cabbage, red peppers, plums, and red

apples—contain antioxidants that prevent the formation of blood clots.

* **Yellow and green plants**—spinach, collards, corn, green peas, avocado, and honeydew—include the pigments lutein and zeaxanthin, which help heal cataracts and macular degeneration and also reduce the risk of developing these eye problems.

* **Orange plants**—carrots, sweet potatoes, winter squash, and mangoes—have alpha carotene, a cancer fighter, and beta carotene, which helps repair damaged DNA. Oranges, peaches, papaya, and nectarines support the transmission of nerve impulses between cells and strengthen the cardiovascular system.

* **Green vegetables**—broccoli, brussels sprouts, cabbage, kale, and bok choy—have anticancer properties.[34]

Vegetables also help raise mineral levels in the body—provided there are enough fat-soluble vitamins A and D in the diet to assimilate the minerals. Because individuals who have excessive levels of some minerals are usually deficient in others, they need to eat more of the vegetables that will normalize their deficient mineral levels and less of those that contain large amounts of the minerals in which they are oversupplied. Because it is in the pigment of plants that many of the minerals and other nutrients in plants are stored, the choice of vegetables depends to some extent upon color. For example, anyone with a potassium deficiency needs green, leafy plants because the dark green pigment in these leafy plants contains high levels of potassium; on the other hand, eating white, orange, yellow, and light green plants increases calcium levels in the body. When we lack a particular nutrient, we also lack one of the pigments that store this nutrient. (See the sidebar "Fruit and Vegetable Choices for Grain and Meat Eaters.")

Fruit and Vegetable Choices for Grain and Meat Eaters

Your choice of fruits and vegetables should be based on your metabolism.

- Grain eaters should satisfy their need for red/purple, yellow, and orange pigment by eating more fruit containing these pigments than vegetables: blueberries, strawberries, plums, red apples, honeydew melon, mangoes, oranges, and peaches. Their need for green pigment is satisfied by eating kale, spinach, and collards.
- Meat eaters should satisfy their need for red/purple, yellow/green, and orange pigment by eating more vegetables than fruit with these pigments: beets, eggplant, red cabbage, red peppers, corn, green peas, avocados, carrots, sweet potatoes, winter squash, broccoli, brussels sprouts, green cabbage, and bok choy.

How to Lose Weight

Practical Suggestions for

Taking Off Pounds

This chapter offers guidance and suggestions that can help you lose weight after you have discovered what type of eater you are—meat eater, grain eater, or omnivore—and have started the appropriate diet. You'll find three potato recipes that reduce the appetite by neutralizing acidity in the body; suggestions for achieving regularity and ending your caffeine addiction (which takes off pounds by eliminating excess acid); a discussion of minerals that cause weight loss; practical tips on how to maximize your body's production of energy in order to burn excess fat; short and easy fasts that take off weight by cleaning out the body; and a raw food that absorbs fat molecules.

Our Paleolithic Ancestors Didn't Have Weight Problems

The Ice Age peoples who hunted and gathered food, like people today who buy their food in supermarkets, experienced elevations in their blood acid levels. Then, as now, enzymes converted the acid overload into fat molecules (fatty acids). But the conversion of acid into fat didn't cause obesity until people stopped eating the foods that nature provided and began growing their own.

In hunting and foraging cultures, the rise in blood acid levels was triggered by fear and anxiety—not by the wrong foods. Blood hyperacidity was advantageous to survival because it accelerated energy production. But while the resulting escalation in energy enabled the hunter-gatherer to respond quickly to danger, its by-product, acetic acid, caused blood acid levels to spike even higher. To prevent acidification of the blood's acid-alkaline pH, acetic acid is converted to fatty acid and stored in fat molecules. Still the hunter-gatherer never had a weight problem because blood hyperacidity occurred only during crises. Once life returned to normal, blood acid levels dropped. Thus any weight gain due to the conversion of acid particles to fat would have been temporary. Proof that weight problems were unknown to the hunter-gatherer can be found in the isolated groups of hunting peoples living in remote areas of the world today. There are no obese people among them.

In today's world, high blood acid levels have a different cause: the routine consumption of inappropriate food. This makes hyperacidity a chronic condition and results in the unending conversion of acid waste into fat. Excess weight is thus directly related to elevated acid waste levels caused by eating the wrong foods. (Emotional stress can also cause acid levels to rise. See the section "Control Your Stress Levels" later in this chapter.)

Individuals who eat foods they can't digest, as they get older, gain weight so rapidly that regular, vigorous exercise can't burn up the fat as fast as it is generated. Their excessive weight is of course stored in fat cells. As long as the individual eats moderately and eats foods that are digested well, fat cells serve a useful purpose—they store fat, for which the body has many uses.[1] But the fat cells of individuals who binge on junk food become like autoimmune cells; they trigger actions that destroy body tissue.

Enlarged Fat Cells Cause Health Problems

Long thought to be nothing more than storage units for fatty acids, fat cells have been found recently by medical researchers to be extremely complex, acting in concert like independent life forms.[2] They try to heal the "injuries" they perceive the body has sustained but take actions that have the opposite effect.

This happens because as fat cells multiply and become enlarged, their judgment becomes skewed, causing them to view their own multiplication and swelling as a response to a life-threatening injury. One of the "therapeutic" chemicals the fat cells trigger causes an increase of blood flow to the site where the fat cells perceive an injury to be located. The immune cells, taking their cue from the fat cells, also respond as though the body had sustained an injury, by inducing the production of macrophages, which augment the inflammatory condition caused by the fat cells. Because in reality there are no injuries, the inflammation induced by the fat cells and macrophage cells doesn't go away. It becomes chronic. As long as the fat cells are too numerous and inflated out of proportion, the tissues remain inflamed and begin breaking down.

Fat cells also secrete estrogen and activate cortisol. These stress-promoting hormones gear the body for fighting off the imagined enemy by causing the heart and breathing rate to increase and by sharpening the mental processes. But when the anticipated physical action doesn't take place, some of the acid particles in the blood are converted into fatty acids and stored in the fat cells, causing the number and size of the fat cells in the body to increase further. Another problem with an elevated fat cell population in the body is that it triggers lower than normal amounts of leptin, a hormone that lessens hunger.

Here is where a diet customized to the individual's unique digestive requirements comes in. Because it is digested handily, it keeps acid waste levels to a minimum so less acid waste is converted to fat. It also normalizes mineral levels, allowing the body to absorb and utilize fats so there is less leftover fat to be stored in the fat cells. (You can also reduce acid waste by taking enzyme supplements to improve digestion. A few drops of alkaline water added to liquids or to rice or other grains also helps neutralize acidity.)

Eating Metabolically Controls Hunger and Takes Off Weight

Using gimmicks to take off pounds, such as keeping a diary of everything you eat, weighing your food, counting calories or points, joining a support group, or writing about the foods you long for to "get them out of your system" seldom works for long. Food cravings reassert themselves, sometimes even more insistently because they've been suppressed. Reducing calories by eating less food doesn't work either because when weight is lost, the genes interpret this to be a sign of starvation. So they alert glands in the stomach to secrete the hormone ghrelin, which increases hunger, causing the dieter to eat greater quantities of food than he or she did before going on a diet. That's why yo-yo dieting is so prevalent.

Hunger pangs eventually overcome the desire to lose weight. The individual on a diet can only hold back the desire to eat for so long, and then the dam bursts. She or he says, in effect, "the heck with it" and goes on a binge. Going on diets, losing weight, and then gaining it back, when it becomes cyclical, is dangerous to health. A recent study shows that it can damage the immune system. Dr. Cornelia M. Ulrich of the Fred Hutchinson Cancer Research Center in Seattle questioned 114 overweight but otherwise healthy women over the age of fifty. The women who had gone on a diet five or more times had fewer immune cells; the highest level of immune cells was found among women whose weight had been stable for several years. Even women who had only twice lost large amounts of weight showed a decrease in the immune cells.[3]

> **"** Hunger pangs eventually overcome the desire to lose weight. **"**

Eating too much at a time is also unhealthy because it can damage the esophageal valve. This is the valve that separates the stomach from the esophagus. When this valve is continually stretched open by unnaturally large masses of food in the stomach, it loses its elasticity. The result is a backup of acid from the stomach into the esophagus, acid reflux, which inflames the esophagus because it doesn't have a thick mucous lining like the stomach. (The stomach needs a lining to protect it from the irritating effect of digestive acids.)

Night Binging: The Greatest Deterrent to Losing Weight

Most people are overweight because they experience such ravenous hunger that even the most disciplined are unable to resist eating. They crave food for the same reason that alcoholics crave whiskey or wine—they feel restless and tense. These symptoms occur most often at night. Many people with appetite problems can't get to sleep unless they binge before going to bed. Some people wake up in the middle of the night and can't get back to sleep unless they raid the refrigerator first. Only mounds of junk food satisfy the appetite when hunger is so powerful that it's impossible not to give in to it.

When you eat the wrong foods during the day, by nighttime the buildup of acid waste has become so extensive that it sets the appetite raging. Food bingers tell me that an acid feeling in the throat or stomach is often the spark that ignites hunger. Gorging on crackers, cheese, chips, and cookies takes the acid feeling away for a time and relieves the hunger pangs. But a junk food binge causes a renewal of acidity in the throat and stomach that fuels another eating spree.

The symptoms of indigestion caused by eating the wrong foods are not always easily recognized as such. Restlessness, itchiness, headaches, a stuffy nose, painful muscles, dizziness, and eye aches are just as often signs of hyperacidity as stomachaches, acid reflux, and nausea. Given the health problems that result from binging, how can the desire to binge be put to rest?

Because calorie-dense foods, especially those made with refined flour and sugar, set up a craving for more of the same, experts tell us to replace rich, heavy foods with large amounts of fruit and vegetables. Dr. Barbara J. Rolls, a professor of Behavioral Health at Pennsylvania State University, writes that because people tend to eat foods that are the same total weight at every meal, all they need do to lose weight is eat foods whose weight, while the same as that of denser foods, is due to their water content rather than their calories.[4] Many people find, however, that when they replace the calorie-rich foods they're used to eating with large volumes of fruit and vegetables, their hunger is not satisfied. That's why so many dieters have turned to the Atkins diet. Meat protein and fat, especially when carbohydrate intake is low, reduce appetite, at least for a time.

There is only one way to eliminate food cravings permanently, and that is to eliminate the acid waste that is their major cause. (Hippocrates, the celebrated ancient Greek physician, in 400 B.C. wrote in his book *Antiqua Medicina* that the best solution to stomach acidity is regurgitation.) To lower the acid waste levels in the digestive tract that are responsible for igniting ravenous hunger, eat foods that suit your metabolism and alkalinize your body with the three potato recipes I outline later in this chapter. (See the next section, "Alkalinize Your Body to Eliminate

Food Cravings.") The potato recipes sometimes work by doing away with the desire to binge; or they spread the hunger pangs out over the entire day, preventing the highs and lows—the lack of desire for food in the morning and the ungovernable food cravings late at night.

When acidity is no longer a problem, the craving for junk food lessens and the level of the appetite-stimulating hormone ghrelin falls because the body is getting all the nutrients it needs. When an overload of acid waste is not generated, there is no excess acid waste to be converted to fatty acids and stored in fat cells. And when food is digested well, the body's ideal weight can be maintained over a long period of time.

Keep in mind, however, that food cravings are sometimes sparked by the body's need for a specific nutrient. For example, an individual who is eating right but who has a problem utilizing calcium might develop a craving for cheese and by eating large amounts of it satisfy his or her body's calcium requirements. Therefore, in order to successfully lose weight it's important to make sure you are getting all the nutrients your body needs.

Dieting shouldn't be about eating low-calorie foods or small portions—"portion control" as it is sometimes referred to—or reducing fats or carbohydrates. It's about eating foods that are easily digested, which lessen the appetite and eliminate food cravings. When you're eating appropriately and have worked one of the potato appetite quenchers into your diet, which almost never fails to take away food cravings, you'll have achieved the objectives of this book: weight loss, good health, and good prospects for a long life.

Alkalinize Your Body to Eliminate Food Cravings

There is only one way to eliminate food cravings permanently, and that is to eliminate the acid waste that causes them. Customizing your diet to your own digestive metabolism is the first step in lowering the acid waste levels in the digestive tract that are responsible for igniting the appetite. The second step is to alkalinize your body regularly.

Of all foods, the greatest alkalinizer is the white potato when prepared in such a way that the alkaline compounds are made available to the body. That's why it's such a potent appetite quencher. Prepared in a special way, it reduces and sometimes completely eliminates the excess hunger that can defeat the most dedicated of dieters.

There are three ways of fixing potatoes, each one yielding slightly different health benefits, but all having a dampening effect on appetite: semi-raw (lightly cooked), grated raw and cooked in a minimum amount of water, and sliced raw and then simmered in water to form a highly alkaline watery soup. (See the upcoming sections "Semi-Raw Potatoes," "Grated Potatoes," and "Alkalinizing Potato Water" for the three recipes.) A regular diet of one or more of these potato recipes will lessen hunger by neutralizing acid waste in the digestive tract.

Potatoes prepared in the three ways mentioned are easily digested by both the grain eater and the meat eater, even though potatoes, cooked until they are soft, are considered good for grain eaters because they speed up their sluggish digestion and bad for meat eaters because they cause their overly rapid digestion to speed up even more. When, however, they are prepared semi-raw or grated raw and then cooked, or made into a watery drink, they have no effect one way or the other on the rate of digestion. Semi-raw potatoes and the grated potato mixture take a little longer to digest, but not long enough to slow the sluggish rate of digestion of the grain eater or speed the too rapid digestion of the meat eater.

Reducing acidity in the body using the potato recipes, and by doing so eliminating food cravings, is far more conducive to weight loss than any of the following: cutting down on carbohydrates, eating less red meat, reducing the intake of fats and oils, or curbing the consumption of natural sugars (honey and fruit). In fact you should eat generous portions of those fats and oils in your metabolic food category if you want to keep the weight you lost off. And if you're a grain eater you can eat all the fruit you want and still lose weight.

The alkaline nature of white potatoes, whether prepared in the special ways described here or eaten raw—due to mucilage and starch as well as to high levels of potassium and other alkaline minerals in the outer pulp and skin—not only decreases hunger but also eliminates acid indigestion. Eating a piece of raw potato just before consuming a food that causes hyperacidity can prevent indigestion. Even eating a chunk or two of raw potato after you get acid reflux can neutralize the acid feeling in your throat and stomach. The acid taste that sometimes forms in the mouth after drinking a cup of coffee or tea is also eliminated by a slice or two of a raw potato, because the alkaline particles in raw potatoes restore the alkaline pH balance of the mouth. Remember, any time acid levels in the body are reduced, weight is lost.

> " Eating a piece of raw potato just before consuming a food that causes hyperacidity can prevent indigestion. "

Semi-raw potatoes, grated potatoes, and potato alkalinizing water eliminate the abnormally high levels of acid in the digestive tract that cause excessive weight and obesity—as well as serious digestive disorders such as ulcers, colitis, diverticulitis, and Crohn's disease. After being on the semi-raw potatoes or grated potatoes for a few months, weight drops and health problems vanish.

The best way to alkalinize the whole body is to drink one or more glasses of potato water every day because, being a fluid, it gets into every nook and cranny in the body. As this highly alkaline water circulates in the blood and lymph vessels and in the interstitial fluid surrounding the cells, and then flows into the fluid inside the cells, it neutralizes acid waste particles from undigested foods and from metabolic waste products. It also eliminates the acids triggered by allergy-induced histamines, thus reducing allergic symptoms. By reducing acid particles in the body and thus preventing their conversion into fatty acids, you will automatically lose weight.

Each of the three potato recipes yields slightly different health benefits and takes a different amount of time to become effective. You'll add semi-raw potatoes to your diet for a few months before you notice you're not as hungry as you had been, but stomach pain and acid reflux lessen in a much shorter time. The healing effects of grated potatoes, including a decrease in hunger pangs, can begin in as short a time as three or four days. This is also true of alkalinizing potato water. The regular consumption of raw potato chunks or slivers has the same dampening effect on the appetite.

Semi-Raw Potatoes

The beneficial effects of semi-raw potatoes are long term. You need to make them a regular part of the diet for two to five months before they decrease hunger, but they heal inflamed gastrointestinal tissues and acid reflux sometimes in a few weeks. You can add vegetable to make a more nutritious and filling meal. (For many people with acid reflux, this is about the only food they can digest.)

A small frying pan is preferable to a pot because the potatoes can be cooked in much less water. This makes for a greater concentration in the water of potato flavor—as well as nutrients—so that it is has a very pleasant taste. This makes it easier to drink the cooking water, so you are less likely to pour it down the drain.

Cut the desired number of potatoes into chunks, preferably leaving the skin on, and place in a small, heavy frying pan. Add water. It should not quite cover the potato chunks. Cover and cook over low heat. The potatoes are finished cooking when they have begun to soften but are still crisp.

Grated Potatoes

Grated potatoes make a good side dish at dinner. They are worth the trouble that preparing them entails because they contain so much mucilage, and this curbs the appetite, sometimes in as little as three or four days.

First peel the potatoes. This releases more mucilage. Then grate. Grating the potatoes splits open the fiber so the heat can release the mucilage. Place the potato slivers in an 8-inch frying pan. Add water, but don't quite cover the potato slivers. (If you add too much water to the potato, not as much mucilage is released.) Put a lid on the pan. Turn the heat to medium high, and after the mixture starts to bubble, keep the heat medium high for 2 or 3 minutes and then turn to medium or low and continue cooking for 5 to 10 minutes. It is sometimes necessary to add a little more water. In 10 to 15 minutes, but sometimes sooner, a gummy mass should form. The potato slivers should be soft, because the point of the cooking is not to preserve enzymes and vitamins but to release as much mucilage as possible.

Variation of Grated Potato Recipe

Peel one large potato and grate. Melt 3 teaspoons butter in an 8-inch frying pan. Add the grated potato slivers and 8 teaspoons of water. Cook at medium heat for 3 to 4 minutes. Turn down the heat and cook for about 4 more minutes or until the potato slivers are soft.

Alkalinizing Potato Water

Drink one or more glasses of this potato water daily. After drinking the potato water for two or three months, excessive hunger disappears.

Slice two medium-sized potatoes with the skins left on, and place in a small pan. Cover with more than enough water to fill a mug, because some of the water vaporizes. Bring to a boil, turn down the heat, and simmer for 15 minutes. Drain the water into a mug and throw out the potatoes because all the nutrients in the potatoes have leached into the water.

Eating the grated potato mixture and/or drinking alkalinizing potato water has the advantage of not only normalizing weight, but also healing any health problems that the semi-raw potatoes haven't taken care of. Using some or all of these potato recipes should result in most symptoms vanishing.

Weight Loss Tips

This section contains more tips on choosing foods, reducing and eliminating toxins, increasing calorie burning, changing eating habits, and making lifestyle changes that will help you control your appetite and balance your body to promote weight loss.

Use Hot Baths and Sour or Bland Foods to Reduce Appetite

When you're ravenous, soaking in a bathtub filled with hot water takes the edge off the appetite by alkalinizing the urine and the lymph fluids.

There are also foods that reduce hunger pangs. Eating sour-tasting foods such as yogurt, vinegar, and lemon or lime juice before a meal cuts the appetite by shrinking the taste buds. Sour-tasting foods do not cause hyperacidity—unless you have a problem handling them. Grain eaters, who don't have enough stomach acid, can eat more sour foods than meat eaters, who have too much stomach acid.

    ❝ When you're ravenous, soaking in a bathtub filled with hot water takes the edge off the appetite by alkalinizing the urine and the lymph fluids. **❞**

You can prevent exciting the taste buds by avoiding foods containing spices and herbs and by choosing bland foods as often as possible. The only bland foods that don't quell hunger, and in fact have the opposite effect, are refined carbohydrates such as spaghetti, breads, and desserts made with white flour and/or refined sugar. By spiking blood sugar levels, they cause the appetite to skyrocket.

Eat Meat Free of Pesticides, Antibiotics, and Hormones

There are measures you can take to lose weight that don't involve eating foods that are low in calories. If you are a meat eater and eat agribusiness meat, that is, meat you bought in the supermarket that is not labeled either organic or natural, you will have a hard time losing weight. But if you switch to beef, lamb, pork, and veal that come from grass-fed animals, you can lose as much as 20 percent of your total weight. Both natural and organic meat come from animals that have been fed on grass or grains such as corn or soy that contain no antibiotics, hormones, or insecticides.

Burn More Calories

You lose weight by burning up the fat stored in the fatty layers under the skin. Eating small amounts of food frequently instead of three big meals a day gets rid of fat because when digestion is constant, stored fat is being continuously burned.

You can also increase the rate at which food is burned up by drinking a glass of ice water right before you eat. Food is burned up faster because the ice water reduces body temperature, and in order to bring the temperature back to normal the body has to burn additional calories.

Probably the best way to burn up excess calories is to eat two tablespoons of coconut oil daily. Coconut oil is the most efficient fuel because it doesn't need to be broken down and detoxified in the liver so none of the energy potential of the oil is wasted. All the coconut oil you eat will be burned up as fuel, so that none of it will add to your weight or stick to your arteries. Furthermore, as the coconut oil in your body is being oxidized, it burns up excess body fat. Two tablespoons of coconut oil a day usually takes off fifteen to twenty pounds in two to three months.

Exercising causes weight loss by speeding up the metabolism, which burns additional fat. Like diet, exercise is an individual matter. Nevertheless, just as there are certain foods that are unhealthy, so there are unhealthy forms of exercise, like jogging and other high-intensity exercise that affect the cartilage, muscles, and bones. Walking up and down hills or stairs as well as on flat ground for one hour five times a week is one of the safest, healthiest, and most weight loss effective forms of exercise. Start out walking at a leisurely pace and gradually build up speed.

Detoxify Your Liver

When the liver is functioning efficiently, it neutralizes more acid waste—which can then be eliminated from the body—than it does when it is congested with toxic waste. This is especially important for anyone wishing to lose weight because cleaning out the liver reduces the body's load of acid waste that would otherwise be converted by enzymes into fat. The best detox program for the liver I know of uses blackstrap lemon drink. To prepare it, mix two heaping tablespoons of blackstrap molasses and the juice of one lemon in a glass of hot water. Drink nothing but this concoction for three days running. Repeat the protocol every few months.

Eliminate Caffeine

Some people never take a drink of an alcoholic beverage because of a family history of alcoholism. They know that even one drink may lead them down the road to alcoholism. Caffeine, like alcohol, is habit forming. Caffeinated soft drinks are also addictive. So if you come from a family that drinks coffee or tea or soft drinks to excess, it would probably be wise to take a lesson from those alcoholism-prone people who stay away from hard drinks and avoid caffeinated beverages altogether.

But who thinks as they drink their first cup of coffee or take their first swig of cola that they may end up addicted to it? Most people, by the time they are in their early twenties, have already "crossed the Rubicon," so to speak, and become hooked on coffee, tea, or soft drinks.

As people age, more than two cups of coffee or tea a day progressively becomes harder for the digestive system to process. The high level of acid in coffee, tea, and soft drinks like colas acidifies the foods in the digestive tract that are exposed to it, and the resulting acid waste sparks hunger. People who give up caffeine by substituting decaffeinated coffee or tea for the real thing are only getting rid of part of the problem. They are still loading up on acid. Caffeine, being an alkaloid, isn't the problem. It's the other ingredients in coffee, tea, and colas that are acid producing. If you do choose to drink decaffeinated coffee or tea, however, it is best to decaffeinate them yourself because toxic metals are used in the commercial decaffeination process. See the sidebar "How to Decaffeinate Coffee or Tea."

> **"** As people age, more than two cups of coffee or tea a day progressively becomes harder for the digestive system to process. **"**

Some people use coffee in an effort to lose weight. In young adults it may work for a time. But when the effect of the coffee wears off, hunger returns, often more persistent than it would have been had the individual not gotten into the habit of drinking coffee. In middle-aged and older people, caffeine is even more likely to stimulate the appetite. No research studies have been done, as far as I know, on the question of whether coffee and tea actually have this effect on appetite in older people. I'm convinced, however, that caffeine becomes an appetite stimulant later on in life for two reasons: first, it acidifies the digestive tract, and second, people who gain excess weight as they get older tend to be big coffee drinkers.

How to Decaffeinate Coffee or Tea

If you drink decaffeinated coffee or tea, decaffeinate it yourself. That way you avoid contamination from the toxic metals used commercially to separate the caffeine out of the tea and coffee. Soak a tea bag or coffee grounds in a small amount of boiled water for about 30 seconds, squeeze the tea bag or coffee grounds with a spoon against the side of the container, and then throw the water out. This removes about 90 percent of the caffeine, leaving just enough to give you a lift.

The best thing to do is to eliminate caffeine from your diet altogether. See the sidebar "Kick the Caffeine Habit" for help in doing this.

Eat More Roughage

Some people think they weigh more than they should because they're chronically constipated. This is true, but not for the rea-

---

Kick the Caffeine Habit

The only way to lose an addiction to caffeine and thus remove one of the major factors in weight gain is to quit drinking caffeinated drinks altogether. Even a little coffee or tea maintains the addiction. If you have sworn off coffee or tea and are having withdrawal symptoms, don't drink a small amount of coffee or tea to ease the symptoms. A few sips is all it takes to keep the addiction alive. It's very hard to stop drinking a caffeinated beverage when you're addicted to it, but exercise helps. A friend, Susan, had been a coffee drinker for thirty years. Then one day she took up swimming. Shortly after that she gave up coffee. Years later, in thinking back on how she was suddenly able to stop drinking coffee, she realized it was because she had taken up swimming twice a week. She concluded that the swimming relaxed her enough that she no longer needed to drink coffee to unwind.

If you can't kick the coffee or tea drinking habit, or can't resist drinking it before breakfast on an empty stomach, you can partially eliminate its weight-producing effects by eating a few pieces of a raw potato or by drinking a glass of potato water. (See the sidebar "Alkalinizing Potato Water" for the recipe.) The alkaline particles in the mucilage and starch in the potato water neutralize the acidic residue from the coffee or tea.

son they think. They don't weigh more because the huge amount of waste in their colon has put on extra pounds. Their excess weight is caused by the toxic nature of the waste. The colon is the body's toxic waste dump. It is so filled with disease-causing bacteria that more than 60 percent of the immune cells in the body are located in the intestines. But even this great defense system can't destroy all the disease-carrying invaders if the waste in the colon is not eliminated regularly. And what isn't eliminated or detoxified by the immune system, the liver, or the lungs is converted to fatty acid and stored in the fatty layers under the skin. This is one of the major reasons that people put on weight. Toxins can also cross the colon into the bloodstream and inflame the tissues exposed to them.

Good health and a slim body are both promoted by regular bowel movements. How is this achieved? Foods high in insoluble fiber such as whole grains can prevent constipation. As fiber is transported through the digestive tract, peristalsis, the pulsating motion in the muscles that moves the fiber along, increases. This keeps the intestinal tract muscles in shape so waste is eliminated more easily. And because cellulose fibers pass through the intestines unaffected by any of the digestive juices, they are still in good enough shape to transport nonfibrous waste to the colon.

Soluble fibers also play a role in maintaining the health of the colon. Starch and dextrin fibers, which are soluble, are found in fruits, vegetables, seeds, rye, barley, and rice bran. They achieve their healing power when they're dissolved by the digestive process into a gel-like (mucilaginous) substance. In its gelatinous state soluble fiber absorbs poisonous acids, thus preventing their conversion into fatty acids that, incorporated in fat cells, put on extra pounds. Soluble fiber also helps rebuild the mucous lining of the colon, small intestine, and stomach. It also keeps blood sugar levels at an equilibrium, enables digestion in the stomach to take place, lubricates the organs, and provides the insulation on the enzymes that transport energy to the cells.

Not all fibrous foods work for everyone. What makes good elimination possible for some may have no effect or actually make constipation worse for others. In part, the kind of roughage that works depends upon your metabolism. A grain eater is more likely to be able to maintain regularity by eating whole grains, fruit, and raw green leafy vegetables such as spinach, chard, and kale. Obtaining the appropriate roughage is more of a problem for the meat eater. The latter has to go easy on fruit and grains, and the root vegetables the meat eater digests well don't contain good roughage. But lettuce, especially romaine and iceberg lettuce, and raw celery are effective roughage for the meat eater. Some meat eaters find that lightly cooked endive and big helpings of cooked beets keep bowel function regulated.

Drinking four or five glasses of water a day is also important for bowel regularity. Water is essential for good bowel function, first, because regularity is dependent on good digestion and enzymes can't digest the food mass in the stomach unless it contains enough water. Second, purine, a nitrogenous waste, the toxic by-product of protein, must be dissolved in water before it can be eliminated along with other waste matter from the colon.

Be Mindful of Calcium and Zinc

Calcium and zinc are important for anyone who wishes to lose weight. Calcium is the only nutrient—with the exception of digestive enzymes—that in large amounts causes a loss of weight. The ability of a calcium-rich diet to promote the metabolism of fat and by doing so reduce weight is shown in a research study conducted in the 1990s in which a small group of hypertensive men ate two cups of low-fat yogurt a day. On this calcium-rich diet, the men lost, on average, eleven pounds at the end of one year. According to Dr. Robert P. Heaney, the author of this study and a professor of medicine at Creighton University in Omaha, Nebraska, three to four servings of calcium-rich food a day could cause the loss of fifteen pounds in one year.[5] (None of these servings should include milk, however, as explained in Chapter 3 in the section "Milk Can Sabotage Your Diet.")

While calcium-rich foods take off weight, eating foods that contain insufficient amounts of zinc causes weight to go up because a zinc-deficient diet increases the appetite. Liver, seafood, dairy products, and eggs are good sources of zinc. While grain products contain zinc in fairly high levels, it is in a less-available form than in animal products.

Eat Raw Foods to Increase Digestive Enzyme Levels

Weight gain caused by hyperacidity is partially offset by eating raw foods. Cooked foods raise stress hormone levels thereby causing the body to produce more nutrients than it needs. The nutrients the body can't use are converted into fat molecules and stored in the fatty tissues, thus adding unwanted pounds.

The fat-inducing effects of cooked foods can be reversed by eating enzyme-rich raw foods. Raw foods normalize stress hormone blood levels, and by doing so guarantee that the exact quantity of food molecules needed by the cells to function will be produced—and no more. Thus a healthy level of enzymes in the digestive tract—the result of consuming raw foods with each meal—ensures that no excess nutrients will be produced and converted into fat.

> " The nutrients the body can't use are converted into fat molecules and stored in the fatty tissues, thus adding unwanted pounds. "

That enzymes play a pivotal role in preventing the accumulation of fat is supported by an experiment in which one group of pigs were fed enzyme-free cooked potatoes, while the control group received raw potatoes. The pigs fed on cooked potatoes gained weight, while the pigs who ate potatoes raw, and therefore received the full complement of enzymes, didn't gain an ounce. Clearly then, all diet plans should include raw foods at each meal and, if possible, some between meals as well. (See menu plans in Part II.) Raw carrots are particularly effective in causing weight loss because they absorb fat molecules.

Raw foods that are high in calories are also high in enzymes. These include avocados, bananas, grapes, dates, pineapples, kiwi, mangoes, figs, papayas, white potatoes, unfiltered honey, and raw nuts. Juicing vegetables and fruit is another way of obtaining a good supply of enzymes because a large number of vegetables and/or fruit are needed to produce one glass of juice. (Use a juicer, such as the Champion juicer, that doesn't extract the juice from the pulp by using centrifugal force, which destroys enzymes.)

Except for raw nuts, the other enzyme-rich foods mentioned in the preceding paragraph don't contain high levels of protein-digesting enzymes. You can add to your protein enzyme levels by eating some raw protein foods. Many people are afraid that raw meat, fish, and eggs are contaminated with bacteria. In fact they are safe to eat provided certain precautions are taken. (See the sidebar "Is It Safe to Eat Raw Eggs?") Do not eat raw fish, meat, or eggs unless you know their source. Raw beef should come from steers that have been fed on grass or organic grains, but preferably on grass. They should also be free of antibiotics and hormones. Avoid all agribusiness meat and farmed fish, raw or cooked. Salmon should be wild, that is, from the ocean, not raised in man-made ponds loaded with antibiotics, pollutants, and sea lice. Even ocean fish shouldn't be eaten raw unless it has been disinfected. You can do this by coating both sides of the fish with salt, much as you would roll fish and chicken in flour or bread crumbs before baking. Let the salted fish stand at room temperature for two or three hours and then refrigerate overnight. Once the salt is dissolved in the watery part of the fish, it kills any infectious microorganisms that might be present, and the dissolved salt loses its salty taste. If you don't like the taste of raw fish, you can pre-

> ### Is It Safe to Eat Raw Eggs?
>
> As to whether or not raw eggs are safe to eat, the American Egg Board reports that research studies conducted by food scientists have found that the average consumer might encounter a salmonella-infected egg once in eighty-four years.[6] Because organic eggs weren't used in the research studies, the chance of eating a salmonella-infected egg laid by environmentally safe hens would probably be even more remote. The oft-repeated warning not to eat the white of a raw egg because a protein called avidin in the white destroys the B vitamin biotin is without any basis in fact. A compound in the yolk neutralizes the offending protein so the biotin isn't eliminated.

pare it by marinating it in lime juice. This kills the germs without destroying the enzymes. Marinate for two to three hours at room temperature, and then in the refrigerator for about fifteen hours.

Eat at the Right Time of Day

One to two hours after eating dinner at 6:30 in the evening, Bob and Amy Gerahty used to come down with acid indigestion. Although they didn't go to bed until 11:00 P.M., the symptoms lingered, preventing them from getting to sleep. They blamed their indigestion and insomnia on the food they ate for dinner. Their typical evening meal consisted of red meat, mashed potatoes with butter, salad, and a vegetable. Having heard so much about the harm a diet heavy in red meat and saturated fat can do to the heart and arteries, they became convinced that the food they had for dinner was at the root of their digestive problems. So they switched to chicken, fish, and polyunsaturated oils, but it didn't ease their indigestion. No matter what they ate for dinner they got acid reflux afterward. The years passed and they continued to lie awake at night with painful esophageal and stomach problems.

Finally it dawned on Amy that because they could eat just about anything for breakfast and lunch without experiencing any indigestion, maybe it wasn't what they ate for dinner but what time they had dinner that was the cause of their indigestion. So she moved their dinner back three and a half hours to three o'clock in the afternoon. They haven't had acid reflux since; their weight problems have also vanished.

Why is it that Bob and Amy have no trouble digesting a big dinner in the middle of the afternoon, but the same meal eaten three and a half hours later at 6:30 P.M. gave them indigestion? This is not unusual. Acid indigestion is far more common in the evening after dinner than at any other time of the day. It is quite likely that the cause is depressed energy levels. This is nature's way of preparing the body for sleep. With less than normal energy, fewer digestive enzymes are generated. The result is that in some individuals, the evening meal remains undigested and gives rise to a whole range of symptoms—including the most common, acid reflux. Amy and Bob have no gastric problems now that they eat their last meal of the day in the midafternoon, because it falls within the time period—between ten in the morning and five thirty in the afternoon—when the body's energy level is highest, indicated by a body temperature of 98.6 degrees Fahrenheit. When energy production in the body goes up, more digestive enzymes are produced.

Amy and Bob's story points out the fact that for many individuals food is more easily digested at lunchtime than at any other time of the day. If you want to continue eating foods that you are allergic or sensitive to, you're less likely to react to them between twelve and three o'clock in the afternoon. This is when the thyroid is at its most active and enzyme levels are highest. Enzyme levels are low in the morning because thyroid function is sluggish then, and they level off in the evening when thyroid function again begins to slow down.

> 66 If you want to continue eating foods that you are allergic or sensitive to, you're less likely to react to them between twelve and three o'clock in the afternoon. 99

If it were possible for everyone to eat the last meal at three o'clock in the afternoon—which amounts to a partial fast—many health problems, including obesity, would disappear. I recommended to an elderly couple, both of whom were very ill with cancer, that they have dinner in midafternoon and not eat anything else for the rest of the day. Although at the time I made the recommendation their doctor had told them that neither would live more than one year, they are still alive and enjoying life—ten years after they began eating dinner at three o'clock in the afternoon.

An offense to good health is eating badly at dinner, but even worse is eating unhealthy snacks late at night. Not only have digestive enzyme and thyroid function slowed to a crawl by then, when you sleep they slow down even more. People are most likely to get acid indigestion in the evening because at the end of the day hydrochloric acid, bile, and enzyme levels fall.

Remember, high acid waste levels in the body lead to weight gain. That's one good reason why liquids that become acidic in the digestive tract shouldn't be drunk in the morning on an empty stomach. Even if coffee and/or tea don't give you acid reflux, don't drink them before breakfast. When there is no food in the stomach, coffee and tea acidify. On the other hand, the best time of the day to eat fruit or drink fruit juice is in the morning when the stomach is empty, because fruit has an alkalinizing effect when the stomach is empty. When fruit is eaten later in the day when the stomach is full, it has an acidifying effect.

Control Your Stress Levels

If you have a sudden scare, an alarm response in your brain sends a signal to the body's adrenal glands. The glands, in turn, release a surge of stress-promoting hormones. This induces feelings of anxiety even after the stressful event is over, which can drive you to binge on calorie-rich foods. But once stress hormone levels return to normal, nervous tension subsides and your impulse to gorge on junk food dies out.

According to a study in which rats were used as subjects, eating calorie-rich foods to calm the nerves in stressful situations is a natural response that is biologically driven. Dr. Pecoraro, the author of the study, states that energy-rich food "provides a brake on the brain's chronic stress response. . . . Once energy stores are replenished, a signal, probably from fat, flows back to the brain saying it is all right to calm down. The chronic stress cycle is then turned off."[7]

For those, however, who feel tense most of the time, stress-promoting hormone levels in the blood remain elevated, driving such individuals into binging on a regular basis. The chronically anxious individual falls into the habit of eating junk foods, most often ice cream, pastries, and chips, because, by stimulating the pleasure sites in the brain, these foods have a calming effect. Scientists claim that there is a feedback loop in the brain that impels some anxiety-ridden people to binge.

The persistent eating of high-calorie junk foods ultimately has the same harmful effect on the body as the stress itself, because the wrong foods—like fear and anxiety—elevate the acid levels in the blood. This triggers the resurgence of the stress-promoting hormones, and the binging starts all over again. The acid produced by emotional stress as well as the acid waste from the junk food binges are converted to fatty acids that are stored in fat cells. This is how emotional stress can cause weight gain.

But emotional stress and indigestion from eating the wrong foods are not the only factors that increase acidity levels and fat in the body. So does vigorous exercise—bad news for those who try to lose weight by jogging, engaging in fitness programs, or other strenuous forms of working out. A study of 319 athletes presented at a meeting of the American College of Gastroenterology in Phoenix in 1999 found that exercising on treadmills, weight lifting, and riding on stationary bicycles increased acid levels in different parts of the digestive tract depending on what muscles got the most workout. Seventy percent of the athletes who got lower bowel symptoms such as diarrhea from excess acidity were those whose lower abdominal muscles were stretched the most and therefore received the greatest blood flow. Furthermore, 43 percent of the athletes who tensed their stomach muscles while exercising got heartburn from increased levels of acidity in the stomach. The study also found that athletes who exercised only on weekends were just as likely to suffer from the effects of hyperacidity as those who exercised four or five times a week.

Given that many people, despite getting acid indigestion after vigorous exercise, won't stop, and people who are anxious and fearful can't control their junk food sprees, how can the harmful effects of the resulting hyperacidity and weight gain be minimized? By eating an alkaline food substance. The most effective food, because of its high mucilage, starch, and alkaline mineral content, is the white potato—if properly prepared. (See recipes in the "Alkalinize Your Body to Eliminate Food Cravings" section in this chapter.) Bananas, because of their soft, starchy pulp, can also absorb and neutralize acids.

Eat 60 Percent Carbohydrates, 25 Percent Fat, and 15 Percent Protein

Although people differ in the kinds of protein, carbohydrates, and fat they can eat, almost everyone needs approximately the same proportion in terms of volume of these three food groups: 60 percent carbohydrates, 25 percent fat, and 15 percent protein.

If you consume complex carbohydrates, fats, and protein in the ratio of 60-25-15, you are far more likely to lose weight than if you don't observe this ratio. By providing your body with the quantities of carbohydrates, fat, and protein it needs to function most efficiently, there will be fewer acid waste by-products left over. When acid waste is minimal, none of it is converted to fat.

A different scenario unfolds if your carbohydrate intake is considerably under 60 percent. Your body lacks the fuel (carbohydrates) necessary to satisfy its enormous energy needs. As a result, your body functions slow down and can't eliminate the acid waste by-products of their metabolic functions. The elevated levels of acid waste, converted into fatty acid and incorporated into your fat cells, will cause the figures on the scale to go up. So, if you are a grain eater, be sure that 60 percent of your diet consists of mostly whole grains such as bread, brown rice, oatmeal, and so on, as well as a few root vegetables. And if you're a meat eater, make certain that 60 percent of your diet consists of mostly lightly cooked and raw potatoes and other root vegetables, as well as a few grain products. (See menu plans in Part II.)

Cleanse Your Body Through Fasting Before You Begin

Brief fasting can be a safe and effective way to lose weight and detoxify the body. Like being too thin, fasting for long periods is not conducive to good health. It can cause an upset in the body's potassium balance. Furthermore, the rapid melting of fat releases toxins stored in the fat molecules at too rapid a rate. These toxins are carried by the blood to the liver to be neutralized and eliminated from the body, but because of the excessive amount, the liver can't neutralize them, so they remain in the liver, impairing its ability to function. Also, those who lose the most weight in the shortest amount of time by severely reducing their fat intake are in danger of developing gallstones.[8]

The safest and healthiest way to fast, if you are doing it on your own, is to either go on a one-day fast every week or ten days during which you drink only water, or on a two- to three-day fast once a month, eating a single type of fruit, either apples or grapes. Edgar Cayce suggested that the cleansing effect of this fast is enhanced when, after eating the last apple or bunch of grapes, you drink a half cup of olive oil.[9] The best way to alkalinize the body is to go on a potato water fast for a few days. Short fasts are very good for taking off a few pounds quickly.

Before you make the switch from your old eating habits to your new metabolically appropriate lifestyle with the delicious and metabolically appropriate meal plans and recipes in the next section, start clean and fresh with any of the fasts described in the sidebar "Three Safe, Effective Fasts."

Three Safe, Effective Fasts

The following fasts can be used to cleanse your body prior to changing your eating habits or to help you detoxify your body and lose weight on a regular basis.

- A one-day fast every week or ten days during which you drink only water.
- A two- to three-day fast once a month eating a single type of fruit, either apples or grapes. Enhance the detoxifying effect of this fast by drinking a half cup of olive oil at the end of the fast.
- A two- to three-day fast once a month drinking only potato water. Drink five to eight glasses daily. Sip the potato water slowly.

PART II

Eat Right to Lose Weight and Regain Health

Menu Plans

6

Lose Weight

Grain Eater

This chapter contains menu plans for people with grain-eater metabolisms who want to lose weight. You don't have to follow these weight-loss menu plans to the letter to get results—as long as you eat as many of the healing foods in the menus as you can. If, however, there are some healing foods you don't like or that don't agree with you, you can replace them with others. For example, if you don't care for almonds and hazelnuts, two nuts that take off pounds because they are high in calcium, substitute other nuts, because all nuts are good diet foods. Or if you don't want to go to the trouble of making Alkalinizing Potato Water or Grated Potatoes, you can leave them out of the diet and still lose weight. These potato recipes, however, are well worth the trouble because they reduce hunger and prevent binging. Also, you can replace the entrées with simpler foods if you like. The recipes followed by an asterisk (*) are in Part III.

There are four menu plans of seven days each, which adds up to twenty-eight days. I've found that people are more likely to stay on a diet plan if it is one month long. This allows enough time for the appetite to diminish—the key to staying on a weight-loss program. The ultimate purpose of these weight-loss menu plans is to bring attention to a way of eating that takes off weight, increases energy, and improves health.

These are the special weight-reducing foods incorporated into the grain-eater menu plans:

* Beans, nuts, seeds, and lentils satiate the appetite by giving a feeling of fullness. Grain eaters, however, should limit their intake of nuts.
* Almonds, hazelnuts, and yogurt cause weight loss because they are high in calcium.
* The Alkalinizing Potato Water and Grated Potatoes recipes reduce the appetite, usually in no time at all. (See Chapter 5 for these recipes.)
* Coconut oil, used for cooking, salad dressing, and flavoring, can help you take off fifteen to twenty pounds in a couple of months. It maintains healthy arteries because all of it is burned up as fuel. (One tablespoon of coconut oil daily, in addition to the coconut oil in the menu plans, will take off weight even faster.)
* Extra-virgin olive oil takes off weight by reducing acidity that the body would otherwise convert to fat. Use plain olive oil for cooking because extra-virgin olive oil turns toxic at high heat.
* Figs help you take off weight because they are an energy-producing food.
* Bland foods don't excite the appetite. (Some of the special recipes in these menu plans, however, contain spices and herbs. If they increase your appetite, add less of them.)
* Raw foods help you take off weight because they produce only the food molecules needed by the body.

Menu Plan 1

I didn't specify amounts of servings in these menu plans for the same reason that I don't recommend a standardized diet. Each individual has unique dietary needs—not only in terms of kinds of protein, carbohydrates, and fats, but also in terms of amounts of foods. My other reason for not recommending specific amounts is that these menu plans are designed to regulate the appetite so that people will naturally eat the amount of food that will keep their weight down and improve their health. Have fun and be creative!

Day 1

BREAKFAST
Fruit smoothie with banana, plain low-fat yogurt, and coconut
  juice
1 or 2 slices whole-grain toast with 1 or 2 pats butter
Alkalinizing Potato Water (see index for recipe)

LUNCH
Tabbouleh salad with sliced tomato, mango, red onion, orange
  bell peppers, chunks of tofu, and crushed walnuts tossed in
  Coconut Oil Dressing* and sprinkled with flaxseeds or sesame
  seeds

DINNER
Grilled or roasted chicken breast
White Bean and Kale Salad*
Carrot and celery sticks

Day 2

BREAKFAST
Eggs scrambled in coconut oil on a bed of chopped raw baby
  spinach
1 or 2 slices whole-grain toast with fruit-sweetened jam
Alkalinizing Potato Water

LUNCH

Raw vegetable sandwich with sliced tomato, cucumber, lettuce, and green onion on whole-grain bread with hummus sprinkled with extra-virgin olive oil

DINNER

Filet of salmon (preferably wild) with 1 pat butter

Garlic Mashed Yams*

Steamed Swiss chard drizzled with extra-virgin olive oil and lemon juice

Green salad with sliced tomato, mango, and red cabbage tossed in Coconut Oil Dressing* and sprinkled with flaxseeds or sesame seeds

Carrot sticks

Day 3

BREAKFAST

Whole-grain cereal with soy milk, sliced banana, fresh blueberries, a few chopped walnuts, and flaxseeds or sesame seeds

Alkalinizing Potato Water

LUNCH

Mixed green salad with lightly cooked diced potato, sliced tomato, avocado, cucumber, mango, and grated carrot topped with sardines and sliced almonds and tossed in Coconut Oil Dressing*

DINNER

Chicken Corn Chowder* (substitute whole milk for cream)

Green salad with sliced tomato, carrot, red cabbage, and garbanzo beans tossed in extra-virgin olive oil and apple cider vinegar

Day 4

BREAKFAST
Oatmeal topped with fresh seasonal fruit, chopped walnuts,
hazelnuts, and a dollop of plain low-fat yogurt sprinkled with
flaxseeds or sesame seeds
Alkalinizing Potato Water

LUNCH
Mediterranean Lentil Stew* with sliced almonds
Green salad with mango chunks topped with hazelnuts and
tossed in Coconut Oil Dressing*

DINNER
Salmon Filet with Mango Cilantro Salsa* (preferably wild
salmon) topped with toasted unsweetened coconut
Steamed spinach drizzled with coconut oil or extra-virgin
olive oil
Roasted Vegetables* (potatoes)
Carrot sticks

Day 5

BREAKFAST
Soft-boiled eggs on a bed of raw or lightly cooked baby spinach
1 or 2 slices whole-grain toast with 1 or 2 pats butter
Alkalinizing Potato Water

LUNCH
Baby spinach salad with lightly cooked diced potato, grated
carrot, and sliced hard-boiled eggs, mushrooms, and
avocado tossed in Apple Cider Vinaigrette* or Coconut Oil
Dressing*

DINNER
Broiled steak
Sweet Potato and Green Bean Salad*
Carrot and celery sticks

Day 6

BREAKFAST
Fresh seasonal berries
Eggs or tofu scrambled in coconut oil
1 or 2 slices whole-grain bread with 1 or 2 pats butter
Alkalinizing Potato Water

LUNCH
Quinoa or couscous salad with garbanzo beans, sliced tomato,
    mushrooms, and radishes tossed in Coconut Oil Dressing* on
    a bed of arugula and sprinkled with flaxseeds or sesame seeds

DINNER
Chicken Chili* on a bed of brown rice sprinkled with coconut
    oil
Crunchy Coleslaw*

Day 7

BREAKFAST
Whole-grain cereal with soy milk, dried figs, chopped almonds,
    hazelnuts, sprinkled with flaxseeds or sesame seeds
Alkalinizing Potato Water

LUNCH
Golden Beet Soup*
Green salad with sliced avocado, tomato, and garbanzo beans
    tossed in Coconut Oil Dressing*

DINNER
Chicken Stroganoff* (substitute yogurt for sour cream)
Whole-grain pasta
Steamed broccoli sprinkled with extra-virgin olive oil and
    lemon juice
Carrot sticks and sliced cucumbers

Menu Plan 2

Day 1

BREAKFAST
Oatmeal topped with fresh seasonal fruit, sliced almonds,
    hazelnuts, dried figs, and a dollop of plain low-fat yogurt
Alkalinizing Potato Water

LUNCH
Mediterranean Lentil Stew* topped with sliced almonds
Green salad with sliced tomato and avocado tossed in Balsamic
    Vinaigrette* and sprinkled with flaxseeds or sesame seeds

DINNER
Salmon Filet with Mango Cilantro Salsa* (preferably wild
    salmon) topped with toasted unsweetened coconut
Steamed Swiss chard sprinkled with coconut oil and lemon juice
Roasted Vegetables* (sweet potatoes)

Day 2

BREAKFAST
Soft-boiled eggs on a bed of chopped raw or lightly cooked baby
    spinach
1 or 2 slices whole-grain toast with almond butter and fruit-
    sweetened jam
Grated Potatoes (see index for recipe)

LUNCH

Raw vegetable sandwich with sliced tomato, cucumber, mushrooms, and green onion on whole-grain bread spread with black bean hummus drizzled with extra-virgin olive oil

DINNER

Filet of salmon (preferably wild) with 1 pat butter

Lightly steamed carrots and Swiss chard drizzled with extra-virgin olive oil and lemon juice

Green salad with cherry tomatoes and sliced orange bell pepper tossed in Coconut Oil Dressing* and sprinkled with flaxseeds and/or sesame seeds

Day 3

BREAKFAST

Eggs scrambled in coconut oil topped with black beans and a dollop of plain low-fat yogurt

Grated Potatoes

LUNCH

Golden Beet Soup*

Brown rice salad with sliced tomato, mushrooms, green pepper, onion, and chopped walnuts tossed in extra-virgin olive oil and apple cider vinegar and sprinkled with flaxseeds or sesame seeds

DINNER

Chicken Stroganoff* (substitute yogurt for sour cream)

Short-grain brown rice sprinkled with coconut oil

Steamed broccoli sprinkled with extra-virgin olive oil, garlic, and lemon juice

Carrot and celery sticks

Day 4

BREAKFAST
Fresh seasonal berries
Eggs or tofu scrambled in coconut oil
1 or 2 slices whole-grain bread with 1 or 2 pats butter
Alkalinizing Potato Water

LUNCH
Whole-grain pasta on a bed of arugula topped with garbanzo
    beans and sliced almonds drizzled with extra-virgin olive oil
    and a few drops lemon juice

DINNER
Chicken Chili*
1 slice whole-grain bread with 1 pat butter
Grated carrot and sliced celery tossed in Coconut Oil
    Dressing*

Day 5

BREAKFAST
Fruit smoothie with pineapple, berries, banana, plain low-fat
    yogurt, and coconut juice
1 or 2 slices whole-grain toast with 1 or 2 pats butter
Alkalinizing Potato Water

LUNCH
Tabbouleh salad with cherry tomatoes, sliced onion, chopped
    garlic, tofu, and grated raw beets tossed in Coconut Oil
    Dressing* and topped with chopped almonds and flaxseeds or
    sesame seeds
2 or 3 fresh figs

DINNER
Grilled or roasted chicken breast
White Bean and Kale Salad*
Carrot and celery sticks

Day 6

BREAKFAST
Low-fat vanilla yogurt with fresh seasonal fruit, sliced almonds,
   and hazelnuts topped with granola, flaxseeds, and sesame
   seeds
Alkalinizing Potato Water

LUNCH
Baby spinach salad with sliced red cabbage, avocado, hard-
   boiled eggs, mushrooms, and grated carrot tossed in Honey-
   Yogurt Dressing*
1 or 2 slices whole-grain bread with 1 or 2 pats butter

DINNER
Grilled or broiled lamb chops with Spicy Curried Lentils* (see
   Halibut with Spicy Curried Lentils* recipe)
Watercress salad with sliced avocado and orange tossed in
   Coconut Oil Dressing* and sprinkled with flaxseeds or sesame
   seeds

Day 7

BREAKFAST
Whole-grain cereal with plain low-fat yogurt, sliced banana,
   fresh blueberries, and a few chopped almonds and
   hazelnuts
Alkalinizing Potato Water

Lunch

Mixed green salad with sliced tomato, avocado, cucumber, carrot, and mango topped with sardines and almonds and drizzled with extra-virgin olive oil and apple cider vinegar
1 slice whole-grain bread with 1 pat butter

Dinner

Chicken Corn Chowder* (substitute whole milk for cream)
Raw cabbage salad with sliced tomato, grated carrot, zucchini, and celery tossed in Coconut Oil Dressing*

Menu Plan 3

Day 1

Breakfast

Whole-grain cereal with plain low-fat yogurt, sliced banana, fresh blueberries, and a few chopped walnuts, and sprinkled with flaxseeds or sesame seeds
Alkalinizing Potato Water

Lunch

Fresh crabmeat atop mixed greens, sliced tomato, avocado, cucumber, mango, and almonds tossed in Balsamic Vinaigrette*
1 or 2 slices whole-grain bread with 1 or 2 pats butter

Dinner

Chicken Corn Chowder* (substitute whole milk for cream)
Green salad with sliced tomato, carrot, red cabbage, and garbanzo beans tossed in Coconut Oil Dressing*
Alkalinizing Potato Water

Day 2

BREAKFAST
Oatmeal topped with chopped figs, walnuts, and plain low-fat
 yogurt or soy milk
Alkalinizing Potato Water

LUNCH
Mediterranean Lentil Stew* with sliced almonds
Sliced tomato and cucumber on a leaf of romaine lettuce
 sprinkled with Honey-Yogurt Dressing* and topped with
 chopped mint

DINNER
Broiled or grilled thick-cut lean pork chops with Mango
 Cilantro Salsa* (see Salmon Filet with Mango Cilantro Salsa*
 recipe) topped with toasted unsweetened coconut
Steamed Swiss chard sprinkled with extra-virgin olive oil and
 lemon juice
Grated Potatoes
Carrot sticks and sliced cucumber

Day 3

BREAKFAST
Sliced papaya or mango
Chopped raw or lightly cooked baby spinach omelet cooked in
 coconut oil and topped with plain low-fat yogurt
Grated Potatoes

LUNCH
Sardine sandwich with sliced tomato, cucumber, lettuce, and
 green onion on whole-grain bread spread with hummus and
 drizzled with extra-virgin olive oil

DINNER
Filet of salmon (preferably wild) with 1 pat butter
Garlic Mashed Yams*
Steamed Swiss chard sprinkled with coconut oil and lemon juice
Green salad with raw zucchini chunks, mushrooms, and carrots
tossed in Apple Cider Vinaigrette* and sprinkled with
flaxseeds or sesame seeds

Day 4

BREAKFAST
Plain low-fat yogurt with fresh seasonal fruit
1 or 2 slices whole-grain bread with 1 or 2 pats butter
Alkalinizing Potato Water

LUNCH
Baby spinach salad with sliced hard-boiled eggs, mushrooms,
avocado, tomato, grated carrot, and garbanzo beans topped
with sliced almonds and tossed in Honey Yogurt Dressing*

DINNER
Chicken Stroganoff* (substitute yogurt for sour cream) on a
bed of whole-grain pasta sprinkled with coconut oil
Steamed broccoli sprinkled with extra-virgin olive oil and lemon
juice
Carrot sticks

Day 5

BREAKFAST
Fresh seasonal berries
Eggs with mushrooms and green onions scrambled in coconut
oil
Grated Potatoes

LUNCH
Tabbouleh or couscous salad with sliced tomato, red onion, and
    red cabbage on a bed of arugula topped with garbanzo beans,
    tossed in Coconut Oil Dressing*, and sprinkled with flaxseeds
    or sesame seeds

DINNER
Chicken Chili*
Brown basmati rice with a dollop of plain low-fat yogurt
Crunchy Coleslaw*

Day 6

BREAKFAST
Whole-grain granola topped with vanilla low-fat yogurt or soy
    milk, dried figs, chopped almonds, and hazelnuts
Alkalinizing Potato Water

LUNCH
Golden Beet Soup*
Green salad with sliced tomato, avocado, and mango topped
    with sliced almonds and drizzled with Coconut Oil Dressing*

DINNER
Halibut with Spicy Curried Lentils*
Green salad with cherry tomatoes and grated carrot tossed in
    Balsamic Vinaigrette*

Day 7

BREAKFAST
Fruit smoothie with mango, banana, plain low-fat yogurt, and
    coconut juice
1 or 2 slices whole-grain toast with 1 or 2 pats butter
Alkalinizing Potato Water

LUNCH
Wild rice or tabbouleh salad with sliced hard-boiled eggs,
    tomato, and mango tossed in Coconut Oil Dressing* and
    topped with poached prawns, fresh figs, crushed hazelnuts,
    and flaxseeds or sesame seeds

DINNER
Broiled or grilled steak
White Bean and Kale Salad*
Carrot sticks

Menu Plan 4

Day 1

BREAKFAST
Oatmeal topped with fresh seasonal fruit, crushed or chopped
    hazelnuts, and plain low-fat yogurt or soy milk
Alkalinizing Potato Water

LUNCH
Mediterranean Lentil Stew* topped with a dollop of plain
    low-fat yogurt and chopped green onion
Green salad with sliced tomato, mushrooms, and red bell pep-
    pers topped with sliced almonds and tossed in Coconut Oil
    Dressing*

DINNER
Chicken Corn Chowder* (substitute whole milk for cream)
Green salad with sliced tomato, grated red cabbage, carrot, and
    garbanzo beans tossed in extra-virgin olive oil and apple cider
    vinegar

Day 2

BREAKFAST
Plain low-fat yogurt with fresh seasonal fruit
1 or 2 slices whole-grain toast with 1 or 2 pats butter
Alkalinizing Potato Water

LUNCH
Tabbouleh salad with brown rice, raw baby spinach, sliced
    tomato, avocado, mushrooms, and grated carrot topped with
    crabmeat and tossed in Coconut Oil Dressing*

DINNER
Trout with Spicy Curried Lentils* (see Halibut with Spicy
    Curried Lentils* recipe)
Carrot and celery sticks

Day 3

BREAKFAST
Fresh seasonal berries
Eggs scrambled in coconut oil topped with black beans and
    plain low-fat yogurt
Grated Potatoes with 1 pat butter

LUNCH
Couscous or brown rice salad with sliced tomato, mango, and
    red onion on a bed of watercress tossed in Coconut Oil
    Dressing*

DINNER
Grilled or roasted chicken breast
White Bean and Kale Salad*
Carrot sticks and cucumber slices

Day 4

BREAKFAST
Eggs fried over easy in 1 pat butter and pure olive oil on a bed of
    chopped raw or lightly cooked baby spinach and grated carrot
1 slice whole-grain toast with almond butter
Alkalinizing Potato Water

LUNCH
Raw vegetable sandwich with sliced tomato, cucumber,
    lettuce, and red onion on whole-grain pita bread spread with
    hummus, and sprinkled with coconut oil

DINNER
Filet of salmon (preferably wild) with extra-virgin olive oil and
    lemon juice
Steamed Swiss chard with 1 pat butter or sprinkled with
    coconut oil
Green salad with cherry tomatoes and orange bell peppers
    tossed in Balsamic Vinaigrette* and sprinkled with flaxseeds
    or sesame seeds
Carrot sticks

Day 5

BREAKFAST
Fresh seasonal fruit
Poached eggs
Grated Potatoes with 1 pat butter

LUNCH
Golden Beet Soup*
Green salad with sliced carrot, lightly steamed peas and lima
    beans, and walnuts, drizzled with extra-virgin olive or
    coconut oil and lemon juice, and sprinkled with flaxseeds or
    sesame seeds

DINNER

Beef Stroganoff (substitute beef for chicken and yogurt for sour cream in the Chicken Stroganoff* recipe)

Whole-grain pasta tossed in coconut oil

Steamed broccoli with 1 pat butter and lemon juice

Carrot sticks and sliced cucumber

Day 6

BREAKFAST

Fruit smoothie with berries, banana, plain low-fat yogurt, and coconut juice

1 or 2 slices whole-grain bread with 1 or 2 pats butter

Alkalinizing Potato Water

LUNCH

Tabbouleh or brown rice salad with cherry tomatoes, raw grated broccoli stem, and blanched cauliflower florets tossed in Coconut Oil Dressing* and topped with shrimp, fresh figs, and flaxseeds or sesame seeds

DINNER

Chicken Chili*

1 slice whole-grain bread with 1 pat butter

Crunchy Coleslaw*

Carrot sticks

Day 7

BREAKFAST

Whole-grain cereal with soy milk, sliced banana, fresh blueberries, papaya, and a few chopped walnuts

Alkalinizing Potato Water

LUNCH

Mixed green salad with lightly cooked diced potato, sliced tomato, avocado, cucumber, carrot, and mango topped with sardines and toasted almonds and tossed in Coconut Oil Dressing*

DINNER

Salmon Filet with Mango Cilantro Salsa* (preferably wild salmon) topped with toasted unsweetened coconut

Steamed baby spinach sprinkled with coconut oil and lemon juice

Roasted Vegetables* (potatoes and carrots)

7

Lose Weight

Meat Eater

The menu plans in this chapter are designed for the person with a meat-eater metabolism who wants to take off pounds. You can follow these weight-loss menu plans to the letter, if all the food items and recipes agree with you and are to your liking, or you can use them as guidelines. But whichever way you approach this diet plan, note the following special weight-loss foods that you will find in the menus and eat as many of them as possible. If you don't like some of them, don't eat them—foods that you don't like don't digest well. If, for example, nuts don't appeal to you, eat seeds instead. Seeds, like nuts, satisfy the appetite for a long time. Or if coconut oil doesn't appeal to you, use olive oil. It's also good for weight loss—although not nearly as effective as coconut oil. Also, you can substitute your own preparation methods for the healthy and slimming entrées, which are included principally to add spark and taste to the menus. Recipes for dishes followed by an asterisk (*) are in Part III.

The four menu plans, each for seven days, add up to twenty-eight days, enough time for the appetite to diminish—the key to staying on a weight-loss program indefinitely. The ultimate purpose of these weight-loss menu plans is to present a way of eating that takes off weight, increases energy, and improves health.

The following special weight-reducing foods are incorporated into the meat-eater menu plans:

* Nuts and seeds satiate the appetite by giving a feeling of fullness, and the meat eater can eat a lot of them.
* Almonds, hazelnuts, and yogurt cause weight loss because they are high in calcium.
* The Alkalinizing Potato Water and Grated Potatoes recipes reduce the appetite, usually in no time at all. (See Chapter 5 for these recipes.)
* Coconut oil, used for cooking, salad dressing, and flavoring, takes off fifteen to twenty pounds in a couple of months—and keeps the arteries healthy because all of it is burned up as fuel. (One tablespoon of coconut oil daily, in addition to the coconut oil in the menu plans, will take off weight even faster.)
* Extra-virgin olive oil can be used as a dressing for salads and vegetables. Use pure olive oil for cooking because extra-virgin olive oil becomes toxic at high heat. Extra-virgin olive oil has less than 1 percent acidity and is produced by the first pressing of olives. Pure olive oil for cooking comes from the second pressing and has fewer nutrients than extra-virgin olive oil, so it's a safer oil to use for cooking.
* Figs take off weight because of their high levels of calcium. A single fig contains 12 mg of calcium.
* Bland foods don't excite the appetite. (Some of the special recipes in these menu plans, however, contain spices and herbs. If they increase your appetite, add less of them.)
* Raw foods take off weight because they produce only the food molecules needed by the body, so there are no acid waste by-products to turn into fat.

Menu Plan 1

I don't specify amounts of servings in these menu plans for the same reason that I don't recommend a standardized diet. Each individual has unique dietary needs—not only in terms of kinds of protein, carbohydrates, and fats, but also in terms of amounts of foods. My other reason for not recommending specific amounts is that these menu plans are designed to regulate the appetite so that people will naturally eat the amount of food that will keep their weight down and improve their health. Have fun and be creative!

Day 1

BREAKFAST
Coconut juice
Whole-grain flour tortilla filled with eggs scrambled in
    coconut oil topped with grated carrot and chopped green
    onion
Alkalinizing Potato Water (see index for recipe)

LUNCH
Sweet Potato and Green Bean Salad*
Celery and carrot sticks
A few mixed nuts and seeds

DINNER
Beef Curry with Minted Cucumber Yogurt Sauce* (substitute
    plain low-fat yogurt for whole-milk yogurt)
1 or 2 slices whole-grain bread with 1 or 2 pats butter
Carrot and celery sticks
1 or 2 fresh or dried figs

Day 2

BREAKFAST
Coconut juice
1 or 2 whole-grain waffles with unsweetened peanut or almond
   butter and sprinkled with fresh seasonal berries
Alkalinizing Potato Water

LUNCH
Tabbouleh salad with green onion, figs, grated carrot, and
   chopped red bell pepper tossed in Apple Cider Vinaigrette*
   and topped with chopped almonds and flaxseeds or sesame
   seeds

DINNER
Pork Tenderloin with Apple-Onion Compote*
Roasted Vegetables* (potatoes and parsnips)
Blanched cauliflower florets tossed in extra-virgin olive oil and
   apple cider vinegar

Day 3

BREAKFAST
Eggs fried over easy in butter
1 or 2 slices whole-grain toast with unsweetened apple butter
A few raw almonds and hazelnuts
Alkalinizing Potato Water

LUNCH
Salmon (preferably wild) topped with Walnut-Basil Butter* and
   a scattering of capers
Steamed peas and carrots
Crunchy Coleslaw* with sliced pecans

DINNER
Lamb Stew*
Green salad with chunks of carrots, lightly cooked diced pota-
    toes, and lightly steamed green beans tossed in Coconut Oil
    Dressing* and sprinkled with flaxseeds and sesame seeds
A few mixed nuts

Day 4

BREAKFAST
Whole-grain cereal with chunks of papaya, banana, and mango;
    raw almond slivers; and unsweetened coconut
Alkalinizing Potato Water

LUNCH
Green salad with cooked diced beets, lightly cooked diced pota-
    toes, and chopped orange or red bell peppers tossed in Apple
    Cider Vinaigrette* and topped with mint, toasted walnuts,
    and flaxseeds or sesame seeds
Raw sugar snap peas

DINNER
Grilled or roasted chicken breast
Steamed whole artichoke with melted butter for dipping
Lightly steamed green beans
Sliced tomato, avocado, and fresh mushrooms on a bed of let-
    tuce drizzled with Coconut Oil Dressing*

Day 5

BREAKFAST
Oatmeal topped with butter, sliced dried figs, chopped hazel-
    nuts, walnuts, and flaxseeds or sesame seeds with almond milk
    or plain low-fat yogurt
Alkalinizing Potato Water

Lunch

Lamb burger topped with raw yellow onion on a bed of baby
   spinach salad with sliced avocado, mango, and chopped
   pecans drizzled with Coconut Oil Dressing*

Dinner

Grilled New York steak
Lightly steamed green beans topped with slivered almonds
Roasted Vegetables* (potatoes and orange bell peppers)
Blanched broccoli and cauliflower florets tossed in extra-virgin
   olive oil and apple cider vinegar

Day 6

Breakfast

Poached egg
1 slice whole-grain toast with butter
Small portion of blanched, chopped asparagus and grated carrot
   sprinkled with coconut oil and lemon juice and topped with
   green onion and parsley
Alkalinizing Potato Water

Lunch

Vegetable Beef Soup*
Green salad with sliced tomato and cucumber topped with walnuts and almonds and tossed in Coconut Oil Dressing*

Dinner

Grilled Lamb Chops with Purée of Rutabaga and Tart Apple*
   (substitute whole milk for cream)
Brown rice with butter
Steamed baby spinach sprinkled with extra-virgin olive oil
Celery and carrot sticks

Day 7

BREAKFAST
Fresh fruit salad with banana, figs, and pineapple topped with
   sliced almonds, hazelnuts, and flaxseeds or sesame seeds and a
   dollop of plain low-fat yogurt
1 slice whole-grain toast with butter
Alkalinizing Potato Water

LUNCH
Lamb and Black Bean Chili with Adobo*
Green salad with grated raw carrot, zucchini, and sliced orange
   or red bell pepper tossed in Coconut Oil Dressing*

DINNER
Thick-cut, lean pork chop, grilled or broiled, with Mango
   Cilantro Salsa* (see Salmon Filet with Mango Cilantro Salsa*
   recipe)
Mashed potatoes with butter topped with chopped green onion
Steamed carrots sprinkled with coconut oil
Blanched broccoli and cauliflower florets tossed in Coconut Oil
   Dressing*

Menu Plan 2

Day 1

BREAKFAST
Whole-grain cereal with butter and chunks of papaya, banana,
   mango, raw almonds, flaxseeds or sesame seeds, unsweetened
   coconut, and plain low-fat yogurt or soy milk
Alkalinizing Potato Water

LUNCH

Green salad with cooked diced beets and a little brown rice
  tossed in Coconut Oil Dressing* and topped with chopped
  mint and a handful of almonds
Raw sugar snap peas

DINNER

Sautéed or roasted duck breast
Steamed whole artichoke with melted butter for dipping
Lightly steamed green beans
Salad of sliced tomato, avocado, and raw mushrooms on a bed
  of lettuce drizzled with Apple Cider Vinaigrette*
Carrot sticks

Day 2

BREAKFAST

Oatmeal with butter, fresh seasonal fruit, plain low-fat yogurt,
  and a sprinkling of raw walnuts, almonds, and flaxseeds or
  sesame seeds
Alkalinizing Potato Water

LUNCH

Lamb burger topped with raw green onion on a bed of green
  salad with sliced avocado, mango, and chopped almonds
  drizzled with Balsamic Vinaigrette*
Grated Potatoes (see index for recipe)

DINNER

Grilled New York steak
Steamed green beans topped with grated raw carrot and slivered
  almonds and drizzled with coconut oil
Roasted Vegetables* (potatoes and carrots)
Sliced fresh cucumber

Day 3

BREAKFAST

Fruit salad with figs, pineapple, and fresh seasonal berries
   topped with almonds, walnuts, and flaxseeds or sesame seeds
   and a dollop of plain low-fat yogurt
1 or 2 slices whole-grain toast with 1 or 2 pats butter
Alkalinizing Potato Water

LUNCH

Brown rice or tabbouleh salad with cherry tomatoes, grated
   carrot, sliced zucchini, green bell pepper, and avocado tossed
   in Balsamic Vinaigrette*

DINNER

Thick-cut, lean pork chop, grilled or broiled, with Mango
   Cilantro Salsa* (see Salmon Filet with Mango Cilantro Salsa*
   recipe)
Mashed potatoes with butter topped with chopped green
   onion
Blanched broccoli and cauliflower florets tossed in coconut oil
   and apple cider vinegar

Day 4

BREAKFAST

Eggs fried over easy in butter
Small portion of blanched, chopped asparagus and grated carrot
   sprinkled with coconut oil, lemon juice, green onion, and
   parsley
1 or 2 slices whole-grain toast
Grated Potatoes with butter

LUNCH
White Bean and Kale Salad*
1 slice whole-grain bread with butter
Green salad with cherry tomatoes and carrot strips tossed in
    Balsamic Vinaigrette*

DINNER
Vegetable Beef Soup*
Green salad with sliced tomato, blanched broccoli and
    cauliflower florets, and walnuts tossed in Coconut Oil
    Dressing*
A few almonds and sunflower seeds

Day 5

BREAKFAST
Coconut juice
1 or 2 whole-grain waffles with unsweetened peanut or almond
    butter sprinkled with fresh berries
Alkalinizing Potato Water

LUNCH
Romaine lettuce salad with green onion, figs, grated carrot,
    sliced red bell pepper, and chopped almonds tossed in
    Balsamic Vinaigrette* and sprinkled with sunflower seeds
1 or 2 slices whole-grain bread with 1 or 2 pats butter

DINNER
Pork Tenderloin with Apple-Onion Compote*
Roasted Vegetables* (potatoes, carrots, and parsnips)
Fresh raw zucchini slices drizzled with coconut oil or extra-
    virgin olive oil and apple cider vinegar and sprinkled with
    flaxseeds or sesame seeds

Day 6

BREAKFAST
Coconut juice
Whole-grain flour tortilla filled with eggs scrambled in coconut
oil topped with grated carrot and chopped green onion
Alkalinizing Potato Water

LUNCH
Sweet Potato and Green Bean Salad*
Celery and carrot sticks
A handful of sunflower seeds

DINNER
Beef Curry with Minted Cucumber Yogurt Sauce* (substitute
plain low-fat yogurt for whole-milk yogurt)
Brown rice with butter
Sliced tomato and avocado drizzled with Coconut Oil Dressing*
Carrot sticks

Day 7

BREAKFAST
Soft-boiled eggs
1 slice whole-grain toast with butter and unsweetened apple
butter
A few almonds
Grated Potatoes with butter

LUNCH
Salmon (preferably wild) topped with Walnut-Basil Butter* and
a scattering of capers
Steamed peas and carrots sprinkled with coconut oil
Crunchy Coleslaw* with sliced pecans

DINNER
Lamb Stew*
Green salad with lightly cooked diced potatoes, snow peas,
 carrot strips, and cherry tomatoes tossed in Coconut Oil
 Dressing*

Menu Plan 3

Day 1

BREAKFAST
Eggs fried over easy in butter
1 slice whole-grain toast with butter
A few almonds
Alkalinizing Potato Water

LUNCH
Salmon (preferably wild) topped with Walnut-Basil Butter* and
 a scattering of capers
Steamed peas and carrots sprinkled with coconut oil
Crunchy Coleslaw* with sliced pecans and sprinkled with
 flaxseeds and sesame seeds

DINNER
Lamb Stew*
1 or 2 slices whole-grain bread with butter
Bibb or romaine lettuce salad with sliced tomato, avocado, and
 snow peas tossed in coconut oil and apple cider vinegar

Day 2

BREAKFAST
Whole-grain cereal with chunks of papaya, banana, mango, raw
 almonds, unsweetened coconut, and almond milk
Alkalinizing Potato Water

LUNCH
Whole-wheat pita filled with sliced avocado, tomato, green
    onion, cucumber, and crabmeat
Raw sugar snap peas

DINNER
Grilled or roasted chicken breast or thighs
Steamed whole artichoke with melted butter for dipping
Steamed green beans, sliced tomato, avocado, and fresh
    mushrooms on a bed of lettuce drizzled with Coconut Oil
    Dressing*
Carrot sticks

Day 3

BREAKFAST
Oatmeal topped with butter, sliced dried figs, and a sprinkling
    of chopped hazelnuts or walnuts with almond milk or plain
    low-fat yogurt
Alkalinizing Potato Water

LUNCH
Lamb or beef burger mixed with capers, garlic, and raw red
    onion and then grilled
Romaine lettuce salad with sliced avocado, mango, and chopped
    pecans drizzled with Coconut Oil Dressing*

DINNER
Pork Tenderloin with Apple-Onion Compote*
Lightly steamed broccoli with slivered almonds
Roasted Vegetables* (potatoes and red bell peppers)
Raw snow peas and carrot strips

Day 4

BREAKFAST
Coconut juice
Whole-grain flour tortilla filled with eggs scrambled in coconut
    oil topped with grated carrot and chopped green onion
Alkalinizing Potato Water

LUNCH
Sweet Potato and Green Bean Salad*
Celery and carrot sticks
A handful of sunflower seeds

DINNER
Beef Curry with Minted Cucumber Yogurt Sauce* (substitute
    plain low-fat yogurt for whole-milk yogurt) with sliced
    almonds and hazelnuts
1 slice whole-grain bread with butter
Celery and carrot sticks

Day 5

BREAKFAST
Omelet with chopped raw or blanched asparagus and grated
    carrot, cooked in coconut oil and topped with chopped green
    onion and parsley
Grated Potatoes with butter

LUNCH
Vegetable Beef Soup*
Green salad with cherry tomatoes, sliced orange bell pepper, red
    onion, and almonds tossed in Apple Cider Vinaigrette*

DINNER
Grilled or broiled lamb chops
Roasted Vegetables* (yams or sweet potatoes and eggplant)
Crunchy Coleslaw* with sliced pecans and sprinkled with
    flaxseeds or sesame seeds
Carrot sticks and sliced cucumbers

Day 6

BREAKFAST
Fruit salad with banana, figs, and pineapple topped with
    almonds, hazelnuts, a dollop of plain low-fat yogurt and
    sprinkled with flaxseeds or sesame seeds
1 or 2 slices whole-grain toast with butter
Alkalinizing Potato Water

LUNCH
Tabbouleh salad with grated carrot, sliced zucchini, chopped
    sweet onion, green bell pepper, and peas drizzled with
    coconut oil and apple cider vinegar

DINNER
Venison or beef steak with Mango Cilantro Salsa* (see Salmon
    Filet with Mango Cilantro Salsa* recipe)
Mashed sweet potatoes with butter and chopped chives
Lightly steamed asparagus
Carrot and celery sticks

Day 7

BREAKFAST
Coconut juice
1 or 2 whole-grain waffles with unsweetened peanut or almond
    butter topped with sliced apple
Alkalinizing Potato Water

LUNCH

Shrimp salad with sliced green onion, lightly cooked diced
   potatoes, red bell peppers, figs, and grated carrot tossed in
   Apple Cider Vinaigrette* or Coconut Oil Dressing* and
   sprinkled with chopped almonds and sunflower seeds

DINNER

Chicken Stroganoff* (substitute plain low-fat yogurt for sour
   cream)
Apple-Onion Compote* (see Pork Tenderloin with Apple-
   Onion Compote* recipe)
Boiled whole potato rolled in butter
Raw snow peas and carrot sticks

Menu Plan 4

Day 1

BREAKFAST

Whole-grain cereal with butter, almond milk, papaya chunks,
   dried chopped figs, sliced pecans, hazelnuts, and unsweetened
   coconut
Alkalinizing Potato Water

LUNCH

Watercress salad with lightly cooked diced potatoes and cooked
   diced beets tossed in Coconut Oil Dressing* and topped with
   chopped mint and toasted walnuts
Raw sugar snap peas and carrot strips

DINNER

Grilled or roasted chicken or duck breast
Salad of cooked rutabaga chunks, sliced sweet onion, avocado,
   tomato, artichoke hearts, and fresh mushrooms on a bed of
   lettuce drizzled with Apple Cider Vinaigrette*

Day 2

BREAKFAST
Coconut juice
Whole-grain flour tortilla filled with eggs scrambled in coconut
    oil topped with grated carrot and chopped green onion
Alkalinizing Potato Water

LUNCH
Sweet Potato and Green Bean Salad* on a bed of chopped
    romaine lettuce

DINNER
Beef Curry with Minted Cucumber Yogurt Sauce* (substitute
    plain low-fat yogurt for whole-milk yogurt), sprinkled with
    walnuts and almonds
1 slice whole-grain bread with butter
Carrot sticks

Day 3

BREAKFAST
Poached eggs
1 slice whole-grain toast with butter
Small portion of blanched, chopped asparagus and grated carrot
    sprinkled with coconut oil and lemon juice and topped with
    green onion and parsley
Grated Potatoes with butter

LUNCH
Vegetable Beef Soup*
Crunchy Coleslaw* with sliced pecans sprinkled with flaxseeds
    or sesame seeds
1 slice whole-grain bread with butter

DINNER
Grilled Lamb Chops with Purée of Rutabaga and Tart Apple*
    (substitute sweet potato for rutabaga)
Lightly steamed spinach sprinkled with coconut oil
Celery and carrot sticks

Day 4

BREAKFAST
Oatmeal sprinkled with cinnamon and topped with butter,
    diced apple, raw almonds, and almond milk
Alkalinizing Potato Water

LUNCH
Mexican-style lamb burger seasoned with cilantro, ground
    cumin, garlic, and mild chili powder and topped with raw
    sweet onion and green bell pepper on a mixed lettuce
    salad with sliced avocado and mango, drizzled with
    Coconut Oil Dressing* and sprinkled with flaxseeds or
    sesame seeds

DINNER
Grilled Steak
Steamed snow peas topped with chopped hazelnuts and butter
Roasted Vegetables* (potatoes and carrots)
Sliced cucumbers

Day 5

BREAKFAST
Fruit salad with papaya, figs, and pineapple topped with
    almonds, hazelnuts, and a dollop of plain low-fat yogurt
Grated Potatoes with butter

LUNCH
Lamb and Black Bean Chili with Adobo*
Steamed or boiled potatoes rolled in butter
Green salad with grated carrot, sliced zucchini, and red bell
　pepper tossed in Coconut Oil Dressing*

DINNER
Grilled or broiled thick-cut, lean pork loin chop with Mango
　Cilantro Salsa* (see Salmon Filet with Mango Cilantro Salsa*
　recipe)
Mashed potatoes with butter topped with chopped green onion
Grated raw carrots and raw zucchini tossed in Apple Cider
　Vinaigrette*

Day 6

BREAKFAST
Coconut juice
1 or 2 whole-grain waffles with unsweetened peanut or almond
　butter topped with sliced pear
Alkalinizing Potato Water

LUNCH
Shrimp salad with sliced red onion, figs, grated carrot, and
　chopped red bell pepper tossed in Apple Cider Vinaigrette*
　and topped with sliced almonds

DINNER
Pork Tenderloin with Apple-Onion Compote*
Roasted Vegetables* (potatoes, zucchini, and red and yellow bell
　peppers)
Baby spinach salad with carrot strips, snow peas, and sliced
　tomato tossed in Coconut Oil Dressing*

Day 7

BREAKFAST

Eggs scrambled in coconut oil with sliced raw mushrooms
1 or 2 slices whole-grain toast with butter and fruit-sweetened
    jam
A few almonds and hazelnuts
Alkalinizing Potato Water

LUNCH

Salmon (preferably wild) topped with Walnut-Basil Butter*
    (substitute hazelnuts for walnuts) and a scattering of capers
Steamed peas and carrots sprinkled with coconut oil
Green salad with cherry tomatoes and sliced cucumber tossed in
    Balsamic Vinaigrette* and sprinkled with flaxseeds or sesame
    seeds

DINNER

Lamb Stew*
Arugula salad with grated carrot and sliced celery tossed in
    extra-virgin olive oil or coconut oil and a squeeze of lemon
    juice

8

Regain Health

Grain Eater

Each grain-eater menu plan in this chapter is designed to relieve a particular health problem. There are menu plans for arthritis; asthma, bronchitis, and emphysema; cancer prevention; cardio-vascular disorders; circulatory disorders; diabetes; hepatitis; hyper-thyroid; hypothyroid; migraine; prostate problems; and stomach, esophageal, and intestinal problems.

The menu plans work in two stages. Because they include the kinds of protein, carbohydrates, and fats and oils that the grain eater can digest, they detoxify the body and balance the pH. This clears the way for the healing foods to act on the body and restore it to health.

Recipes followed by an asterisk (*) are in Part III. Recipes for Alkalinizing Potato Water and Grated Potatoes are in Chapter 5.

Arthritis

The healing foods in the following list are incorporated in the grain eater's menu plan for arthritis. The food items in this plan that have proven most effective for eliminating pain are the Alka-linizing Potato Water and the raw potato slivers. The key foods in the grain-eater's menu plan that help heal arthritis are as follows:

* Alkalinizing Potato Water and raw potato slivers eliminate or reduce pain.
* Okra and celery make joints more flexible because they are high in sodium.
* Powdered ginger, cloves, and garlic lessen joint pain.
* Organic raw eggs are high in pantothenic acid, a B vitamin deficient in most arthritics.
* Whey (found in health food stores) and liver are also high in B vitamins: eat 3 or 4 tablespoons per week.
* Citrus fruit and cherry juice break up calcium deposits. Cherry juice is especially effective for bursitis.
* Salmon, mackerel, and sardines are rich in vitamin D, which the body needs to absorb calcium.

Day 1

BREAKFAST
½–1 ounce gelatin powder dissolved in 2 tablespoons boiling water and mixed with cherry juice or Alkalinizing Potato Water (see index for recipe)

Eggs scrambled in butter and pure olive oil on a bed of chopped raw baby spinach

2 slices whole-grain toast with fruit-sweetened jam

Chai tea brewed from a tea bag and sweetened, if desired, with honey (preferably unfiltered) or stevia (see index)

LUNCH
Raw vegetable sandwich with sliced tomato, cucumber, lettuce, and green onion on whole-grain bread spread with hummus and drizzled with extra-virgin olive oil

Celery sticks

Alkalinizing Potato Water

DINNER
Filet of salmon (preferably wild) drizzled with extra-virgin olive oil
Garlic Mashed Yams*
Steamed Swiss chard with 1 pat butter or sprinkled with extra-
virgin olive oil and served with a wedge of lemon
Raw potato slivers (use peeler to make slivers)

Day 2

BREAKFAST
½–1 ounce gelatin powder dissolved in 2 tablespoons boiling
water and mixed with cherry juice or Alkalinizing Potato
Water
Oatmeal with fresh seasonal berries, melon, and ground flaxseed
Organic Raw Egg Soy Milk Shake*

LUNCH
Baby spinach salad with sliced hard-boiled eggs, mushrooms,
celery, avocado, soybeans, pickled okra, sardines, and minced
garlic tossed in Honey-Yogurt Dressing*

DINNER
Chicken Stroganoff* on a bed of whole-grain pasta
Lightly steamed broccoli sprinkled with extra-virgin olive oil,
lemon juice, and sunflower seeds
Raw potato slivers and carrot sticks

Day 3

BREAKFAST
Whole-grain cereal with plain low-fat yogurt, raisins, chopped
dried apricots, dates, and a sprinkling of almonds
Organic Raw Egg Soy Milk Shake*
Chai tea brewed from a tea bag and sweetened, if desired, with
honey (preferably unfiltered) or stevia

LUNCH
½–1 ounce gelatin powder dissolved in 2 tablespoons boiling
    water and mixed with cherry juice or Alkalinizing Potato
    Water
Golden Beet Soup*
1 or 2 slices whole-grain bread with 1 or 2 pats butter
Green salad with sliced celery, tomato, and minced garlic tossed
    in Balsamic Vinaigrette*

DINNER
Halibut with Spicy Curried Lentils*
Lightly steamed celery with 1 pat butter
Red or green bell pepper slices

Day 4

BREAKFAST
½–1 ounce gelatin powder dissolved in 2 tablespoons boiling
    water and mixed with cherry juice
Eggs or tofu scrambled in butter and pure olive oil or coconut
    oil
Grated Potatoes (see index for recipe) topped with 1 pat butter
Chai tea brewed from a tea bag and sweetened, if desired, with
    honey (preferably unfiltered) or stevia

LUNCH
Tabbouleh salad with sliced avocado, mango, and cucumber on
    a bed of arugula sprinkled with extra-virgin olive oil, apple
    cider vinegar, and flaxseeds
Salmon filet (preferably wild) drizzled with extra-virgin olive oil
Orange wedges

DINNER
Chicken Chili* topped with sliced pickled okra
1 or 2 slices whole-grain bread with 1 or 2 pats butter
Raw potato slivers and carrot sticks

Day 5

BREAKFAST
Oatmeal with fresh seasonal berries, chunks of kiwi, ⅛ cup
   wheat germ, a dollop of whole-milk yogurt, and sprinkled
   with flaxseeds
Organic Raw Egg Soy Milk Shake*
Chai tea brewed from a tea bag and sweetened, if desired, with
   honey (preferably unfiltered) or stevia

LUNCH
½–1 ounce gelatin powder dissolved in 2 tablespoons boiling
   water and mixed with cherry juice
Mediterranean Lentil Stew* on a bed of barley sprinkled with
   sliced almonds
Celery sticks

DINNER
Salmon Filet with Mango Cilantro Salsa*
Steamed Swiss chard sprinkled with minced garlic, extra-virgin
   olive oil, and lemon juice
Roasted Vegetables* (potatoes and carrots)
Sliced tomato and avocado drizzled with extra-virgin olive oil
   and apple cider vinegar and sprinkled with sunflower seeds
Raw potato slivers

Day 6

B REAKFAST

½–1 ounce gelatin powder dissolved in 2 tablespoons boiling
water and mixed with cherry juice or Alkalinizing Potato
Water

Whole-grain cereal with sliced banana and a few chopped
walnuts

Chai tea brewed from a tea bag and sweetened, if desired, with
honey (preferably unfiltered) or stevia

Organic Raw Egg Soy Milk Shake*

L UNCH

Mixed green salad with sliced tomato, avocado, celery, cucumber, and mango tossed in Balsamic Vinaigrette* and topped
with sardines, sliced almonds, and sesame seeds

D INNER

Beef Curry with Minted Cucumber Yogurt Sauce* on a bed of
brown rice

Green salad with sliced tomato and garbanzo beans tossed in
extra-virgin olive oil and apple cider vinegar

Raw potato slivers and celery sticks

Day 7

B REAKFAST

Fruit smoothie with pineapple, banana, plain low-fat yogurt,
whey protein powder and 1 beaten raw organic egg in
unsweetened apple juice

1 or 2 slices whole-grain toast with 1 or 2 pats butter

Chai tea brewed from a tea bag and sweetened, if desired, with
honey (preferably unfiltered) or stevia

LUNCH

Salad with greens, brown rice, sliced onion, avocado, cherry tomatoes, pickled okra, and steamed peas tossed in extra-virgin olive oil and vinegar and topped with chopped walnuts and flaxseeds

A side dish of smoked mackerel

DINNER

Grilled or roasted chicken breast

White Bean and Kale Salad* topped with shaved celery

1 slice whole-grain bread with 1 pat butter

Raw potato slivers and carrot sticks

Asthma, Bronchitis, and Emphysema

A combination of the following healing foods has proven effective in restoring the lungs to health.

* Garlic, cayenne, mustard, coffee, and hot chili pepper several times weekly open up the bronchial tubes and heal inflammation.
* Onion should be eaten as often as possible. Onions (and garlic) contain a substance called Allium that has an anti-inflammatory effect.
* Orange juice and cantaloupe are high in vitamin C. As vitamin C courses through the blood it picks up and disposes of acid waste, which inflames the joints.
* Dark green leafy vegetables are excellent for asthma because they are high in omega-3 fatty acids, which build strong cell membranes.
* Ground flaxseed is rich in omega-3 fatty acids.
* Saturated fat to build cellular membranes in the lungs should be eaten in a limited amount by the grain eater. (See index; fats and oils for the grain eater.)
* An apple daily makes it easier for the asthmatic to breathe.

Day 1

BREAKFAST
Orange juice
Eggs scrambled in butter and coconut oil or pure olive oil on a
    bed of chopped raw or lightly cooked baby spinach
1 or 2 slices whole-grain toast with fruit-sweetened jam
1 cup coffee

LUNCH
Raw vegetable sandwich with sliced tomato, cucumber, red
    onion, and lettuce on whole-grain bread spread with hummus
    and mustard

DINNER
Filet of salmon (preferably wild) with 1 pat butter
Garlic Mashed Yams*
Steamed Swiss chard sprinkled with extra-virgin olive oil,
    chopped onion, sesame seeds, and lemon juice
A few flaxseed crackers

Day 2

BREAKFAST
Chunks of apple, cantaloupe, sliced almonds, and flaxseeds on
    whole-milk yogurt sweetened with honey (preferably unfil-
    tered) or stevia
1 or 2 slices whole-grain toast with 1 or 2 pats butter
1 cup coffee

LUNCH
Baby spinach salad with cooked diced potatoes, sliced hard-
    boiled eggs, red onion, mushrooms, and avocado tossed in
    Honey-Yogurt Dressing*
Alkalinizing Potato Water (see index for recipe)

DINNER
Chicken Stroganoff* on bed of whole-grain pasta
Steamed Swiss chard onion with garlic butter
Raw potato slivers and carrot sticks (use peeler to make slivers)

Day 3

BREAKFAST
Orange juice
Whole-grain cereal with soy milk, raisins, cantaloupe, dates,
   and a sprinkling of walnuts and sesame seeds
1 cup coffee

LUNCH
Golden Beet Soup*
1 or 2 slices whole-grain bread with 1 or 2 pats butter
Carrot sticks
Alkalinizing Potato Water

DINNER
Red snapper with 1 pat butter and Spicy Curried Lentils* (see
   Halibut with Spicy Curried Lentils* recipe) topped with
   chopped sweet onion
Steamed spinach sprinkled with extra-virgin olive oil, minced
   garlic, and lemon juice
Raw potato slivers and carrot sticks

Day 4

BREAKFAST
Cantaloupe and apple slices
Eggs or tofu scrambled in coconut oil or pure olive oil
Alkalinizing Potato Water

LUNCH
1 apple
Mixed salad with cooked diced beets, lightly cooked diced
    potatoes, walnuts, chopped celery, and sliced green onion
    tossed in Apple Cider Vinaigrette* and sprinkled with
    sunflower seeds on a bed of arugula
A few flaxseed crackers

DINNER
Chicken Chili* topped with chopped pickled jalapeno
1 or 2 slices whole-grain bread with 1 or 2 pats butter
Celery sticks and raw potato slivers

Day 5

BREAKFAST
Orange juice
Oatmeal with cantaloupe, fresh seasonal berries, walnuts, a
    dollop of whole-milk yogurt, and sprinkled with flaxseeds
1 cup coffee

LUNCH
1 apple
Mediterranean Lentil Stew* topped with almonds and chopped
    sweet onion
1 slice whole-grain bread with 1 pat butter

DINNER
Salmon Filet with Mango Cilantro Salsa*
Roasted Vegetables* (potatoes and carrots)
Sliced avocado and tomato drizzled with extra-virgin olive oil
    and apple cider vinegar
Alkalinizing Potato Water

Day 6

BREAKFAST
Orange juice
Whole-grain cereal with soy milk, sliced banana, and a few
  chopped walnuts
1 cup coffee

LUNCH
Mixed green salad with sliced tomato, avocado, cucumber, and
  mango topped with sliced almonds, sesame seeds, and a tiny
  sprinkling of cayenne pepper drizzled with extra-virgin olive
  oil and apple cider vinegar
1 or 2 slices whole-grain bread with 1 or 2 pats butter
Alkalinizing Potato Water

DINNER
1 apple
Lamb and Black Bean Chili with Adobo* topped with minced
  jalapeño
Green salad with sliced tomato, red onion, and garbanzo beans
  tossed in Balsamic Vinaigrette*
Raw potato slivers

Day 7

BREAKFAST
Fruit smoothie with cantaloupe, orange, banana, whole-milk
  yogurt, and unsweetened apple juice
1 or 2 slices whole-grain bread with 1 or 2 pats butter
1 cup coffee

LUNCH
Tabbouleh salad with chunks of tofu, raw baby spinach, chopped onion, and chopped walnuts drizzled with extra-virgin olive oil and lemon juice
Alkalinizing Potato Water

DINNER
1 apple
Grilled chicken breast served with Dijon mustard
White Bean and Kale Salad*
Raw potato and carrot strips

Cancer Prevention

The foods that stand out as cancer preventatives are orange vegetables and berries. There are other foods as well that protect against cancer. These anticancer foods, included in the menu plans, are as follows:

* Brussels sprouts, cabbage, bok choy, and green pepper have high levels of folic acid that block the formation of cancer tumors.
* Carrots, sweet potatoes, squash, pumpkin, and mango contain beta carotene, which fights cancer by repairing damaged DNA.
* Strawberries and black raspberries depress growth of cancer cells.
* Sunflower seeds and wheat germ are cancer preventives because of their high levels of vitamin B_6.
* Ground flaxseed increases anticancer hormones.
* Yogurt lowers risk of intestinal cancer.
* Cooked tomatoes help prevent prostate cancer.
* Raw apples decrease risk of lung cancer.
* Almonds are a general cancer preventive.

Day 1

BREAKFAST
1 apple
2 tablespoons ground flaxseed stirred into black raspberry juice
Eggs scrambled in pure olive oil and butter on a bed of chopped
    raw baby spinach
1 or 2 slices whole-grain toast with fruit-sweetened jam

LUNCH
Raw vegetable sandwich with sliced tomato, avocado, cucum-
    ber, grated carrot, lettuce, green pepper, and green onion on
    whole-grain bread spread with hummus and drizzled with
    extra-virgin olive oil

DINNER
Filet of salmon (preferably wild) with 1 pat butter
Garlic Mashed Yams*
Steamed kale sprinkled with extra-virgin olive oil or coconut oil
Carrot sticks
A few flaxseed crackers

Day 2

BREAKFAST
2 tablespoons ground flaxseed stirred into black raspberry juice
Whole-milk yogurt with fresh strawberries, sliced almonds, and
    sweetened with honey (preferably unfiltered) or stevia
1 or 2 slices whole-grain toast with 1 or 2 pats butter

LUNCH
Baby spinach salad with brown rice, sliced hard-boiled eggs,
    mushrooms, grated carrot, avocado, and mango tossed in
    Honey-Yogurt Dressing*
A handful of sunflower seeds

DINNER
1 apple
Chicken Stroganoff* on a bed of whole-grain pasta
Steamed brussels sprouts sprinkled with extra-virgin olive oil
    and lemon juice
Orange bell pepper slices

Day 3

BREAKFAST
2 tablespoons ground flaxseed stirred into black raspberry juice
Whole-grain cereal with soy milk, raisins, wheat germ, chopped
    dried mango, dates, and a sprinkling of almonds

LUNCH
Golden Beet Soup*
Green pepper slices drizzled with extra-virgin olive oil
1 or 2 slices whole-grain bread with 1 or 2 pats butter

DINNER
Halibut with Spicy Curried Lentils* with 2 cups chopped Swiss
    chard added to lentil recipe 10 minutes before it is done
Romaine lettuce salad with cherry tomatoes and sliced orange
    bell pepper tossed in Balsamic Vinaigrette*

Day 4

BREAKFAST
1 apple
2 tablespoons ground flaxseed stirred into black raspberry juice
Eggs or tofu scrambled in butter and pure olive oil or coconut
    oil
Grated Potatoes (see index for recipe) with 1 pat butter

LUNCH
Couscous or tabbouleh salad with sliced avocado, cherry toma-
    toes, sesame seeds, sliced almonds, and grated carrot on a bed
    of arugula and drizzled with Apple Cider Vinaigrette*
A small handful of sunflower seeds

DINNER
Chicken Chili*
1 or 2 slices whole-grain bread with 1 or 2 pats butter
Carrot sticks
A few flaxseed crackers

Day 5

BREAKFAST
2 tablespoons ground flaxseed stirred into black raspberry juice
Oatmeal with fresh strawberries and black raspberries topped
    with a dollop of whole-milk yogurt and sprinkled with wheat
    germ and ground flaxseed

LUNCH
1 apple
Mediterranean Lentil Stew* with sliced almonds
1 or 2 slices whole-grain bread with 1 or 2 pats butter
A small handful of sunflower seeds

DINNER
Salmon Filet with Mango Cilantro Salsa* (preferably wild
    salmon)
Steamed baby spinach sprinkled with coconut oil or extra-virgin
    olive oil and lemon juice
Roasted Vegetables* (sweet potatoes and green bell peppers)
Sunflower seeds

Day 6

BREAKFAST
2 tablespoons ground flaxseed stirred into favorite juice
Whole-grain cereal with soy milk, sliced banana, and strawberries topped with wheat germ, a few chopped walnuts, and
   almonds

LUNCH
Brown rice salad with sliced tomato, avocado, green pepper,
   cucumber, and mango tossed in Apple Cider Vinaigrette* and
   topped with sardines and sliced almonds
A handful of sunflower seeds

DINNER
Vegetable Beef Soup*
Green salad with sliced tomato and garbanzo beans tossed in
   extra-virgin olive oil and apple cider vinegar
Carrot and celery sticks and sliced cucumber
A few flaxseed crackers

Day 7

BREAKFAST
Fruit smoothie with pineapple, mango, strawberries, whole-milk
   yogurt, unsweetened apple juice, and 2 tablespoons ground
   flaxseed

LUNCH
1 apple
Chunks of tofu and crushed walnuts tossed in Apple Cider
   Vinaigrette*
Brown rice salad with sliced cucumber and green pepper
Roasted Vegetables* (sweet potatoes)
Carrot sticks

DINNER
Grilled or roasted chicken breast
White Bean and Kale Salad* topped with chopped almonds
Whole canned tomatoes heated and drizzled with extra-virgin
   olive oil
A small handful of sunflower seeds

Cardiovascular Disorders

This menu plan contains foods that lower the incidence of aneurysms (weakened blood vessel walls), heal thrombosis (blood clots), reduce high blood pressure, normalize elevated uric acid, strengthen weak heart muscle, and lower high cholesterol. These foods include:

* ❖ Nuts, seeds, green olives, and olive oil due to their monounsaturated oils, and in the case of nuts, their high levels of vitamin E and selenium.
* ❖ Fish, particularly sardines, mackerel, salmon, lobster, and oysters because of their high omega-3 fatty acid levels.
* ❖ Grapes, blueberries, strawberries, plums, and red apples prevent blood clots because of their high levels of carotene and antioxidants.
* ❖ Green tea, because of its high level of antioxidants, and avocadoes and olive oil, because they are high in monounsaturated oils, which lower cholesterol.
* ❖ Olives, endive, green leafy vegetables, and white clover honey strengthen the heart muscle due to their antioxidants and, in the case of vegetables and fruit, their high levels of carotene.

Day 1

BREAKFAST
Eggs scrambled in butter and pure olive oil or coconut oil on a
  bed of chopped raw or lightly cooked baby spinach
1 or 2 slices whole-grain toast with fruit-sweetened strawberry
  jam
Green tea with white clover honey

LUNCH
1 apple
Raw vegetable sandwich with sliced tomato, cucumber, lettuce,
  green onion, avocado, and black olives on whole-grain bread
  spread with hummus and drizzled with extra-virgin olive oil

DINNER
Filet of salmon (preferably wild) with 1 pat butter
Garlic Mashed Yams*
Steamed Swiss chard sprinkled with extra-virgin olive oil or
  coconut oil and lemon juice
A few flaxseed crackers

Day 2

BREAKFAST
Blueberries, papaya, and apricots with a dollop of whole-milk
  yogurt sprinkled with wheat bran
1 or 2 slices whole-grain toast with 1 or 2 pats butter
Green tea with white clover honey

LUNCH
Red grapes and sliced apples
Lettuce and endive salad with lobster tail sprinkled with extra-
  virgin olive oil and apple cider vinegar
Lightly cooked diced potatoes

DINNER
Halibut with Spicy Curried Lentils*
Blanched cauliflower florets tossed in extra-virgin olive oil or
   coconut oil and apple cider vinegar
A few flaxseed crackers

Day 3

BREAKFAST
Whole-grain cereal with soy milk, fresh blueberries, dried
   apricots, raisins, dates, and a sprinkling of almonds
Green tea with white clover honey

LUNCH
Golden Beet Soup*
Smoked oysters on whole-grain crackers
Sliced avocado and papaya drizzled with extra-virgin olive oil
   and apple cider vinegar

DINNER
Chicken Stroganoff* on a bed of whole-grain pasta
Lightly steamed broccoli sprinkled with extra-virgin olive oil
   and lemon juice
Carrot sticks and sliced red bell pepper

Day 4

BREAKFAST
Papaya, plums, and strawberries sprinkled with wheat bran
Eggs or tofu scrambled in butter and coconut oil or pure olive
   oil
Grated Potatoes (see index for recipe)
Green tea with white clover honey

LUNCH
A handful of red grapes and sliced apples
Quinoa salad with dried apricots on a bed of arugula drizzled
    with Apple Cider Vinaigrette*
Smoked oysters on whole-grain crackers

DINNER
Chicken Chili*
1 or 2 slices whole-grain bread with 1 or 2 pats butter
Green salad with avocado, green onion, and fresh blueberries
    tossed in extra-virgin olive oil and a dash of lemon juice

Day 5

BREAKFAST
Oatmeal with fresh strawberries, papaya, and apricots topped
    with a dollop of whole-milk yogurt and sprinkled with wheat
    bran and flaxseeds
Green tea with white clover honey

LUNCH
Mediterranean Lentil Stew* on a bed of barley
Carrot sticks and sliced orange bell peppers

DINNER
Salmon steak or filet (preferably wild) with plum cilantro salsa
    (substitute plum for mango in Salmon Filet with Mango
    Cilantro Salsa* recipe)
Steamed Swiss chard sprinkled with coconut oil or extra-virgin
    olive oil
Creamy Polenta*
Raw sugar snap peas

Day 6

BREAKFAST

Whole-grain cereal with soy milk, sliced banana, fresh strawberries or blueberries, and wheat bran topped with a few chopped walnuts, flaxseeds, and sunflower seeds
Green tea with white clover honey

LUNCH

Mixed green salad with sliced tomato, avocado, cucumber, and papaya tossed in extra-virgin olive oil and lemon juice and topped with poached lobster tail and sliced almonds
1 or 2 slices whole-grain bread with 1 or 2 pats butter

DINNER

Shrimp corn chowder (substitute shrimp for chicken in Chicken Corn Chowder* recipe)
1 or 2 slices whole-grain bread with 1 or 2 pats butter
Green salad with sliced tomato, green olives, and garbanzo beans tossed in Balsamic Vinaigrette* and sprinkled with sunflower seeds

Day 7

BREAKFAST

Fruit smoothie with blueberries, strawberries, papaya, banana, whole-milk yogurt, wheat bran, and unsweetened apple juice
1 or 2 slices whole-grain bread with 1 or 2 pats butter
Green tea with white clover honey

LUNCH

Brown rice salad with sliced avocado, tomato, red onion, cooked diced beets, tofu chunks, and crushed walnuts tossed in Apple Cider Vinaigrette* and served on a bed of raw spinach
Smoked oysters on whole-wheat crackers

Dinner
Grilled chicken breast
White Bean and Kale Salad* topped with sliced black olives
Creamy Polenta* topped with grated carrot and sesame seeds
Celery sticks

Circulatory Disorders

This menu plan contains foods that heal hardened arteries, elevated homocysteine levels, and poor circulation.

* Garlic, garlic juice, raw potatoes, and Alkalinizing Potato Water clear the arteries of fatty plaques.
* Romaine lettuce, dark green leafy vegetables, lentils, wheat germ, orange juice, and egg yolk lower homocysteine levels.
* Grated Potatoes, Alkalinizing Potato Water, and dark green leafy vegetables contain nitrate, which dilates the blood vessels, increases circulation, and alkalinizes the blood.

Day 1

Breakfast
Orange juice
Eggs scrambled in butter and pure olive oil or coconut oil on a
    bed of chopped raw or lightly cooked baby spinach
Grated Potatoes (see index for recipe)
1 slice whole-grain toast with fruit-sweetened jam

Lunch
Raw vegetable sandwich with sliced tomato, green pepper,
    cucumber, lettuce, black olives, and green onion on whole-
    grain bread spread with hummus and sprinkled with extra-
    virgin olive oil
Alkalinizing Potato Water (see index for recipe)

DINNER

Salmon Filet with Mango Cilantro Salsa* (preferably wild salmon)

Garlic Mashed Yams*

Steamed Swiss chard sprinkled with extra-virgin olive oil or coconut oil

Cucumber slices

A few flaxseed crackers

Day 2

BREAKFAST

1 beaten raw organic egg in orange juice

Oatmeal topped with plain low-fat yogurt, fresh seasonal fruit, wheat germ, and sweetened with honey (preferably unfiltered)

LUNCH

Baby spinach salad with cooked diced potato, sliced hard-boiled eggs, mushrooms, and avocado tossed in Honey-Yogurt Dressing* with minced garlic

A small handful of sesame seeds

DINNER

Filet of flounder or sole with Spicy Curried Lentils* (see Halibut with Spicy Curried Lentils* recipe)

Cucumber slices drizzled with extra-virgin olive oil and lemon juice

Carrot sticks

Day 3

BREAKFAST

1 beaten raw organic egg in orange juice

Whole-grain cereal with soy milk, raisins, dried apricots, dates, wheat germ, and a sprinkling of almonds

LUNCH
1 apple
Golden Beet Soup*
1 or 2 slices whole-grain bread with 1 or 2 pats butter
Baby spinach salad tossed in Apple Cider Vinaigrette* and
  sprinkled with walnuts
Alkalinizing Potato Water

DINNER
Chicken Stroganoff* on a bed of whole-grain pasta
Lightly steamed broccoli sprinkled with extra-virgin olive oil
  and lemon juice
Carrot sticks

Day 4

BREAKFAST
Orange juice
Eggs scrambled in butter and pure olive oil or coconut oil on a
  bed of steamed Swiss chard
Grated Potatoes

LUNCH
Tabbouleh vegetable salad with sliced avocado, cucumber,
  orange or yellow bell pepper, and tomato on a bed of arugula
  sprinkled with sesame seeds and wheat germ and drizzled
  with Balsamic Vinaigrette*
Carrot sticks

DINNER
Pork Tenderloin with Apple-Onion Compote*
Streamed spinach and minced garlic sprinkled with extra-virgin
  olive oil and lemon juice
1 or 2 slices whole-grain bread with 1 or 2 pats butter
Celery sticks
A few flaxseed crackers

Day 5

BREAKFAST
1 beaten organic raw egg in orange juice
Oatmeal with fresh seasonal berries, chunks of kiwi, and a
    dollop of plain low-fat yogurt and sprinkled with wheat germ
    and sliced almonds

LUNCH
Mediterranean Lentil Stew* with walnuts and sliced almonds
1 or 2 slices whole-grain bread with 1 or 2 pats butter
Alkalinizing Potato Water

DINNER
Salmon Filet with Mango Cilantro Salsa* (preferably wild
    salmon)
Steamed carrots and peas sprinkled with extra-virgin olive oil
Roasted Vegetables* (potatoes and onions)
A few flaxseed crackers

Day 6

BREAKFAST
1 beaten raw organic egg in orange juice
Whole-grain cereal with soy milk, sliced banana, wheat germ,
    sesame seeds, and a few chopped walnuts

LUNCH
Mixed green salad with sliced tomato, avocado, cucumber, and
    mango tossed in Balsamic Vinaigrette* with minced garlic
    and topped with sardines and sliced almonds
Grated Potatoes

DINNER
Chicken Corn Chowder*
A side dish of barley sprinkled with extra-virgin olive oil
Green salad with cherry tomatoes and orange bell pepper tossed
   in Honey Yogurt Dressing*
Carrot sticks

Day 7

BREAKFAST
Fruit smoothie with pineapple, banana, plain low-fat yogurt,
   wheat germ, and orange juice
Eggs scrambled in pure olive oil or coconut oil sprinkled with
   parsley and stuffed in a whole-wheat croissant

LUNCH
Brown rice salad with sliced avocado, tomato, cucumber, onion,
   and radishes on a bed of baby spinach drizzled with extra-
   virgin olive oil and apple cider vinegar and topped with
   chopped walnuts
Alkalinizing Potato Water

DINNER
Lamb Stew*
White Bean and Kale Salad*
Carrot sticks
A few flaxseed crackers

Diabetes

The foods listed here in the diabetic grain-eater's menu plan lower
blood sugar and help prevent kidney damage:

❖ Nuts, eggs, green pepper, broccoli, brussels sprouts, pork, raw or cooked onion, raw string beans, and fish lower blood sugar.

❖ Eggs, preferably raw (if eaten raw eat only organic eggs), nuts, and whole grains—foods high in vitamin B_1 complex—help prevent kidney damage.

Diabetics should limit carbohydrates to 40 percent of the diet.

For diabetics and others who want to find a sweetener that is healthy and won't put on weight, *stevia* is a good choice. It's an herbal plant that grows in South America and is 100 to 300 times sweeter than sugar. For that reason, use it sparingly until you find the amount that gives you the right degree of sweetness. It can be purchased in health food stores and organic food supermarkets.

Day 1

BREAKFAST
Eggs scrambled in coconut oil on a bed of chopped raw baby spinach
1 or 2 slices whole-grain toast with 1 or 2 pats butter

LUNCH
Raw vegetable sandwich with sliced tomato, avocado, cucumber, green pepper, lettuce, and green onion on whole-grain bread spread with hummus and sprinkled with extra-virgin olive oil

DINNER
Filet of salmon (preferably wild) with 1 pat butter
Garlic Mashed Yams*
Steamed broccoli sprinkled with coconut oil or extra-virgin olive oil
Celery sticks

Day 2

BREAKFAST
Fresh seasonal fruit with whole-milk yogurt and chopped
    pecans and almonds
1 or 2 slices whole-grain toast with 1 or 2 pats butter

LUNCH
Baby spinach salad with sliced red onion, hard-boiled eggs,
    mushrooms, blanched string beans, and sliced avocado tossed
    in extra-virgin olive oil and apple cider vinegar and sprinkled
    with sesame seeds
A few flaxseed crackers

DINNER
Pork Stroganoff (substitute pork tenderloin for chicken in
    Chicken Stroganoff* recipe) on a bed of whole-grain pasta
Lightly steamed brussels sprouts sprinkled with extra-virgin
    olive oil and lemon juice
Celery sticks

Day 3

BREAKFAST
Whole-grain cereal with soy milk, raisins, and a sprinkling of
    almonds and walnuts

LUNCH
Golden Beet Soup*
Lightly steamed brussels sprouts tossed in extra-virgin olive oil
Carrot and celery sticks and sliced cucumber

DINNER

Halibut with Spicy Curried Lentils*

Green salad with sliced green bell pepper tossed in extra-virgin
   olive oil and apple cider vinegar

A few flaxseed crackers

Day 4

BREAKFAST

Eggs or tofu scrambled in butter and pure olive oil or coconut
   oil

1 slice whole-grain bread with 1 pat butter

LUNCH

Quinoa or tabbouleh salad with sliced avocado, green peppers,
   cherry tomatoes, celery, blanched string beans, and radishes
   on a bed of arugula, drizzled with extra-virgin olive oil and
   lemon juice, and topped with flaked white tuna

DINNER

Chicken Chili*

1 or 2 slices whole-grain bread with 1 or 2 pats butter

Raw string beans

Day 5

BREAKFAST

Oatmeal with fresh seasonal berries, walnuts, and chunks of
   kiwi topped with a dollop of whole-milk yogurt

Alkalinizing Potato Water (see index for recipe)

LUNCH

Mediterranean Lentil Stew* on a bed of barley

Salad of sliced avocado, green pepper, and tomato sprinkled with
   sesame seeds, extra-virgin olive oil, and a dash of lemon juice

DINNER
Pork Tenderloin with Apple-Onion Compote*
Lightly steamed brussels sprouts
Roasted Vegetables* (eggplant, zucchini, and green bell peppers)
Green salad with sliced orange, red, and green bell peppers
    tossed in Balsamic Vinaigrette*
A few flaxseed crackers

Day 6

BREAKFAST
Whole-grain cereal with soy milk, sliced banana, and a few
    chopped walnuts and almonds

LUNCH
Mixed green salad with brown rice, lightly cooked brussels
    sprouts, sliced tomato, avocado, cucumber, green onion,
    green bell pepper, and mango tossed in Balsamic Vinaigrette*
A small handful of sesame seeds

DINNER
Tabbouleh salad with sliced tomato, red onion, and garbanzo
    beans tossed in extra-virgin olive oil and apple cider vinegar
    and topped with sardines

Day 7

BREAKFAST
Fruit smoothie with banana, whole-milk yogurt, ground
    flaxseed, and raw egg, in unsweetened apple juice
1 or 2 slices whole-grain bread with 1 or 2 pats butter

LUNCH
Brown rice salad with chunks of tofu and crushed walnuts
    tossed in extra-virgin olive oil and apple cider vinegar

DINNER
Cod, baked or lightly broiled, with 1 pat butter
White Bean and Kale Salad*
Green bell pepper slices

Hepatitis

Hepatitis B and C cause liver damage that can become chronic, making cirrhosis of the liver or cancer more likely. Foods that help to heal the inflamed liver reduce the chances of this happening. The following foods are included in the menu plan for grain eaters with hepatitis.

* Potato soup heals inflammation.
* Garlic, onions, carrots, brussels sprouts, artichoke hearts, and dark green leafy vegetables improve liver function because they are high in vitamin K_1.
* Liver, meat, yogurt, and cheese heal liver inflammation because they are high in vitamin K_2.

Day 1

BREAKFAST
Fresh seasonal berries
Eggs scrambled in pure olive oil or coconut oil and butter on a
    bed of chopped raw or lightly cooked baby spinach
1 or 2 slices whole-grain toast with fruit-sweetened jam

LUNCH
Potato Soup*
Raw vegetable sandwich with slices of tomato and avocado,
    grated carrots, lettuce, chopped garlic, and green onion on
    whole-grain bread spread with hummus and drizzled with
    extra-virgin olive oil

DINNER

Filet of salmon (preferably wild) with 1 pat butter

Garlic Mashed Yams*

Steamed Swiss chard and onion sprinkled with extra-virgin olive
   oil and lemon juice

A few almonds and walnuts

Day 2

BREAKFAST

Oatmeal with fresh seasonal fruit and walnuts topped with a
   dollop of whole-milk yogurt and sweetened with honey
   (preferably unfiltered)

LUNCH

Baby spinach salad with sliced hard-boiled eggs, mushrooms,
   avocado, red onion, and artichoke hearts, and minced garlic
   tossed in Honey-Yogurt Dressing* and topped with sautéed
   shrimp and sesame seeds

Potato Soup*

DINNER

Calf's liver and onions sautéed in butter and pure olive oil

Lightly steamed brussels sprouts sprinkled with extra-virgin
   olive oil or coconut oil and lemon juice

Caesar salad tossed in extra-virgin olive oil and apple cider
   vinegar to which a beaten organic raw egg has been added

Cucumber slices and raw green onions

Day 3

BREAKFAST

Whole-grain cereal with soy milk, raisins, chopped dried
   apricots, dates, and a sprinkling of almonds

Alkalinizing Potato Water* (see index for recipe)

LUNCH
Golden Beet Soup*
1 or 2 slices whole-grain bread with 1 or 2 pats butter
Green salad with sliced peaches, green onion, and sautéed bay
shrimp tossed in Balsamic Vinaigrette*

DINNER
Potato Soup*
Chilean sea bass with Spicy Curried Lentils* (see Halibut with
Spicy Curried Lentils* recipe)
Steamed artichokes with melted butter for dipping
Baby spinach salad with grated carrots, almonds, and walnuts
tossed in extra-virgin olive oil and apple cider vinegar and
topped with sesame seeds
Celery sticks

Day 4

BREAKFAST
Sliced melon
Eggs or tofu scrambled in butter and/or coconut oil or pure olive
oil
1 or 2 slices whole-grain bread with 1 or 2 pats butter
Alkalinizing Potato Water

LUNCH
Quinoa or tabbouleh salad with cherry tomatoes, goat cheese,
sliced onion, minced garlic, and black olives tossed in Apple
Cider Vinaigrette*, topped with artichoke hearts and sesame
seeds, and served on a bed of arugula
Potato Soup*

DINNER
Chicken livers sautéed in butter and topped with diced red
  onion
1 or 2 slices whole-grain bread with 1 or 2 pats butter
Carrot and celery sticks
A few flaxseed crackers

Day 5

BREAKFAST
Oatmeal with fresh seasonal berries, chunks of kiwi, a few
  walnuts, and sesame seeds topped with a dollop of whole-
  milk yogurt

LUNCH
Mediterranean Lentil Stew* topped with grated carrot and
  chopped almonds
Alkalinizing Potato Water

DINNER
Grilled prawns with Mango Cilantro Salsa* (see Salmon Filet
  with Mango Cilantro Salsa* recipe)
Steamed artichokes with melted butter for dipping
Potato Soup*

Day 6

BREAKFAST
Whole-grain cereal topped with soy milk, sliced banana, fresh
  seasonal berries, a few chopped walnuts, and sprinkled with
  ground flaxseed

LUNCH
Mixed green salad with sliced tomato, red onion, avocado,
   minced garlic, cucumber, and mango tossed in Balsamic
   Vinaigrette* and topped with sardines and slivered almonds
Potato Soup*

DINNER
Calf's liver sautéed in butter and sprinkled with parsley
Baby spinach salad with sliced tomato, avocado, carrot slivers,
   and artichoke hearts
Grated Potatoes (see index for recipe)
A few flaxseed crackers

Day 7

BREAKFAST
Fruit smoothie with pineapple, banana, whole-milk yogurt, raw
   organic egg, and unsweetened apple juice
1 or 2 slices whole-grain bread with 1 or 2 pats butter
Alkalinizing Potato Water

LUNCH
Brown rice salad with sliced avocado, tomato, radishes, grated
   carrots, minced garlic, chunks of tofu, and chopped walnuts
   tossed in extra-virgin olive oil and apple cider vinegar
Potato Soup*

DINNER
Calf or chicken liver sautéed in butter and topped with chopped
   green onion
White Bean and Kale Salad*
1 or 2 slices whole-grain bread with 1 or 2 pats butter
A few flaxseed crackers

Hyperthyroid

When a hyperthyroid can't be controlled with drugs, the thyroid is destroyed with radioactive iodine. To make sure this doesn't happen to you, and to help your body heal when you have a hyperthyroid condition, make the following foods a regular part of your diet.

- Raw cabbage, broccoli, and cauliflower prevent absorption of iodine.
- Cooked liver (or raw liver juice) heals the thyroid gland. It should be eaten daily if possible.
- Distilled water eliminates the industrial chemicals found in most tap water that speed up thyroid function.
- Avoid commercial puddings, yogurt, and food additives—they contain iodine emulsifiers.

Day 1

BREAKFAST
Eggs scrambled in coconut oil or pure olive oil on a bed of
    chopped raw or lightly cooked baby spinach
2 slices whole-grain toast with fruit-sweetened jam
Distilled water

LUNCH
Raw vegetable sandwich with sliced tomato, cucumber, lettuce,
    green onion, red cabbage, and sardines on whole-grain bread
    spread with hummus and drizzled with extra-virgin olive oil
Distilled water

DINNER
Filet of salmon (preferably wild) with 1 pat butter
Garlic Mashed Yams*

Steamed Swiss chard and onion sprinkled with extra-virgin olive
   oil
Raw broccoli florets tossed in extra-virgin olive oil and apple
   cider vinegar
Distilled water

Day 2

BREAKFAST
Oatmeal topped with fresh seasonal fruit, soy milk, and sweet-
   ened with honey (preferably unfiltered)
Distilled water

LUNCH
Baby spinach salad with sliced hard-boiled eggs, mushrooms,
   avocado, grated raw broccoli stems, and raw cauliflower
   florets tossed in Apple Cider Vinaigrette*
Distilled water

DINNER
Calf's liver and onion sautéed in butter and pure olive oil
Spicy Curried Lentils* (see Halibut with Spicy Curried Lentils*
   recipe) topped with shredded raw cabbage
Distilled water

Day 3

BREAKFAST
Whole-grain cereal with soy milk, raisins, chopped dried
   apricots, dates, and a sprinkling of almonds and flaxseeds
Distilled water

LUNCH
Golden Beet Soup*
1 or 2 slices brown rice bread dipped in extra-virgin olive oil
Green salad with cherry tomatoes, sliced cucumber, grated raw
    broccoli stems, and cauliflower florets tossed in Balsamic
    Vinaigrette* and sprinkled with sunflower seeds
Distilled water

DINNER
Chicken livers and onion sautéed in butter and pure olive oil
Whole-grain pasta drizzled with extra-virgin olive oil and
    melted butter
Crunchy Coleslaw*
Distilled water

Day 4

BREAKFAST
Eggs or tofu scrambled in butter and pure olive oil
Grated Potatoes (see index for recipe)
Distilled water

LUNCH
Tabbouleh salad with grated cabbage, raw cauliflower florets,
    sliced green onion, and sliced hard-boiled eggs tossed in
    Apple Cider Vinaigrette*
A few flaxseed crackers
Distilled water

DINNER
Chicken Chili*
1 or 2 slices whole-grain bread dipped in extra-virgin olive oil
Crunchy Coleslaw*
Distilled water

Day 5

BREAKFAST
Oatmeal with fresh seasonal berries and chunks of kiwi topped
with soy milk
Distilled water

LUNCH
Mediterranean Lentil Stew* with chopped almonds on a bed of
barley or brown rice
Raw cauliflower florets tossed in extra-virgin olive oil and apple
cider vinegar and sprinkled with sesame seeds
Distilled water

DINNER
Salmon Filet with Mango Cilantro Salsa* (preferably wild
salmon)
Steamed spinach sprinkled with extra-virgin olive oil and lemon
juice
Roasted Vegetables* (potatoes and carrots)
Raw cauliflower and broccoli florets tossed in Apple Cider
Vinaigrette*
Distilled water

Day 6

BREAKFAST
Whole-grain cereal with soy milk, sliced banana, and a few
chopped walnuts
Distilled water

LUNCH
Mixed green salad with lightly cooked diced potatoes, sliced
    tomato, cucumber, avocado, mango, and raw grated broccoli
    stems tossed in Balsamic Vinaigrette* and topped with sar-
    dines and sliced almonds
Distilled water

DINNER
Calf's liver and onion sautéed in butter
Brown rice sprinkled with extra-virgin olive oil and chopped
    parsley
Green salad with shredded cabbage, sliced tomato, raw cauli-
    flower florets, and garbanzo beans tossed in Balsamic
    Vinaigrette*
Distilled water

Day 7

BREAKFAST
Fruit smoothie with pineapple, banana, strawberries, and
    unsweetened apple juice
1 or 2 slices whole-grain toast with 1 or 2 pats butter
Distilled water

LUNCH
Brown rice or tabbouleh salad with grated raw broccoli stems,
    sliced tomato and avocado, chunks of tofu, and crushed
    walnuts tossed in Balsamic Vinaigrette*
Distilled water

DINNER
Chicken livers sautéed in butter and pure olive oil
White Bean and Kale Salad* topped with shredded raw cabbage
    and raw cauliflower florets
Distilled water

Hypothyroid

A vast majority of individuals have underactive thyroids by the time they are middle aged. While food allergies are sometimes the cause (see the sidebar "Pulse Test to Uncover Food Allergies" in Chapter 2), nutritional deficiencies should also be considered. The following foods incorporated in the hypothyroid menu plan can give a slow-acting thyroid a jump start.

* Coconut oil increases energy production and repairs the energy factories (mitochondria) in the cells, which helps normalize thyroid function.
* Coconut meat and juice, figs, chicken skin and hearts, organic eggs (preferably raw), and butter (in limited amounts for the grain eater) increase energy levels by normalizing thyroid function.
* Foods to avoid include beans (except string beans); peanuts; polyunsaturated oils; raw broccoli, cabbage, and cauliflower; and seaweed because they prevent the thyroid from absorbing iodine.

Day 1

BREAKFAST
Coconut juice
Eggs scrambled in coconut oil and butter on a bed of chopped raw or lightly cooked baby spinach
1 or 2 slices whole-grain toast with fruit-sweetened jam
Spring water

LUNCH
Raw vegetable sandwich with sliced tomato, cucumber, lettuce, and green onion on whole-grain bread spread with hummus and drizzled with coconut oil
2 whole-wheat fig cookies

DINNER
Filet of salmon (preferably wild) with 1 pat butter
Garlic Mashed Yams*
Steamed Swiss chard sprinkled with coconut oil
Fresh or dried figs
Cucumber slices

Day 2

BREAKFAST
Fresh or dried figs with whole-milk yogurt sweetened with
    honey (preferably unfiltered) and topped with unsweetened
    shredded coconut and sunflower seeds
1 or 2 slices brown rice or other grain bread with butter

LUNCH
Baby spinach salad with sliced hard-boiled eggs, mushrooms,
    avocado, and pear or melon tossed in Honey-Yogurt
    Dressing*
Fresh or dried figs

DINNER
Baked red snapper or other fish with 1 pat butter and shredded
    unsweetened coconut
Brown rice with butter
Lightly steamed green beans sprinkled with coconut oil
Cucumber slices

Day 3

BREAKFAST
Whole-grain cereal with rice milk, raisins, chopped dried apri-
    cots, figs, a sprinkling of almonds, and shredded unsweetened
    coconut

Carrot sticks
Spring water

LUNCH
Golden Beet Soup*
1 or 2 slices whole-grain bread with 1 or 2 pats butter
Carrot sticks
Spring water

DINNER
Broiled chicken breast with skin
Whole-grain pasta tossed in extra-virgin olive oil
Whole canned tomatoes (heated) and steamed broccoli with
    butter, a few drops lemon juice, and a sprinkling of sesame
    seeds
Green salad with sliced fresh figs and avocado tossed in
    Balsamic Vinaigrette*
Spring water

Day 4

BREAKFAST
Fresh or dried figs
Eggs or tofu scrambled in coconut oil
Grated Potatoes (see index for recipe)
Spring water

LUNCH
Quinoa or couscous salad with sliced avocado, tomato, and
    radishes on a bed of arugula
1 or 2 slices multigrain bread with butter
A few flaxseed crackers
Spring water

DINNER
Lamb Stew* with brown rice
Green salad with sliced figs and walnuts tossed in Balsamic
  Vinaigrette*
Carrot sticks
Spring water

Day 5

BREAKFAST
Oatmeal with fresh seasonal berries, dried figs, kiwi, shredded
  coconut, and walnuts topped with a dollop of whole-milk
  yogurt
Spring water

LUNCH
Mediterranean Lentil Stew* with chopped almonds and grated
  coconut on a bed of brown rice or barley
Carrot sticks
A small handful of sunflower seeds

DINNER
Salmon filet coated with unsweetened shredded coconut,
  sautéed in butter, and served with Mango Cilantro Salsa* (see
  Salmon Filet with Mango Cilantro Salsa* recipe)
Steamed Swiss chard sprinkled with extra-virgin olive oil
Roasted Vegetables* (potatoes and carrots)
Cucumber slices and carrot sticks
Spring water

Day 6

BREAKFAST
Coconut juice
Whole-grain cereal with rice milk, sliced banana, a few chopped
  walnuts, and sprinkled with flaxseeds
Distilled water

LUNCH
Mixed green salad with sliced tomato, avocado, cucumber,
  mango, and brown rice or lightly cooked diced potatoes
  drizzled with Apple Cider Vinaigrette* and topped with
  sardines, almonds, and toasted unsweetened coconut

DINNER
Chicken Corn Chowder*
1 or 2 slices whole-grain bread dipped in extra-virgin olive oil
Green salad with sliced tomato, avocado, and dried figs tossed
  in coconut oil and apple cider vinegar
Carrot sticks
Distilled water

Day 7

BREAKFAST
Fruit smoothie with pineapple, banana, yogurt, coconut juice,
  and unsweetened apple juice
1 or 2 slices whole-grain toast with 1 or 2 pats butter

LUNCH
Tabbouleh salad with chopped walnuts, toasted unsweetened
  coconut, and sliced avocado and tomato drizzled with
  coconut oil and apple cider vinegar
Carrot sticks

DINNER
Grilled chicken breast with skin
Mashed sweet potatoes with butter
Green salad with sliced fresh figs tossed in Balsamic
   Vinaigrette* and sprinkled with sesame seeds
Carrot sticks

Migraine

Migraine sufferers are often deficient in B-complex vitamins, magnesium, and omega-3 fatty acids. The foods listed here and in the migraine menu plan help to erase these nutritional deficiencies with the result that the number and severity of migraine headaches are reduced.

* Yogurt and powdered ginger provide B-complex vitamins. Ginger also blocks the production of prostoglandins, which trigger inflammation.
* Root vegetables, apples, bananas, peaches, lima beans, and whole grains are good sources of B vitamins, potassium, and vitamin A.
* Fatty fish including salmon, mackerel, and sardines provide omega-3 fatty acids.
* Avoid the following foods, which appear to trigger migraines: chocolate, coffee, citrus, alcohol, and dairy products unless fermented.

Day 1

BREAKFAST
Sliced apple and banana
Eggs scrambled in pure olive oil or coconut oil on a bed of
   chopped raw or lightly cooked baby spinach
1 or 2 slices whole-grain toast with fruit-sweetened jam

LUNCH
Raw vegetable sandwich with sliced tomato, avocado, cucumber, grated carrot, lettuce, and green onion on whole-grain bread spread with hummus and drizzled with extra-virgin olive oil

DINNER
Filet of salmon (preferably wild) with 1 pat butter
Roasted Vegetables* (yams or sweet potatoes)
Lightly steamed lima beans
Carrot sticks

Day 2

BREAKFAST
Banana, apple, and peach slices with whole-milk yogurt, sprinkled with powdered ginger
1 or 2 slices toasted brown rice or millet bread dipped in extra-virgin olive oil

LUNCH
Filet of mackerel atop a baby spinach salad with sliced hard-boiled eggs, mushrooms, avocado, peaches, and steamed lima beans drizzled with Honey-Yogurt Dressing*

DINNER
Chicken Stroganoff * on a bed of whole-grain pasta
Steamed broccoli sprinkled with extra-virgin olive oil
Carrot sticks

Day 3

BREAKFAST
Whole-grain cereal with whole-milk yogurt, raisins, banana, peaches, and a sprinkling of almonds, flaxseeds, and powdered ginger

LUNCH
Golden Beet Soup*
Steamed lima beans
1 or 2 slices brown rice or millet bread dipped in extra-virgin
    olive oil
Carrot sticks

DINNER
Halibut with Spicy Curried Lentils*
Couscous or quinoa with a dollop of whole-milk yogurt and
    sprinkled with powdered ginger
Steamed lima beans
Carrot sticks

Day 4

BREAKFAST
Sliced apple
Eggs or tofu scrambled in coconut oil or pure olive oil
Grated Potatoes (see index for recipe) with a sprinkling of extra-
    virgin olive oil and walnuts

LUNCH
Quinoa or tabbouleh salad with sliced avocado, tomato,
    radishes, cooked diced beets, and mushrooms on a bed of
    arugula, drizzled with extra-virgin olive oil and apple cider
    vinegar, and topped with filet of mackerel

DINNER
Chicken Chili*
1 or 2 slices whole-grain bread dipped in extra-virgin olive oil
Carrot sticks

Day 5

BREAKFAST
Oatmeal with fresh peach, apple, banana, walnuts, and flaxseeds
  topped with whole-milk yogurt and sprinkled with powdered
  ginger

LUNCH
Mediterranean Lentil Stew* on a bed of barley or brown rice
  topped with a dollop of whole-milk yogurt and chopped
  almonds
Carrot sticks

DINNER
Salmon Filet with Mango Cilantro Salsa* (preferably wild
  salmon)
Creamy Polenta*
Steamed Swiss chard sprinkled with extra-virgin olive oil or
  coconut oil and lemon juice

Day 6

BREAKFAST
Whole-grain cereal with sliced banana, peach, apple, chopped
  walnuts, and sesame seeds topped with whole-milk yogurt
  and sprinkled with powdered ginger

LUNCH
Mixed green salad with sliced tomato, avocado, cucumber, and
  mango tossed in extra-virgin olive oil and a few drops lemon
  juice and topped with sardines and toasted almonds

DINNER
Smoked oysters on whole-wheat crackers
Vegetable Beef Soup*
Lightly steamed lima beans
Green salad with sliced tomato and cucumber tossed in Apple
   Cider Vinaigrette*

Day 7

BREAKFAST
Fruit smoothie with pineapple, banana, peach, apple, whole-
   milk yogurt, and unsweetened apple juice
1 or 2 slices whole-grain bread dipped in extra-virgin olive oil

LUNCH
Brown rice or tabbouleh salad with sliced carrot, pepper, onion,
   and steamed lima beans tossed in Balsamic Vinaigrette* and
   topped with chunks of tofu, a dollop of whole-milk yogurt,
   crushed walnuts, and sprinkled with powdered ginger
Celery sticks

DINNER
Filet of salmon (preferably wild) with 1 pat butter
White Bean and Kale Salad*
Carrot sticks

Prostate Problems

Low-grade infection and prostate enlargement are common problems in middle-aged men, and cancer of the prostate is becoming
more common. Diet is the key to preventing these illnesses and
also in reducing their severity. The foods listed below are included
in the menu plan for prostate problems.

❖ One carrot daily reduces inflammation.
❖ Oysters, preferably smoked, supply zinc. The prostate has six times more zinc than any other organ.
❖ Avocados and tomatoes eaten together can reduce cancer growth by 52 percent. Avocados are high in lutein, which inhibits prostate cancer.
❖ Citrus, especially lemons, which have high levels of anti-cancer nutrients vitamins C and A, and grapefruit, which is high in the powerful antioxidant lycopene. Impressive anecdotal evidence indicates that four lemons or two grapefruits daily have been known to cure prostate cancer.
❖ A handful of pumpkin seeds and a few walnuts daily can shrink an enlarged prostate.
❖ Green tea can prevent cancer recurrence. Drink 1 cup of green tea during the day, preferably at bedtime.

Day 1

BREAKFAST
Lemonade made with the juice of 4 lemons, distilled or spring water, and sweetened with honey (preferably unfiltered) or stevia
Eggs scrambled in pure olive oil or coconut oil and butter on a bed of chopped raw baby spinach
1 or 2 slices whole-grain toast with fruit-sweetened jam

LUNCH
Raw vegetable sandwich with sliced tomato, avocado, cucumber, lettuce, and green onion on whole-grain bread spread with hummus and drizzled with extra-virgin olive oil
A handful of pumpkin seeds

DINNER
Filet of salmon (preferably wild) with 1 pat butter
Garlic Mashed Yams*
Steamed Swiss chard sprinkled with extra-virgin olive oil and
    lemon juice
1 raw carrot
1 cup green tea (preferably at bedtime)

Day 2

BREAKFAST
Fresh grapefruit juice made from the juice of 2 whole
    grapefruits
Whole-milk yogurt with banana, sweetened with honey (prefer-
    ably unfiltered), and sprinkled with walnuts
1 or 2 slices whole-grain toast with 1 or 2 pats butter

LUNCH
Baby spinach salad with sliced hard-boiled eggs, mushrooms,
    avocado, and tomato tossed in Honey-Yogurt Dressing*
A handful of pumpkin seeds

DINNER
Chicken Stroganoff* on a bed of whole-grain pasta or brown
    rice
Steamed broccoli with 1 pat butter and a few drops lemon juice
1 raw carrot
1 cup green tea (preferably at bedtime)

Day 3

BREAKFAST
Whole-grain cereal with soy milk, raisins, chopped dried
    apricots, dates, and a sprinkling of almonds and flaxseeds

LUNCH

Lemonade made with the juice of 4 lemons, distilled or spring
   water, and sweetened with honey (preferably unfiltered) or
   stevia
Golden Beet Soup*
1 or 2 slices whole-grain bread with 1 or 2 pats butter
Green salad with sliced avocado, tomato, and a handful of
   pumpkin seeds tossed in Apple Cider Vinaigrette*
1 whole carrot
A small handful of pumpkin seeds

DINNER

Halibut with Spicy Curried Lentils*
Sliced avocado and tomato drizzled with extra-virgin olive oil
   and apple cider vinegar
Celery sticks
A few walnuts
1 cup green tea (preferably at bedtime)

Day 4

BREAKFAST

Fresh grapefruit juice made from the juice of 2 whole
   grapefruits
Eggs scrambled in coconut oil and butter
Grated Potatoes (see index for recipe) topped with walnuts and
   almonds

LUNCH

Quinoa or tabbouleh salad with sliced tomato and avocado on a
   bed of arugula, drizzled with extra-virgin olive oil and apple
   cider vinegar, and sprinkled with a handful of pumpkin seeds

DINNER
Chicken Chili*
Creamy Polenta*
1 raw carrot
1 cup green tea (preferably at bedtime)

Day 5

BREAKFAST
Lemonade made with the juice of 4 lemons, distilled or spring
    water, and sweetened with honey (preferably unfiltered) or
    stevia
Oatmeal with fresh seasonal berries and banana topped with
    whole-milk yogurt and a sprinkling of walnuts

LUNCH
Mediterranean Lentil Stew* with chopped almonds on a bed of
    brown rice
Green salad with sliced tomato and avocado tossed in Balsamic
    Vinaigrette*
A handful of pumpkin seeds

DINNER
Salmon Filet with Mango Cilantro Salsa* (preferably wild
    salmon)
Steamed spinach sprinkled with coconut oil or extra-virgin olive
    oil
Canned stewed tomatoes heated in a little butter
Roasted Vegetables* (potatoes, green and red bell peppers, and
    eggplant)
1 raw carrot
1 cup green tea (preferably at bedtime)

Day 6

BREAKFAST
Fresh grapefruit juice made from the juice of 2 whole grapefruits
Whole-grain cereal with soy milk, sliced banana, and a few
　chopped walnuts

LUNCH
Smoked oysters on whole-wheat crackers
Mixed green salad with sliced tomato, avocado, mango, and
　cucumber tossed in Apple Cider Vinaigrette* and topped with
　sardines and slivered almonds
A handful of pumpkin seeds

DINNER
Chicken Corn Chowder*
1 or 2 slices whole-grain bread
Green salad with sliced tomato, avocado, and garbanzo beans
　tossed in Apple Cider Vinaigrette*
1 raw carrot
1 cup green tea (preferably at bedtime)

Day 7

BREAKFAST
Fruit smoothie with pineapple, banana, whole-milk yogurt, and
　unsweetened apple juice
1 or 2 slices whole-grain bread with 1 or 2 pats butter

LUNCH
Lemonade made with the juice of 4 lemons, distilled or spring
　water, and sweetened with honey (preferably unfiltered) or
　stevia
Brown rice salad with sliced avocado, tomato, chunks of tofu,
　and crushed walnuts tossed in Honey-Yogurt Dressing*
A handful of pumpkin seeds

DINNER
Smoked oysters on whole-wheat crackers
Lamb Stew*
White Bean and Kale Salad*
Canned stewed tomatoes with chopped raw garlic, heated and
    topped with extra-virgin olive oil
1 raw carrot
1 cup green tea (preferably at bedtime)

Stomach, Esophageal, and Intestinal Problems

Although eating the foods appropriate to your metabolism will
prevent inflammatory digestive tract diseases, they won't heal
existing ones. To do that you need the following special healing
foods, which are included in the diet plan:

* Gelatin, Alkalinizing Potato Water, Grated Potatoes,
  bananas, and raw cabbage juice neutralize acid waste, heal
  inflammation, and rebuild the mucous membranes. (Make
  raw cabbage juice using a juicer, preferably the Champion
  Juicer because it doesn't destroy enzymes, and enough
  cabbage to make one 8-ounce glass of juice.)

Day 1

BREAKFAST
½–1 ounce gelatin powder dissolved in 2 tablespoons boiling
    water and mixed with your favorite fruit juice
Eggs scrambled in pure olive oil or coconut oil and butter on a
    bed of chopped raw or lightly cooked baby spinach
Grated Potatoes (see index for recipe)

LUNCH
Raw vegetable sandwich with sliced tomato, cucumber, grated
   carrots, lettuce, and green onion on whole-grain bread spread
   with hummus and drizzled with extra-virgin olive oil
Raw cabbage juice

DINNER
Filet of salmon (preferably wild) with 1 pat butter
Garlic Mashed Yams*
Steamed Swiss chard with 1 pat butter
Alkalinizing Potato Water (see index for recipe)
Carrot sticks

Day 2

BREAKFAST
½–1 ounce gelatin powder dissolved in 2 tablespoons boiling
   water and mixed with your favorite fruit juice
Sliced banana with whole-milk yogurt, sweetened with honey
   (preferably unfiltered)
1 or 2 slices whole-grain toast with 1 or 2 pats butter

LUNCH
Baby spinach salad with sliced hard-boiled eggs, mushrooms,
   and avocado tossed in Honey-Yogurt Dressing*
Alkalinizing Potato Water

DINNER
Halibut with Spicy Curried Lentils*
Grated Potatoes
Raw cabbage juice

Day 3

BREAKFAST
½–1 ounce gelatin powder dissolved in 2 tablespoons boiling
   water and mixed with your favorite fruit juice
Whole-grain cereal with soy milk, raisins, banana, chopped
   dates, and a sprinkling of almonds

LUNCH
Golden Beet Soup*
1 or 2 slices brown rice or multigrain bread
Raw cabbage juice

DINNER
Chicken Stroganoff*
Grated Potatoes
Steamed broccoli and carrots tossed in extra-virgin olive oil and
   a few drops lemon juice

Day 4

BREAKFAST
½–1 ounce gelatin powder dissolved in 2 tablespoons boiling
   water and mixed with your favorite fruit juice
Eggs or tofu scrambled in pure olive oil or coconut oil and
   butter
Grated Potatoes

LUNCH
Tabbouleh salad with sliced avocado, red or orange bell pepper,
   and mushrooms tossed in extra-virgin olive oil and apple cider
   vinegar and served on a bed of arugula
Raw cabbage juice

DINNER

Salmon Filet with Mango Cilantro Salsa* (preferably wild salmon)

Steamed cabbage and onion with 1 pat butter on a bed of barley or brown rice

Alkalinizing Potato Water

Day 5

BREAKFAST

Oatmeal with fresh seasonal berries, sliced banana, and chunks of kiwi topped with a dollop of whole-milk yogurt

Alkalinizing Potato Water

LUNCH

Mediterranean Lentil Stew* with sliced almonds

1 or 2 slices whole-grain bread with 1 or 2 pats butter

Raw cabbage juice

DINNER

Red snapper or other fish with Mango Cilantro Salsa* (see Salmon Filet with Mango Cilantro Salsa* recipe)

Steamed spinach sprinkled with extra-virgin olive oil

Grated Potatoes

Day 6

BREAKFAST

½–1 ounce gelatin powder dissolved in 2 tablespoons boiling water and mixed with your favorite fruit juice

Whole-grain cereal with soy milk, sliced banana, and a few chopped walnuts

Alkalinizing Potato Water

LUNCH

Mixed green salad with sliced tomato, avocado, cucumber, carrot, cabbage, and mango tossed in Balsamic Vinaigrette* and topped with sardines and almonds

Grated Potatoes

DINNER

Chicken Corn Chowder*

Green salad with sliced tomato and garbanzo beans tossed in Apple Cider Vinaigrette*

Raw cabbage juice

Day 7

BREAKFAST

Fruit smoothie with orange slices, banana, whole-milk yogurt, and unsweetened apple juice

1 or 2 slices whole-grain bread with 1 or 2 pats butter

Alkalinizing Potato Water

LUNCH

½–1 ounce gelatin powder dissolved in 2 tablespoons boiling water and mixed with your favorite fruit juice

Brown rice salad with sliced tomato, avocado, chunks of tofu, and crushed walnuts tossed in extra-virgin olive oil and apple cider vinegar

Grated Potatoes

DINNER

Vegetable Beef Soup*

White Bean and Kale Salad*

Raw cabbage juice

9

Regain Health

Meat Eater

The meat-eater menu plans in this chapter are designed to benefit the following health problems: arthritis; asthma, bronchitis, and emphysema; cancer prevention; cardiovascular disorders; circulatory disorders; diabetes; hepatitis; hyperthyroid; hypothyroid; migraine; prostate problems; and stomach, esophageal, and intestinal problems.

The menu plans work in two stages. First, they detoxify the body by supplying the kinds of protein, carbohydrates, and fats and oils that the meat-eater metabolism requires. After the toxicity is cleared up and the pH is balanced, the healing foods restore the body to health.

Recipes followed by an asterisk (*) are in Part III. Recipes for Alkalinizing Potato Water and Grated Potatoes are in Chapter 5. Almond milk, used in some menus, can be found in health food stores and organic food supermarkets.

Arthritis

The healing foods for meat eaters are the same as those grain eaters incorporate into their menu plans for arthritis. The food items in this plan that have proven most effective for eliminating pain are the Alkalinizing Potato Water and the raw potato slivers. The key foods in the meat-eater's menu plan that help heal arthritis are as follows:

* Alkalinizing Potato Water and raw potato slivers eliminate or reduce pain.
* Okra and celery make joints more flexible because they are high in sodium.
* Powdered ginger, cloves, and garlic lessen joint pain.
* Organic raw eggs are high in pantothenic acid, a B vitamin in which most arthritics are deficient.
* Whey (found in health food stores) and liver are also high in B vitamins: eat 3 or 4 tablespoons per week.
* Citrus fruit and cherry juice break up calcium deposits. Cherry juice is especially effective for bursitis.
* Salmon, mackerel, and sardines are rich in vitamin D, which the body needs to absorb calcium.

Day 1

Breakfast
Oatmeal with sliced oranges, whole-milk yogurt, and sprinkled with powdered ginger and walnuts
Chai tea brewed from tea bag and sweetened with honey (preferably unfiltered)
Organic Raw Egg Almond Milk Shake* with whey protein or Alkalinizing Potato Water

Lunch
Lamb burger topped with minced garlic and grilled onion on a bed of mixed lettuce salad with sliced pickled okra, avocado, mango, and sardines (optional) sprinkled with extra-virgin olive oil and apple cider vinegar
1 or 2 slices spelt or rye bread with butter

DINNER

Calf's liver and onion sautéed in pure olive oil and butter (or if you don't like liver, grilled steak)

Lightly steamed green beans

Roasted Vegetables* (potatoes and carrots)

Raw potato slivers (use peeler to make slivers)

Day 2

BREAKFAST

Whole-grain flour tortilla filled with eggs scrambled in butter, grated carrot, green onion, and goat cheese

Chai tea brewed from tea bag and sweetened with honey (preferably unfiltered)

Organic Raw Egg Almond Milk Shake* with whey protein

LUNCH

Sweet Potato and Green Bean Salad* (add ¼ cup sliced celery to recipe)

Alkalinizing Potato Water (see index for recipe)

DINNER

Beef Curry with Minted Cucumber Yogurt Sauce*

Steamed celery sprinkled with extra-virgin olive oil

1 or 2 slices brown rice or millet bread with butter

Carrot sticks and raw potato slivers

Day 3

BREAKFAST

Fruit salad with banana, pineapple, a dollop of whole-milk yogurt, chopped walnuts, and sprinkled with ½ ounce gelatin powder

1 or 2 slices whole-grain toast with butter

Chai tea brewed from tea bag and sweetened with honey (preferably unfiltered)

LUNCH

Raw vegetable sandwich with sliced cucumber, avocado, tomato, and onion on whole-grain bread spread with mustard or hummus and sprinkled with extra-virgin olive oil

Organic Raw Egg Almond Milk Shake* with whey protein

Celery sticks

DINNER

Mackerel filet with Mango Cilantro Salsa* (see Salmon Filet with Mango Cilantro Salsa* recipe)

Mashed potatoes with butter

Lightly cooked broccoli

Raw potato slivers and celery sticks

Day 4

BREAKFAST

1 or 2 poached eggs on a bed of Grated Potatoes seasoned with green onion, parsley, and butter

Chai tea brewed from tea bag and sweetened with honey (preferably unfiltered)

Organic Raw Egg Almond Milk Shake* with whey protein or Alkalinizing Potato Water

LUNCH

Vegetable Beef Soup* (add ½ cup celery to recipe)

1 or 2 slices whole-grain bread with butter

Cucumber slices

DINNER

Grilled Lamb Chops with Purée of Rutabaga and Tart Apple*

Roasted Vegetables* (potatoes)

Celery sticks and raw potato slivers

Day 5

BREAKFAST
Oatmeal with papaya, banana, mango, almonds, and sprinkled
 with ½–1 ounce gelatin
Chai tea brewed from tea bag and sweetened with honey
 (preferably unfiltered)
Organic Raw Egg Almond Milk Shake* with whey protein

LUNCH
Calf's liver and onion sautéed in butter
Mixed green salad with goat cheese, raw walnuts, and sliced
 peaches or mango tossed in apple cider vinegar and extra-
 virgin olive oil
Celery sticks and raw potato slivers

DINNER
Grilled chicken or duck breast topped with sliced pickled okra
Steamed whole artichoke with melted butter for dipping
Lightly steamed green beans with extra-virgin olive oil and
 wedge of lemon
Alkalinizing Potato Water

Day 6

BREAKFAST
1 or 2 eggs fried over easy in butter
1 or 2 slices whole-grain toast with butter and unsweetened
 apple butter
Chai tea brewed from tea bag and sweetened with honey
 (preferably unfiltered)
Organic Raw Egg Almond Milk Shake* with whey protein or
 Alkalinizing Potato Water

LUNCH

Salmon (preferably wild), grilled, broiled, or baked, with
     Walnut-Basil Butter*
Steamed peas and carrots sprinkled with sesame seeds
1 slice whole-grain bread with butter

DINNER

Lamb Stew* sprinkled with ½–1 ounce gelatin powder
Green salad with cherry tomatoes and sliced celery tossed in
     Balsamic Vinaigrette*
Raw potato slivers

Day 7

BREAKFAST

1 or 2 whole-grain waffles with unsweetened almond butter and
     fruit-sweetened jam
Chai tea brewed from tea bag and sweetened with honey
     (preferably unfiltered)
Organic Raw Egg Almond Milk Shake* with whey protein or
     Alkalinizing Potato Water

LUNCH

Salad with brown rice, green onion, red grapes, sliced red bell
     pepper, and chopped or sliced almonds tossed in Balsamic
     Vinaigrette*
Raw potato slivers

DINNER

Chicken livers and onion sautéed in pure olive oil and butter
     with Apple-Onion Compote* (see Pork Tenderloin with
     Apple-Onion Compote* recipe)
Roasted Vegetables* (potatoes, orange and red bell peppers, and
     zucchini, squash, or eggplant)

Steamed cauliflower with butter
Carrot sticks

Asthma, Bronchitis, and Emphysema

A combination of the following healing foods has proven effective in restoring the lungs to health.

* Garlic, cayenne, mustard, coffee, and hot chili pepper several times weekly open up the bronchial tubes and heal inflammation.
* Onion should be eaten as often as possible. Onions (and garlic) contain a substance called Allium that has an anti-inflammatory effect.
* Orange juice and cantaloupe are high in vitamin C. As vitamin C courses through the blood it picks up and disposes of acid waste, which inflames the joints.
* Dark green leafy vegetables are excellent for asthma because they are high in omega-3 fatty acids, which build strong cell membranes.
* Ground flaxseed is rich in omega-3 fatty acids.
* Saturated fat to build strong cellular membranes in the lungs should be eaten in a limited amount by the grain eater. (See index where fats and oils for the grain eater are listed.)
* An apple daily makes it easier for the asthmatic to breathe.

Day 1

BREAKFAST
Orange juice
Oatmeal with sliced cantaloupe, whole-milk yogurt, and a
   sprinkling of walnuts
1 cup coffee

LUNCH
Lamb burger topped with sliced red onion and jalapeños on a
    mixed lettuce salad with sliced avocado and mango tossed in
    Apple Cider Vinaigrette*
1 or 2 slices whole-grain bread with butter

DINNER
Grilled steak with grilled onion and Dijon mustard
Lightly steamed spinach or chard
Roasted Vegetables* (potatoes and carrots)
Celery sticks

Day 2

BREAKFAST
Whole-grain flour tortilla filled with eggs scrambled in butter,
    grated carrot, green onion, and goat cheese
1 cup coffee

LUNCH
1 apple
Sweet Potato and Green Bean Salad* sprinkled with chopped
    green onion
1 or 2 slices whole-grain bread with butter
A few almonds or walnuts

DINNER
Beef Curry with Minted Cucumber Yogurt Sauce*
A side dish of brown rice with butter
Raw sliced red or yellow bell pepper

Day 3

BREAKFAST
Fruit salad with sliced orange, apple, and cantaloupe topped
   with a dollop of whole-milk yogurt, chopped almonds, and
   walnuts
1 or 2 slices whole-grain toast with butter
1 cup coffee

LUNCH
1 apple
Brown rice salad with diced avocado, sliced onion, cucumber,
   radishes, and mango tossed in Apple Cider Vinaigrette*

DINNER
Thick-cut lean pork chop with Mango Cilantro Salsa* (see
   Salmon Filet with Mango Cilantro Salsa* recipe)
Mashed potatoes with butter
Steamed spinach with a sprinkling of extra-virgin olive oil and
   lemon juice
Cucumber slices

Day 4

BREAKFAST
1 or 2 poached eggs on a bed of Grated Potatoes (see index for
   recipe) seasoned with green onion, parsley, and butter
1 cup coffee

LUNCH
1 apple
Vegetable Beef Soup*
Green salad with sliced onion and cherry tomatoes tossed in
   extra-virgin olive oil and apple cider vinegar

DINNER
Grilled Lamb Chops with Purée of Rutabaga and Tart Apple*
A side dish of brown rice with butter and a tiny dash of cayenne
    pepper (optional)
Cucumber slices

Day 5

BREAKFAST
Orange juice
Oatmeal with sliced cantaloupe, banana, and almonds
1 cup coffee

LUNCH
Mixed salad with cooked diced beet, lightly cooked diced
    potato, and chopped onion tossed in extra-virgin olive oil and
    apple cider vinegar and topped with chopped mint and
    walnuts

DINNER
Dijon marinated grilled or roasted chicken breast
Steamed whole artichoke with melted garlic butter for dipping
Lightly cooked green beans sprinkled with chopped raw red
    onion
Carrot sticks

Day 6

BREAKFAST
Sliced cantaloupe
1 or 2 eggs fried over easy in butter
1 or 2 slices whole-grain toast with unsweetened apple butter
1 cup coffee

LUNCH
Salmon (preferably wild), broiled, grilled, or baked, with
  Walnut-Basil Butter*
Steamed peas, carrots, and potato chunks with butter and a tiny
  dash of cayenne pepper (optional)
Celery sticks

DINNER
1 apple
Lamb Stew*
Lightly steamed green beans with butter
Green salad with walnuts and sesame seeds tossed in Balsamic
  Vinaigrette*

Day 7

BREAKFAST
1 or 2 whole-grain waffles with unsweetened peanut butter and
  fruit-sweetened jam
1 cup coffee

LUNCH
1 apple
Salad with green onion, red grapes, and sliced red bell pepper
  tossed in extra-virgin olive oil and apple cider vinegar
1 or 2 slices whole-grain bread with butter

DINNER
Chicken Chili*
Lightly steamed spinach
1 boiled potato rolled in butter and Dijon mustard
Celery sticks

Cancer Prevention

The foods that stand out as cancer preventives are orange vegetables and berries. There are other foods as well that protect against cancer. These anticancer foods, included in the menu plans, are as follows:

* Brussels sprouts, cabbage, bok choy, and green pepper have high levels of folic acid that block the formation of cancer tumors.
* Carrots, sweet potatoes, squash, pumpkin, and mango contain beta carotene, which fights cancer by repairing damaged DNA.
* Strawberries and black raspberries depress growth of cancer cells.
* Sunflower seeds and wheat germ are cancer preventives because of their high levels of vitamin B$_6$.
* Ground flaxseed increases anticancer hormones.
* Yogurt lowers risk of intestinal cancer.
* Cooked tomatoes help prevent prostate cancer.
* Raw apples decrease risk of lung cancer.
* Almonds are a general cancer preventive.

Day 1

BREAKFAST
Oatmeal with black raspberries, strawberries, walnuts, a dollop of whole-milk yogurt, and sprinkled with 2 tablespoons ground flaxseed

LUNCH
Mixed lettuce salad with lightly cooked diced potato, sliced avocado, mango, and apples tossed in Balsamic Vinaigrette*

DINNER
Grilled steak
Lightly steamed green beans and carrots topped with chopped
   green onion
Roasted butternut squash with butter
Carrot sticks

Day 2

BREAKFAST
2 tablespoons ground flaxseed mixed into black raspberry juice
Whole-grain flour tortilla filled with eggs scrambled in butter,
   grated carrot, green onion, and goat cheese

LUNCH
Sweet Potato and Green Bean Salad* on a bed of raw baby
   spinach
A handful of sunflower seeds

DINNER
Beef Curry topped with Minted Cucumber Yogurt Sauce*
1 slice whole-grain bread with butter
Carrot and celery sticks
A handful of sunflower seeds

Day 3

BREAKFAST
Fruit salad with sliced banana, strawberries or black raspberries,
   a dollop of whole-milk yogurt, and sprinkled with wheat
   germ and flaxseed
1 or 2 slices whole-grain toast with butter

LUNCH

Brown rice with sliced avocado, mango, orange bell pepper, and red cabbage, drizzled with extra-virgin olive oil, a few drops lemon juice, and sprinkled with sunflower seeds

Carrot sticks

DINNER

Thick-cut lean pork chop with Mango Cilantro Salsa* (see Salmon Filet with Mango Cilantro Salsa* recipe)

Roasted Vegetables* (sweet potatoes) with a tiny dash of cayenne pepper (optional)

Steamed spinach with butter

Raw green pepper slices

Day 4

BREAKFAST

2 tablespoons ground flaxseed mixed with black raspberry juice

1 or 2 poached eggs on a bed of Grated Potatoes seasoned with green onion, parsley, and butter

LUNCH

Sliced raw green and orange bell pepper tossed in extra-virgin olive oil and apple cider vinegar

Baked acorn squash with butter

1 or 2 slices whole-grain bread dipped in extra-virgin olive oil

A handful of sunflower seeds

DINNER

Grilled Lamb Chops with Purée of Rutabaga and Tart Apple*

Lightly steamed brussels sprouts tossed in butter or a sprinkling of coconut oil

Carrot sticks

Day 5

BREAKFAST
Oatmeal with whole-milk yogurt, black raspberries, strawberries, banana, and mango topped with chopped almonds and sunflower seeds

LUNCH
Mixed green salad with cooked diced beet, lightly cooked diced potato, and orange bell pepper tossed in Apple Cider Vinaigrette* and topped with goat cheese, chopped mint, and raw walnuts

DINNER
Grilled chicken breast
Steamed whole artichoke with melted garlic butter for dipping
Lightly steamed green beans
Canned whole tomatoes, drained and heated, topped with chopped raw green pepper, grated carrot, and drizzled with extra-virgin olive oil or coconut oil

Day 6

BREAKFAST
Strawberries topped with a dollop of whole-milk yogurt and sprinkled with ground flaxseed
1 or 2 eggs fried over easy in butter
1 or 2 slices whole-grain toast with unsweetened apple butter

LUNCH
Sweet Potato and Green Bean Salad*
Lightly steamed bok choy and carrots with butter or a sprinkling of coconut oil
Raw green pepper slices

DINNER
Lamb Stew*
Green salad with chunks of apple, toasted almonds, and sun-
flower seeds tossed in Balsamic Vinaigrette*

Day 7

BREAKFAST
1 or 2 whole-grain waffles with unsweetened almond butter
topped with sliced strawberries or black raspberries and
sprinkled with sunflower seeds

LUNCH
Salad with green onion, red grapes, sliced orange and green bell
pepper, and chopped walnuts and almonds tossed in Apple
Cider Vinaigrette*
1 or 2 slices whole-grain bread with butter

DINNER
Chicken Corn Chowder*
Lightly steamed brussels sprouts with butter
1 or 2 slices whole-grain bread dipped in extra-virgin olive oil
Carrot sticks
A handful of sunflower seeds

Cardiovascular Disorders

This menu plan contains foods that lower the incidence of
aneurysms (weakened blood vessel walls), heal thromboses (blood
clots), reduce high blood pressure, normalize elevated uric acid,
strengthen weak heart muscle, and lower cholesterol. These foods
include:

❖ Nuts, seeds, green olives, and olive oil due to their monounsaturated oils, and in the case of nuts, their high levels of vitamin E and selenium.

❖ Fish, particularly sardines, mackerel, salmon, lobster, and oysters because of their high omega-3 fatty acid levels.

❖ Grapes, blueberries, strawberries, plums, and red apples prevent blood clots because of their high levels of carotene and antioxidants.

❖ Green tea, because of its high level of antioxidants, and avocadoes and olive oil, because they are high in monounsaturated oils, lower cholesterol.

❖ Olives, endive, green leafy vegetables, and white clover honey strengthen the heart muscle due to their antioxidants and, in the case of vegetables and fruit, their high levels of carotene.

Day 1

BREAKFAST
Oatmeal with whole-milk yogurt, fresh blueberries or strawberries, red grapes, apricots, and a sprinkling of raw walnuts and sunflower seeds
1 cup green tea with white clover honey

LUNCH
Mixed endive and lettuce salad with cooked diced beet and potatoes, green olives, sliced avocado, and papaya tossed in Apple Cider Vinaigrette*

DINNER
Grilled steak
Roasted Vegetables* (potatoes, eggplant, and onion)
Crunchy Coleslaw* made with red cabbage

Day 2

BREAKFAST

Whole-grain flour tortilla filled with eggs scrambled in butter, chopped raw red pepper, green onion, and sliced avocado
1 cup green tea with white clover honey

LUNCH

Sweet Potato and Green Bean Salad* served on a bed of chopped endive drizzled with extra-virgin olive oil and sprinkled with green olives, sesame seeds, and walnuts

DINNER

Beef Curry with Minted Cucumber Yogurt Sauce* topped with sunflower seeds
A side dish of brown rice with butter
Celery and carrot sticks

Day 3

BREAKFAST

Fruit salad with fresh blueberries or strawberries, plums or red apples, and banana topped with whole-milk yogurt, almonds, and sesame seeds
1 or 2 slices whole-grain toast with butter
1 cup green tea with white clover honey

LUNCH

Brown rice salad with sliced red cabbage, avocado, green olives, and endive tossed in Balsamic Vinaigrette*

DINNER
Sautéed duck breast with Mango Cilantro Salsa* (see Salmon
    Filet with Mango Cilantro Salsa* recipe)
Mashed potatoes
Lightly steamed broccoli sprinkled with butter or coconut oil
Carrot sticks

Day 4

BREAKFAST
1 or 2 poached eggs on a bed of Grated Potatoes (see index for
    recipe) seasoned with green onion, parsley, and butter
1 cup green tea with white clover honey

LUNCH
Sliced avocado, cucumber, and fresh blueberries on bed of
    Belgian endive drizzled with extra-virgin olive oil and a dash
    of apple cider vinegar
Baked acorn squash with butter

DINNER
Grilled Lamb Chops with Purée of Rutabaga and Tart Apple*
Roasted Vegetables* (potatoes, red bell pepper, and eggplant)
Carrot sticks
A handful of pumpkin or sesame seeds

Day 5

BREAKFAST
Whole-grain cereal with fresh blueberries or strawberries, sliced
    apple, dried apricots, chopped walnuts, almonds, and almond
    milk
1 cup green tea with white clover honey

LUNCH
Green salad with lightly cooked diced potato and beet, sliced
    raw red cabbage, and red pepper tossed in Apple Cider
    Vinaigrette* and topped with chopped mint, walnuts, and
    flaxseeds

DINNER
Grilled chicken breast with black olives, steamed beets, and
    spaghetti squash sprinkled with extra-virgin olive oil
Green beans marinated in extra-virgin olive oil and apple cider
    vinegar topped with sliced tomato
Celery and carrot sticks

Day 6

BREAKFAST
1 or 2 eggs fried over easy in butter
1 or 2 slices whole-grain toast with unsweetened apple butter
1 cup green tea with white clover honey

LUNCH
Raw vegetable sandwich with sliced avocado, tomato, red
    cabbage, papaya, red pepper, and red onion on whole-grain
    bread spread with mustard and drizzled with extra-virgin
    olive oil

DINNER
Lamb Stew*
Endive salad with cooked diced beets, black olives, green olives,
    and sunflower seeds
1 slice whole-grain or brown rice bread with butter

Day 7

BREAKFAST

1 apple

1 or 2 whole-grain waffles with unsweetened almond butter, or peanut butter, sprinkled with fresh seasonal berries

1 cup green tea with white clover honey

LUNCH

Salad with a little brown rice, sliced green onion, red grapes, red bell pepper, avocado, Belgian endive, red cabbage, chopped almonds, walnuts, and sesame seeds tossed in extra-virgin olive oil and apple cider vinegar

DINNER

Pork Tenderloin with Apple-Onion Compote*

Roasted Vegetables* (sweet potatoes and eggplant)

Red, orange, and/or green bell pepper slices drizzled with Balsamic Vinaigrette*

Circulatory Disorders

This menu plan contains foods that heal hardened arteries, elevated homocysteine levels, and poor circulation.

* ❖ Garlic, garlic juice, raw potatoes, and Alkalinizing Potato Water clear the arteries of fatty plaques.
* ❖ Romaine lettuce, dark green leafy vegetables, lentils, wheat germ, orange juice, and egg yolk lower homocysteine levels.
* ❖ Grated Potatoes, Alkalinizing Potato Water, and dark green leafy vegetables contain nitrate that dilates the blood vessels, increases circulation, and alkalinizes the blood.

Day 1

BREAKFAST
Oatmeal with sliced orange and banana topped with a
   sprinkling of walnuts and wheat germ
Organic Raw Egg Almond Milk Shake*

LUNCH
Lamb burger topped with grilled onion
Romaine lettuce salad with a little minced garlic, sliced avocado,
   and mango drizzled with extra-virgin olive oil or coconut oil
   and apple cider vinegar
Alkalinizing Potato Water (see index for recipe)

DINNER
Calf's liver and onion sautéed in butter
Lightly steamed green beans
Roasted Vegetables* (potatoes and carrots)
Carrot and celery sticks

Day 2

BREAKFAST
Whole-grain flour tortilla filled with eggs scrambled in butter
Salad with grated carrot, cooked grated beet, and chopped
   green onion tossed in extra-virgin olive oil and apple cider
   vinegar
Alkalinizing Potato Water

LUNCH
Sweet Potato and Green Bean Salad* served on a bed of romaine
   lettuce tossed in extra-virgin olive oil, apple cider vinegar, and
   garlic juice

DINNER
Beef Curry with Minted Cucumber Yogurt Sauce*
Brown rice with butter
Steamed Swiss chard sprinkled with extra-virgin olive oil and
    minced garlic
Carrot sticks

Day 3

BREAKFAST
Fruit salad with fresh seasonal berries, sliced apple, banana, and
    plums topped with a dollop of whole-milk yogurt and sprin-
    kled with wheat germ and flaxseeds
1 or 2 slices whole-grain toast with butter
Organic Raw Egg Almond Milk Shake*

LUNCH
Romaine lettuce salad with lightly cooked diced potato, cooked
    diced beet, sliced cucumber, and green onion tossed in extra-
    virgin olive oil, apple cider vinegar, and minced garlic
Alkalinizing Potato Water

DINNER
Chicken Stroganoff* on a bed of whole-grain pasta
Steamed broccoli with butter
Celery and carrot sticks

Day 4

BREAKFAST
Poached eggs on a bed of Grated Potatoes (see index for recipe)
    with green onion, parsley, and butter

LUNCH
Vegetable Beef Soup*
Romaine lettuce salad with grated carrot and raw green pepper
    slices tossed in extra-virgin olive oil and apple cider vinegar,
    and topped with almonds, walnuts, and flaxseeds

DINNER
Thick-cut, lean pork chop with Mango Cilantro Salsa* (see
    Salmon Filet with Mango Cilantro Salsa* recipe)
Mashed potatoes with butter
Lightly steamed broccoli with butter
Celery and carrot sticks

Day 5

BREAKFAST
Whole-grain cereal topped with fresh blueberries or strawber-
    ries; sliced apple, banana, or plums; almonds; and sunflower
    or sesame seeds
Organic Raw Egg Almond Milk Shake*

LUNCH
Salad with shredded iceberg lettuce, cooked diced beet, lightly
    cooked diced potato, sliced avocado, cucumber, and cherry
    tomatoes, tossed in extra-virgin olive oil and apple cider vine-
    gar, and topped with chopped mint and toasted almonds
Alkalinizing Potato Water

DINNER
Calf's liver and onion sautéed in pure olive oil and butter
Steamed whole artichoke with melted garlic butter for dipping
Lightly steamed green beans sprinkled with extra-virgin olive oil
Alkalinizing Potato Water

Day 6

BREAKFAST
1 or 2 eggs fried over easy in butter
1 or 2 slices whole-grain toast with unsweetened apple butter
Alkalinizing Potato Water

LUNCH
Raw vegetable sandwich with sliced tomato, cucumber, green
    onion, and green olives on whole-grain bread with Dijon
    mustard and drizzled with extra-virgin olive oil

DINNER
Lamb Stew*
Raw baby spinach salad with walnuts and sliced pear or melon
    tossed in Apple Cider Vinaigrette*
A handful of pumpkin seeds

Day 7

BREAKFAST
1 or 2 whole-grain waffles with unsweetened peanut butter and
    fruit-sweetened jam
Organic Raw Egg Almond Milk Shake*

LUNCH
Salad with romaine lettuce, brown rice, sliced green onion, red
    grapes, red bell pepper, and tomato tossed in Balsamic Vinai-
    grette* and topped with chopped almonds
Alkalinizing Potato Water

Dinner
Calf's liver sautéed in pure olive oil and butter with Apple-
    Onion Compote* (see Pork Tenderloin with Apple-Onion
    Compote* recipe)
Roasted Vegetables* (sweet potatoes, green and orange bell pep-
    per, and eggplant)
Carrot sticks and cucumber slices

Diabetes

The foods listed here in the diabetic meat-eater's menu plan lower
blood sugar and help prevent kidney damage:

* Nuts, eggs, green pepper, broccoli, brussels sprouts, pork,
  raw or cooked onion, raw string beans, and fish lower blood
  sugar.
* Eggs, preferably raw (if eaten raw eat only organic eggs),
  nuts, and whole grains—foods high in vitamin B_1
  complex—help prevent kidney damage.

Diabetics should limit carbohydrates to 40 percent of the diet.

For diabetics and others who want to find a sweetener that is
healthy and won't put on weight, *stevia* is a good choice. It's an
herbal plant that grows in South America and is 100 to 300 times
sweeter than sugar. For that reason, use it sparingly until you find
the amount that gives you the right degree of sweetness. It can be
purchased in health food stores and organic food supermarkets.

Day 1

Breakfast
Oatmeal with whole-milk yogurt, sliced banana, kiwi, and a
    sprinkling of walnuts

LUNCH
Mixed lettuce salad with sliced avocado, green peppers, blanched green beans, and mango tossed in Balsamic Vinaigrette* and sprinkled with sesame seeds
1 or 2 corn tortillas
Cucumber slices

DINNER
Pork Tenderloin with Apple-Onion Compote*
Steamed broccoli
Brown rice with butter
Celery sticks

Day 2

BREAKFAST
Whole-grain flour tortilla filled with eggs scrambled with butter, grated carrot, chopped green pepper, and green onion

LUNCH
White Bean and Kale Salad*
1 or 2 slices whole-grain bread with butter
Carrot and celery sticks

DINNER
Beef Curry with Minted Cucumber and Yogurt Sauce*
Steamed brussels sprouts
Green pepper slices and carrot sticks

Day 3

BREAKFAST
Fruit salad with sliced apple and banana topped with a dollop of whole-milk yogurt and walnuts
1 egg fried over easy in butter
1 or 2 slices whole-grain bread with butter

LUNCH
Lamb and Black Bean Chili with Adobo*
Brown rice with 1 pat butter and sprinkled with diced avocado
Celery sticks and cucumber slices

DINNER
Thick-cut, lean pork chop with Mango Cilantro Salsa* (see
    Salmon Filet with Mango Cilantro Salsa* recipe)
Small serving brown rice with butter
Steamed brussels sprouts and green beans sprinkled with extra-
    virgin olive oil
Green bell pepper slices

Day 4

BREAKFAST
1 or 2 poached eggs on 1 slice whole-grain toast, topped with
    buttered steamed asparagus, and sprinkled with chopped
    green onion and parsley

LUNCH
Vegetable Beef Soup*
A side dish of brown rice
Blanched broccoli florets tossed in extra-virgin olive oil and
    apple cider vinegar and sprinkled with sesame seeds

DINNER
Grilled or broiled lamb chops
Lightly steamed brussels sprouts
Brown rice with butter
Celery sticks

Day 5

BREAKFAST
Whole-grain cereal with whole-milk yogurt, chunks of papaya
   and banana, and chopped almonds and walnuts

LUNCH
Green salad with cooked diced beet, green pepper, a little
   brown rice, green onion, and tomato, tossed in extra-virgin
   olive oil and apple cider vinegar, and sprinkled with walnuts
   and sesame seeds

DINNER
Grilled chicken breast
Steamed green beans sprinkled with extra-virgin olive oil, apple
   cider vinegar, chopped hard-boiled egg, and parsley
1 slice whole-grain bread with butter
Celery sticks and cucumber slices

Day 6

BREAKFAST
1 or 2 soft-boiled eggs on 1 slice whole-grain toast with butter
   and 1 slice whole-grain toast with unsweetened apple butter

LUNCH
Salmon (preferably wild), grilled, broiled, or baked, with
   Walnut-Basil Butter*
Lightly steamed brussels sprouts and broccoli drizzled with
   extra-virgin olive oil and lemon juice
1 or 2 slices whole-grain bread with butter

DINNER
Black Bean Chili with Adobo*
Green salad with sliced green and orange bell pepper, onion,
and cherry tomatoes tossed in Balsamic Vinaigrette* and
topped with walnuts and sesame or sunflower seeds

Day 7

BREAKFAST
1 or 2 whole-grain waffles with unsweetened peanut butter and
a few fresh seasonal berries

LUNCH
Mixed green salad with green onion, red grapes, sliced avocado,
blanched green beans, and green bell pepper, tossed in extra-
virgin olive oil and apple cider vinegar, and topped with
chopped walnuts and sesame seeds

DINNER
Pork Tenderloin with Apple-Onion Compote*
Roasted Vegetables* (eggplant, green bell pepper, and
onion)
Lightly steamed cauliflower and green beans with butter
Celery sticks

Hepatitis

Hepatitis B and C cause liver damage that can become chronic,
making cirrhosis of the liver or cancer more likely. Foods that help
to heal the inflamed liver reduce the chances of this happening.
These foods are included in the menu plan for meat eaters with
hepatitis:

* Potato soup heals inflammation.
* Garlic, onions, carrots, brussels sprouts, artichoke hearts, and dark green leafy vegetables improve liver function. because they are high in vitamin K_1.
* Liver, meat, yogurt, and cheese heal liver inflammation because they are high in vitamin K_2.

Day 1

BREAKFAST
Oatmeal with sliced apple, chopped dried figs, and a sprinkling of walnuts

LUNCH
Potato Soup*
Romaine lettuce salad with sliced avocado, artichoke hearts, and mango, tossed in Apple Cider Vinaigrette*, and sprinkled with sunflower seeds and walnuts

DINNER
Grilled sirloin steak with sautéed red onion
Roasted Vegetables* (potatoes, red and orange bell pepper, and eggplant)
Lightly steamed green beans and onion with butter
Carrot sticks

Day 2

BREAKFAST
Whole-grain flour tortilla filled with eggs scrambled in butter, grated carrot, and green onion

LUNCH
Sweet Potato and Green Bean Salad*
Potato Soup*
Carrot sticks

DINNER
Grilled or broiled steak sprinkled with chopped raw onion
Baked acorn squash with butter
Steamed whole artichoke with melted butter for dipping
Celery sticks

Day 3

BREAKFAST
Fruit salad with sliced banana, pineapple, a dollop of whole-
milk yogurt, and a sprinkling of walnuts
1 or 2 slices whole-grain toast with butter

LUNCH
Potato Soup*
Sardine sandwich with sliced avocado, onion, and tomato on
whole-grain bread with mustard and sprinkled with extra-
virgin olive oil
Cucumber slices

DINNER
Thick-cut, lean pork chop with Mango Cilantro Salsa* (see
Salmon Filet with Mango Cilantro Salsa* recipe)
Garlic mashed potatoes
Lightly cooked broccoli with butter
Green or orange bell pepper slices

Day 4

BREAKFAST
1 or 2 poached eggs on a bed of Grated Potatoes (see index for
recipe) seasoned with green onion, parsley, and butter

LUNCH
Vegetable Beef Soup*
Green salad with sliced red onion and mango tossed in Balsamic
 Vinaigrette*

DINNER
Potato Soup*
Grilled Lamb Chops with Purée of Rutabaga and Tart Apple*
1 slice whole-grain bread dipped in extra-virgin olive oil
Carrot sticks

Day 5

BREAKFAST
Whole-grain cereal with whole-milk yogurt, sliced papaya,
 banana, and mango, sprinkled with almonds, walnuts, and
 sesame seeds

LUNCH
Potato Soup*
Green salad with cooked diced beet, lightly cooked diced
 potato, goat cheese, sweet onion, mint, and raw walnuts,
 tossed in extra-virgin olive oil, apple cider vinegar, and
 minced garlic

DINNER
Grilled chicken breast
Steamed whole artichoke with melted butter for dipping
Lightly steamed green beans and potato chunks with garlic
 butter
Celery sticks

Day 6

BREAKFAST
Sliced banana, fresh seasonal berries, and sliced apple
1 or 2 soft-boiled eggs on 1 or 2 slices whole-grain toast with
    butter

LUNCH
Potato Soup*
Baked acorn squash with butter and honey
Green salad with artichoke hearts and green onion tossed in
    Honey-Yogurt Dressing*

DINNER
Salmon (preferably wild), grilled, broiled, or baked, with
    Walnut-Basil Butter*
Brown rice with butter
Lightly steamed Swiss chard sprinkled with extra-virgin olive oil
Cucumber slices

Day 7

BREAKFAST
1 or 2 whole-grain waffles with unsweetened peanut butter and
    fruit-sweetened jam, sprinkled with fresh seasonal berries

LUNCH
Potato Soup*
Salad with sliced green onion, red grapes, and red bell pepper
    tossed in Apple Cider Vinaigrette* and topped with chopped
    almonds, walnuts, and sesame seeds

DINNER
Pork Tenderloin with Apple-Onion Compote*
Roasted Vegetables* (potatoes and carrots)
Blanched cauliflower florets and green beans, tossed in extra-
   virgin olive oil and apple cider vinegar

Hyperthyroid

When hyperthyroid can't be controlled with drugs, the thyroid is destroyed with radioactive iodine. To make sure this doesn't happen to you, and to help your body heal when you have a hyperthyroid condition, make the following foods a regular part of your diet.

* Raw cabbage, broccoli, and cauliflower prevent absorption of iodine.
* Cooked liver (or raw liver juice) heals the thyroid gland. It should be eaten daily if possible.
* Distilled water eliminates the industrial chemicals found in most tap water that speed up thyroid function.
* Avoid commercial puddings, yogurt, and food additives—they contain iodine emulsifiers.

Day 1

BREAKFAST
Oatmeal with whole-milk yogurt, sliced melon, banana, apple, and a sprinkling of walnuts and sesame seeds
Distilled water

LUNCH

Mixed lettuce salad with sliced pear, red cabbage, raw broccoli, and avocado tossed in Apple Cider Vinaigrette* and sprinkled with sunflower seeds

Distilled water

DINNER

Calf's liver and onion sautéed in butter

Roasted Vegetables* (potatoes)

Lightly steamed green beans

Raw cauliflower chunks tossed in extra-virgin olive oil and apple cider vinegar

Distilled water

Day 2

BREAKFAST

Whole-grain flour tortilla filled with eggs scrambled in butter, grated carrot, grated raw broccoli stems, green onion, and goat cheese

Distilled water

LUNCH

Chicken livers and onion sautéed in butter

Sweet Potato and Green Bean Salad*

Distilled water

DINNER

Beef Curry with Minted Cucumber Yogurt Sauce* (omit cauliflower from recipe and add the same amount of raw cauliflower just before serving)

Brown rice with butter

Distilled water

Day 3

BREAKFAST
Fruit salad with sliced banana, pineapple, a dollop of whole-
 milk yogurt, and sprinkled with walnuts, almonds, and
 sesame seeds
1 or 2 slices whole-grain toast with butter
Distilled water

LUNCH
Mixed lettuce salad with sliced tomato, avocado, raw cauliflower
 chunks, and lightly cooked diced potato tossed in Honey-
 Yogurt Dressing* and sprinkled with cashews and pine nuts
Distilled water

DINNER
Calf's liver sautéed in butter
Brown rice with butter and topped with diced cucumber
Sliced raw broccoli or cauliflower florets tossed in extra-virgin
 olive oil and apple cider vinegar
Distilled water

Day 4

BREAKFAST
1 or 2 poached eggs on a bed of Grated Potatoes (see index for
 recipe) seasoned with green onion, parsley, and butter
Distilled water

LUNCH
Raw vegetable sandwich with sliced tomato, avocado, cucumber, and grated broccoli stems on whole-grain bread with
 mustard and a sprinkling of extra-virgin olive oil

DINNER
Calf's liver and onion sautéed in butter
Crunchy Coleslaw*
Roasted Vegetables* (potatoes and carrots)
Celery sticks
Distilled water

Day 5

BREAKFAST
Whole-grain cereal with whole-milk yogurt, sliced papaya,
   banana, almonds, and sunflower seeds
Distilled water

LUNCH
Salad greens with cooked diced beet, lightly cooked diced
   potato, sliced cucumber, and cherry tomatoes, tossed in extra-
   virgin olive oil and apple cider vinegar, and topped with goat
   cheese, chopped mint, and toasted walnuts
Distilled water

DINNER
Sardine sandwich with sliced onion, avocado, and tomato on
   whole-grain bread with mustard and a sprinkling of extra-
   virgin olive oil
Raw cauliflower florets
Distilled water

Day 6

BREAKFAST
Fresh seasonal fruit
1 or 2 soft-boiled eggs
1 or 2 slices whole-grain toast with butter
Distilled water

LUNCH
Steamed carrots, peas, and potato chunks and grated raw broccoli stems tossed in Apple Cider Vinaigrette* and sprinkled with flaxseeds
Distilled water

DINNER
Chicken livers and onion sautéed in butter
Green salad with raw broccoli and cauliflower florets and cherry tomatoes tossed in Balsamic Vinaigrette*
Distilled water

Day 7

BREAKFAST
1 or 2 whole-grain waffles with unsweetened peanut butter and fruit-sweetened jam
Distilled water

LUNCH
Mixed lettuce salad with green onion, grated raw cabbage, red and green grapes, and sliced red bell pepper tossed in Balsamic Vinaigrette* and topped with chopped almonds and sesame seeds
1 or 2 slices whole-grain bread dipped in extra-virgin olive oil
Distilled water

DINNER
Chicken livers and onion sautéed in butter
Lightly boiled potatoes rolled in butter
Crunchy Coleslaw*
Distilled water

Hypothyroid

A vast majority of individuals have underactive thyroids by the time they are middle-aged. While food allergies are sometimes the cause (see the sidebar "Pulse Test to Uncover Food Allergies" in Chapter 2), nutritional deficiencies should also be considered. The following foods incorporated in the hypothyroid menu plan can give a slow-acting thyroid a jump start.

* Coconut oil increases energy production and repairs the energy factories (mitochondria) in the cells, which helps normalize thyroid function.
* Coconut meat and juice, figs, chicken skin and hearts, organic eggs (preferably raw), and butter increase energy levels by normalizing thyroid function.
* Foods to avoid include beans (except string beans); peanuts; polyunsaturated oils; raw broccoli, cabbage, and cauliflower; and seaweed because they prevent the thyroid from absorbing iodine.

Day 1

BREAKFAST
Oatmeal with whole-milk yogurt, dried figs, apricots, and a
  sprinkling of walnuts and sesame seeds

LUNCH
Chicken hearts sautéed in butter and coconut oil
Mixed lettuce salad with sliced avocado, mango, lightly cooked
  diced potato, and cooked diced beet tossed in Honey-Yogurt
  Dressing*
Carrot sticks

DINNER
Grilled steak
Lightly steamed green beans sprinkled with coconut oil
Roasted Vegetables* (potatoes and squash)
Cucumber slices

Day 2

BREAKFAST
Fresh or dried figs
Whole-grain flour tortilla filled with eggs scrambled in butter,
  grated carrot, green onion, and goat cheese

LUNCH
Sweet Potato and Green Bean Salad*
1 or 2 corn tortillas
Celery sticks

DINNER
Roasted chicken thigh and leg with skin
Brown rice sprinkled with coconut oil
Steamed broccoli with lemon butter
Carrot sticks

Day 3

BREAKFAST
Fruit salad with sliced banana, pineapple, dried or fresh figs, a
  dollop of whole-milk yogurt, and sprinkled with cashews and
  pine nuts
1 or 2 slices whole-grain toast with butter
Organic Raw Egg Almond Milk Shake*

LUNCH
Flank steak marinated in pure olive oil and lemon juice
Brown rice with butter
Green salad with diced avocado and chopped onion tossed in
   extra-virgin olive oil and apple cider vinegar

DINNER
Thick-cut, lean pork chop with Mango Cilantro Salsa* (see
   Salmon Filet with Mango Cilantro Salsa* recipe)
Mashed potatoes with butter
Lightly steamed broccoli sprinkled with coconut oil
Carrot sticks

Day 4

BREAKFAST
1 or 2 poached eggs on a bed of Grated Potatoes (see index for
   recipe) seasoned with green onion, parsley, and butter

LUNCH
Chicken hearts sautéed in butter and pure olive oil
Green salad with sliced dried figs and mango, grated carrots,
   and sliced almonds tossed in Honey-Yogurt Dressing* and
   sprinkled with sesame seeds

DINNER
Grilled Lamb Chops with Purée of Rutabaga and Tart Apple*
Roasted Vegetables* (potatoes, green pepper, and zucchini)
Celery sticks

Day 5

BREAKFAST
Whole-grain cereal with whole-milk yogurt, sliced papaya, banana, fresh or dried figs, and sprinkled with walnuts and sesame seeds
Organic Raw Egg Almond Milk Shake*

LUNCH
Green salad with cooked diced beet, lightly cooked diced potato, goat cheese, grated carrots, mint, raw walnuts, and fresh or dried figs tossed in coconut oil and apple cider vinegar

DINNER
Grilled chicken breast with skin
Steamed whole artichoke with melted butter for dipping
Lightly steamed green beans and potato chunks sprinkled with coconut oil
Carrot sticks

Day 6

BREAKFAST
Eggs fried over easy in butter
1 or 2 slices whole-grain toast with butter and unsweetened apple butter

LUNCH
Salmon (preferably wild), grilled, broiled, or baked, with Walnut-Basil Butter*
Steamed asparagus and potato chunks sprinkled with coconut oil
Celery sticks

DINNER
Lamb Stew*
Green salad with sliced dried figs, barley, and walnuts tossed in
    Apple Cider Vinaigrette*
Cucumber slices

Day 7

BREAKFAST
1 or 2 whole-grain waffles with almond butter and fruit-
    sweetened jam
Organic Raw Egg Almond Milk Shake*

LUNCH
Salad made with green onion, chopped dried figs, sliced red bell
    pepper, and chopped almonds tossed in Balsamic Vinaigrette*

DINNER
Roasted or grilled chicken breast with skin
Roasted Vegetables* (sweet potatoes, squash, and red bell
    pepper)
Steamed asparagus sprinkled with coconut oil
Celery sticks

Migraine

Migraine sufferers are often deficient in B-complex vitamins, magnesium, and omega-3 fatty acids. The foods listed here and in the
migraine menu plan help to erase these nutritional deficiencies,
with the result that the severity and number of migraine headaches are reduced.

✤ Yogurt and powdered ginger provide B-complex vitamins.
   Ginger also blocks the production of prostoglandins, which
   trigger inflammation.

* Root vegetables, apples, bananas, peaches, lima beans, and whole grains are good sources of B vitamins, potassium, and vitamin A.
* Fatty fish including salmon, mackerel, and sardines provide omega-3 fatty acids.
* Avoid the following foods, which appear to trigger migraines: chocolate, coffee, citrus, alcohol, and dairy products (unless fermented).

Day 1

BREAKFAST
Oatmeal with whole-milk yogurt, sliced banana, apple, peach, and walnuts sprinkled with powdered ginger

LUNCH
Mixed lettuce salad with sliced avocado, mango, and red onion tossed in extra-virgin olive oil and apple cider vinegar and topped with pine nuts and cashews
1 or 2 slices whole-grain bread with butter

DINNER
Grilled steak
Lightly steamed lima beans
Roasted Vegetables* (potatoes, red and orange bell pepper, and eggplant)
Carrot sticks

Day 2

BREAKFAST
Eggs scrambled in butter and sprinkled with grated carrot, sliced green onion, and goat cheese
1 or 2 slices whole-grain toast with butter

LUNCH
Sweet Potato and Green Bean Salad*
Plain whole-milk yogurt sprinkled with powdered ginger
1 or 2 corn tortillas
Carrot sticks

DINNER
Vegetable Beef Soup*
A side dish of brown rice with butter
Green salad with steamed lima beans, cherry tomatoes, and
    radishes tossed in extra-virgin olive oil and apple cider vinegar
Celery sticks

Day 3

BREAKFAST
Fruit salad with sliced banana, peach, and apple, a dollop of
    whole-milk yogurt, and sprinkled with powdered ginger
1 or 2 slices brown rice bread with butter
A handful of walnuts, almonds, and sesame seeds

LUNCH
Baby spinach salad with lightly cooked diced potato, sliced
    tomato, and avocado tossed in extra-virgin olive oil and apple
    cider vinegar and topped with smoked mackerel or sardines
Carrot sticks

DINNER
Salmon Filet with Mango Cilantro Salsa*
Mashed sweet potatoes with butter
Lightly steamed lima beans and broccoli with butter topped
    with chopped cashews and pine nuts
Sliced red, orange, and/or green bell pepper

Day 4

B REAKFAST
Sliced peach or apple
1 or 2 poached eggs on a bed of Grated Potatoes (see index for
recipe) seasoned with green onion and parsley

L UNCH
Sardine sandwich with sliced tomato, avocado, and cucumber
on whole-grain bread with mustard and sprinkled with extra-
virgin olive oil

D INNER
Vegetable Beef Soup* (substitute lima beans for peas in recipe)
1 whole boiled potato rolled in butter and grated carrot

Day 5

B REAKFAST
Whole-milk yogurt with papaya, banana, apple slices, raw
almonds, and sprinkled with powdered ginger
1 or 2 soft-boiled eggs on whole-grain toast with butter

L UNCH
Green salad with cooked diced beet, and lightly cooked diced
potato tossed in extra-virgin olive oil and apple cider vinegar
and topped with goat cheese, chopped mint, and walnuts
Sautéed filet of mackerel

D INNER
Grilled chicken breast
Steamed whole artichoke with melted butter for dipping
Lightly steamed lima beans
Roasted yams or sweet potatoes with butter
Raw celery sticks

Day 6

BREAKFAST
Banana and apple slices
1 or 2 soft-boiled eggs
1 or 2 slices whole-grain toast

LUNCH
Salmon (preferably wild), grilled, broiled, or baked, with
    Walnut-Basil Butter*
Lightly cooked peas
Roasted Vegetables* (sweet potatoes)
Carrot sticks

DINNER
Lamb Stew*
Sliced mango on a bed of lettuce drizzled with Apple Cider
    Vinaigrette* and topped with whole-milk yogurt sprinkled
    with powdered ginger

Day 7

BREAKFAST
Vanilla whole-milk yogurt sprinkled with powdered ginger
Eggs scrambled in butter
1 or 2 slices toasted brown rice bread with unsweetened apple
    butter

LUNCH
Salad with sliced red onion, red bell pepper, lightly cooked
    diced potato, and cooked diced beet tossed in Apple Cider
    Vinaigrette* and topped with whole-milk yogurt sprinkled
    with chopped or sliced almonds and powdered ginger
1 can smoked sardines

DINNER
Pork Tenderloin with Apple-Onion Compote*
1 boiled potato rolled in butter
Steamed Swiss chard or spinach sprinkled with extra-virgin olive
   oil and lemon juice
Carrot sticks

Prostate Problems

Low-grade infection and prostate enlargement are common problems in middle-aged men, and cancer of the prostate is becoming
more common. Diet is the key to preventing these illnesses and
also in reducing their severity. The foods listed below are included
in the menu plan for prostate problems.

* One carrot daily reduces inflammation.
* Oysters, preferably smoked, supply zinc. The prostate has
  six times more zinc than any other organ.
* Avocados and tomatoes eaten together can reduce cancer
  growth by 52 percent. Avocados are high in lutein, which
  inhibits prostate cancer.
* Include citrus in the diet, especially lemons, which have
  high levels of anti-cancer nutrients vitamins C and A, and
  grapefruit, which is high in the powerful antioxidant
  lycopene. Impressive anecdotal evidence indicates that four
  lemons or two grapefruits daily have been known to cure
  prostate cancer.
* A handful of pumpkin seeds and a few walnuts daily shrink
  an enlarged prostate.
* Green tea can prevent cancer recurrence. Drink 1 cup of
  green tea during the day, preferably at bedtime.

Day 1

BREAKFAST

Lemonade made with the juice of 4 lemons, distilled or spring
water, and sweetened with honey (preferably unfiltered) or
stevia

Oatmeal with whole-milk yogurt, dried apricots, sliced apple,
and a sprinkling of raw walnuts

LUNCH

Romaine lettuce salad with sliced avocado, tomato, cucumber,
and radishes tossed in Balsamic Vinaigrette*

1 or 2 slices whole-grain bread with butter

A handful of pumpkin seeds

DINNER

Smoked oysters

Grilled sirloin steak

Lightly steamed green beans

Roasted Vegetables* (potatoes and red and orange bell peppers)

1 raw carrot

Day 2

BREAKFAST

Fresh grapefruit juice made from the juice of 2 whole grapefruits

Whole-grain flour tortilla filled with eggs scrambled in butter,
grated carrot, green onion, and goat cheese

LUNCH

Sweet Potato and Green Bean Salad*

A handful of pumpkin seeds

DINNER

Beef Curry with Minted Cucumber Yogurt Sauce*

Green salad with sliced tomato and avocado tossed in Apple
Cider Vinaigrette

1 raw carrot

Day 3

BREAKFAST

Fruit salad with sliced banana, mango, pear, apple, a dollop of
whole-milk yogurt, walnuts, and sesame seeds

1 or 2 slices whole-grain toast with butter

A handful of pumpkin seeds

LUNCH

Lemonade made with the juice of 4 lemons, distilled or spring
water, and sweetened with honey (preferably unfiltered) or
stevia

Lamb and Black Bean Chili* topped with diced avocado on a
bed of brown rice

1 raw carrot

DINNER

Smoked oysters

Thick-cut, lean pork chop with Mango Cilantro Salsa* (see
Salmon Filet with Mango Cilantro Salsa* recipe)

Mashed potatoes with butter

Lightly cooked broccoli sprinkled with extra-virgin olive oil

Raw celery sticks

Day 4

BREAKFAST

Fresh grapefruit juice made from the juice of 2 whole grapefruits

1 or 2 poached eggs on a bed of Grated Potatoes (see index for
   recipe) seasoned with green onion and parsley

A handful of pumpkin seeds

LUNCH

Vegetable Beef Soup*

Green salad with sliced avocado and tomato tossed in Balsamic
   Vinaigrette*

1 raw carrot

DINNER

Lemonade made with the juice of 4 lemons, distilled or spring
   water, and sweetened with honey (preferably unfiltered) or
   stevia

Grilled Lamb Chops with Purée of Rutabaga and Tart Apple*

1 boiled potato rolled in butter

Sliced tomato and avocado drizzled with extra-virgin olive oil
   and apple cider vinegar

Day 5

BREAKFAST

Fresh grapefruit juice made from the juice of 2 whole
   grapefruits

Whole-grain cereal with whole-milk yogurt, chunks of papaya,
   banana, and mango, topped with chopped raw almonds and
   sesame seeds

Lunch

Green salad with cooked diced beet and lightly cooked diced
potato, tossed in extra-virgin olive oil and apple cider vinegar
and topped with goat cheese, chopped mint, and walnuts
A handful of pumpkin seeds

Dinner

Smoked oysters on whole-grain crackers
Grilled or roasted chicken breast with skin
Steamed whole artichoke with melted butter for dipping
Lightly steamed green beans drizzled with extra-virgin olive oil
or coconut oil
1 raw carrot

Day 6

Breakfast

Lemonade made with the juice of 4 lemons, distilled or spring
water, and sweetened with honey (preferably unfiltered) or
stevia
1 or 2 eggs fried over easy in butter
1 or 2 slices whole-grain toast with unsweetened apple butter

Lunch

Brown rice salad with sliced avocado, tomato, cucumber, and
red onion tossed in Apple Cider Vinaigrette* and topped with
sliced pecans or almonds
A handful of pumpkin seeds

Dinner

Salmon (preferably wild), grilled, broiled, or baked, with
Walnut-Basil Butter*
Stewed canned tomatoes, drained and heated, with butter
Lightly steamed peas, carrots, and potato chunks with butter
1 raw carrot

Day 7

BREAKFAST

Fresh grapefruit juice made from the juice of 2 whole grapefruits
1 or 2 whole-grain waffles with unsweetened peanut butter and
    fruit-sweetened jam

LUNCH

Salad with lightly cooked diced potato, green onion, red or
    green grapes, sliced red bell pepper, tomato, and avocado
    tossed in extra-virgin olive oil and apple cider vinegar and
    topped with pecans and pine nuts
A handful of pumpkin seeds

DINNER

Chicken Stroganoff*
Canned whole tomatoes, drained and heated, with butter
Roasted Vegetables* (potatoes, parsnips, and carrots)
Lightly steamed cauliflower with butter
1 raw carrot

Stomach, Esophageal, and Intestinal Problems

Although eating the foods appropriate to your metabolism will
prevent inflammatory digestive tract diseases, they won't heal
existing ones. To do that you need the following special healing
foods, which are included in the diet plan:

❖ Gelatin, Alkalinizing Potato Water, Grated Potatoes,
   bananas, and raw cabbage juice neutralize acid waste, heal
   inflammation, and rebuild the mucous membranes. (Make
   raw cabbage juice using a juicer, preferably the Champion
   Juicer because it doesn't destroy enzymes, and enough cabbage to make one 8-ounce glass of juice.)

Day 1

BREAKFAST
Oatmeal with sliced banana, dried fruit, walnuts, sprinkled with
    ½–1 ounce gelatin powder
Alkalinizing Potato Water (see index for recipe)

LUNCH
Raw cabbage juice
Mixed lettuce salad with sliced avocado, mango, and lightly
    cooked diced potato tossed in Apple Cider Vinaigrette*

DINNER
Grilled steak
Lightly cooked buttered green beans on top of Grated Potatoes
    (see index for recipe)
Carrot sticks

Day 2

BREAKFAST
Whole-grain tortilla filled with eggs scrambled in butter, grated
    carrot, green onion, and goat cheese
Alkalinizing Potato Water

LUNCH
Raw cabbage juice
Sweet Potato and Green Bean Salad* (add grated carrot)
1 or 2 slices whole-grain bread with butter

DINNER
Salmon Filet with Mango Cilantro Salsa*
White Bean and Kale Salad* with a sprinkling of ½–1 ounce
    gelatin powder
Carrot sticks

Day 3

BREAKFAST
Banana and pineapple fruit salad topped with a dollop of whole-
milk yogurt, sliced almonds, hazelnuts, and sunflower seeds,
and sprinkled with ½–1 ounce gelatin powder
1 or 2 slices whole-grain toast with butter

LUNCH
Raw cabbage juice
Raw vegetable sandwich with sliced tomato, avocado, cucumber, and mango on whole-grain bread with mustard and drizzled with extra-virgin olive oil

DINNER
Thick-cut, lean pork chop with Mango Cilantro Salsa* (see
Salmon Filet with Mango Cilantro Salsa* recipe)
Grated Potatoes
Lightly steamed broccoli with butter
Carrot sticks

Day 4

BREAKFAST
Sliced banana
1 or 2 poached eggs
1 or 2 slices whole-grain toast with butter

LUNCH
Vegetable Beef Soup*
Fruit salad with sliced banana, orange, and apple tossed in
Honey-Yogurt Dressing*

DINNER
Raw cabbage juice
Grilled Lamb Chops with Purée of Rutabaga and Tart Apple*
1 boiled potato rolled in butter
Cucumber slices

Day 5

BREAKFAST
Whole-grain cereal with sliced banana, papaya, and mango,
    topped with sliced almonds and hazelnuts and sprinkled with
    ½–1 ounce gelatin powder
Alkalinizing Potato Water (see index for recipe)

LUNCH
Raw cabbage juice
Green salad with cooked beet and lightly cooked diced potato
    tossed in extra-virgin olive oil and apple cider vinegar and
    sprinkled with goat cheese and walnuts

DINNER
Grilled chicken breast
Steamed whole artichoke with melted butter for dipping
Lightly steamed green beans
Grated Potatoes
Celery sticks

Day 6

BREAKFAST
1 or 2 soft-boiled eggs
1 or 2 slices whole-grain toast with unsweetened apple butter
Alkalinizing Potato Water

LUNCH
Raw cabbage juice
Salmon (preferably wild), grilled, broiled or baked, with
    Walnut-Basil Butter* (substitute pecans for walnuts)
Lightly steamed peas and carrots sprinkled with extra-virgin
    olive oil or coconut oil
Grated Potatoes

DINNER
Lamb Stew* sprinkled with ½–1 ounce gelatin powder
Green salad with grated carrot, sliced avocado, and tomato
    tossed in Balsamic Vinaigrette* and sprinkled with almonds,
    sliced hazelnuts, and pumpkin seeds

Day 7

BREAKFAST
Whole-grain waffles with unsweetened peanut butter and
    banana slices
Alkalinizing Potato Water

LUNCH
Romaine or other lettuce salad with green onion, red grapes,
    sliced red bell pepper, and celery tossed in extra-virgin olive
    oil and apple cider vinegar and topped with sunflower and
    sesame seeds
Grated Potatoes

DINNER
Raw cabbage juice
Pork Tenderloin with Apple-Onion Compote*
Grated Potatoes
Steamed cauliflower and carrots with butter

Recipes

The twenty-six recipes in Part III include twelve entrées (two fish, three chicken, two beef, three lamb, one pork, and one vegetarian), five side dishes (including a walnut-basil butter and a dairy-free milk shake), two soups, three salads, and four salad dressings. These recipes are not fattening. There are no heavy cream dishes that cause a stuffed feeling and put on pounds. The recipes are designed to suit different tastes: some are on the bland side while others are quite spicy. They add variety and flavor to the health-oriented foods in the menu plans and are easy to make. Nutrition information is given per serving.

Entrées

Halibut with Spicy Curried Lentils

1 tablespoon pure olive oil
½ cup chopped onion
2 cloves garlic, minced
½ cup diced rutabaga
¼ cup diced carrot
½ cup green lentils, rinsed and drained
½ cup canned diced tomato with garlic and onion, with
    juice
1 cup vegetable broth, preferably natural
1 tablespoon mild Indian curry paste
4 6-ounce portions halibut filet or steak
1 tablespoon chopped fresh cilantro

In a small saucepan, sauté onion in olive oil until tender. Add garlic, sauté for 30 seconds. Add rutabaga, carrot, lentils, tomato, vegetable broth, and curry paste. Simmer until lentils are tender, stirring occasionally, approximately 40 to 45 minutes. Meanwhile, grill, bake, or broil the halibut. Stir cilantro into lentil mixture to finish. Serve halibut on a bed of lentils.

Yield: 4 servings

Nutrition Information: 361 calories, 10 g fat, 46 g protein, 21 g carbohydrate, 10 g dietary fiber, 55 mg cholesterol, 453 mg sodium

Salmon Filet with Mango Cilantro Salsa

4 6-ounce portions salmon filet

Mango Cilantro Salsa
1 ripe mango, peeled and ½-inch diced
½ cup chopped scallion, green part only
¼ cup diced red bell pepper
1 tablespoon finely diced fresh jalapeño
1 tablespoon chopped fresh cilantro
1 small clove garlic, minced
1 tablespoon freshly squeezed lime juice
¼ teaspoon salt
½ teaspoon extra-virgin olive oil

Bake salmon filet at 400°F for 15 to 20 minutes, depending on the thickness of the salmon. For Mango Cilantro Salsa, lightly toss all ingredients in bowl. Chill in refrigerator for at least 1 hour for flavors to meld. Serve salsa as an accompaniment to salmon. Mango Cilantro Salsa also goes nicely with grilled meat or chicken.

Yield: 4 servings

Nutrition Information: 245 calories, 7 g fat, 35 g protein, 11 g carbohydrate, 2 g dietary fiber, 88 mg cholesterol, 251 mg sodium

Chicken Chili

1 cup white beans, washed and soaked overnight in 3 cups
water
2 cups diced yellow onion
1 tablespoon pure olive oil or butter
2 large cloves garlic, minced
1 15-ounce can diced tomato seasoned with garlic and
onion
1 quart chicken broth, preferably natural
¼ cup dry white wine
1 pound boneless, skinless chicken breast, cut into 1-inch
pieces
2 teaspoons cumin powder
¼ cup mild chili powder
1 4-ounce can chopped green chilies
¼ cup chopped fresh cilantro
Sour cream for topping (optional)
Grated cheddar cheese for topping (optional)

Drain beans. Sauté onion in olive oil over medium-high heat
until soft but not brown, approximately 4 to 5 minutes. Add garlic and sauté for an additional minute. Add soaked beans, tomato,
chicken broth, wine, chicken, cumin, chili powder, green chilies,
and cilantro. Simmer for approximately 1 hour or until beans are
tender. Top chili with sour cream and grated cheddar cheese.

Yield: 4 servings

Nutrition Information: 462 calories, 7 g fat, 48 g protein, 53 g
carbohydrate, 18 g dietary fiber, 53 mg cholesterol, 1037 mg sodium

Chicken Corn Chowder

1 pound boneless, skinless chicken breast, cut into 1-inch
   pieces
1 tablespoon lime juice
1 teaspoon salt
1 cup diced yellow onion
1 cup chopped green onion
2 tablespoons pure olive oil or butter
2 cloves garlic, minced
1 cup diced celery
1 cup diced red bell pepper
1 or 2 jalapeños, seeded and chopped fine
1 16-ounce bag frozen corn kernels
1 4-ounce can green chilies, diced
1 quart chicken broth, preferably natural
1 cup cream
½ teaspoon ground black pepper
1 cup grated potato, preferably Yukon Gold, grated just
   before using
1 teaspoon cornstarch
¼ cup chopped fresh cilantro

Marinate chicken in lime juice and ¼ teaspoon salt. Set aside. In soup pot, sauté yellow and green onions in olive oil over medium-high heat until soft, approximately 4 to 5 minutes. Add garlic and sauté an additional minute. Add celery, bell pepper, jalapeño, corn, green chilies, chicken broth, remaining salt, cream, and black pepper. Bring soup to a simmer. As soon as soup starts to simmer, grate potato and add directly to pot. Mix cornstarch with 2 tablespoons water and add to pot. Continue to simmer for

20 minutes. Add chicken and juice to the pot and simmer for an additional 10 minutes. Stir in cilantro. Serve hot.

Yield: 6 servings

Nutrition Information: 358 calories, 16 g fat, 27 g protein, 31 g carbohydrate, 4 g dietary fiber, 70 mg cholesterol, 870 mg sodium

Chicken Stroganoff

> 1⅓ cup brown rice or 1 pound pasta (to make 4 servings)
> 1 pound skinless chicken thighs, cut into 1-inch strips
> ¼ cup pure olive oil
> ½ teaspoon salt
> ¼ teaspoon ground black pepper
> ½ cup diced yellow onion
> 2 cloves garlic, minced
> 1½ cups chicken broth
> 1 tablespoon tomato paste
> ⅓ cup dry sherry
> ½ teaspoon finely chopped fresh rosemary
> 1 teaspoon cornstarch
> 1 cup sliced mushrooms
> ¼ cup sour cream

Prepare brown rice or pasta according to package directions. Toss chicken with 1 tablespoon olive oil, ¼ teaspoon salt, and pepper and set aside to marinate. Sauté onion over medium-high heat in 1 tablespoon olive oil until tender, approximately 3 to 4 minutes. Add garlic and sauté an additional 30 seconds. Add chicken broth, tomato paste, sherry, rosemary, and ¼ teaspoon salt. Stir until tomato paste is incorporated into broth. Bring to a simmer and cook to reduce for 5 minutes.

In a small bowl, mix cornstarch with 1 teaspoon water to create a smooth paste. Add cornstarch paste to simmering sauce. Simmer for an additional minute to thicken. Remove stroganoff sauce from heat. Heat 1 tablespoon olive oil in sauté pan; add mushrooms and sauté until tender. Put mushrooms in a separate bowl and set aside. In same pan, over medium-high heat, sauté marinated chicken (with marinade) in remaining 1 tablespoon olive oil until cooked through, approximately 5 to 7 minutes. In small bowl, mix ¼ cup stroganoff sauce with sour cream. Add sour cream mixture back into sauce, stirring until incorporated. Place stroganoff sauce, chicken, and sautéed mushrooms all into the same sauté pan. Stirring constantly, heat over medium heat until just hot. Serve over brown rice or pasta.

Yield: 4 servings

Nutrition Information: 291 calories, 19 g fat, 18 g protein, 6 g carbohydrate, 1 g dietary fiber, 60 mg cholesterol, 560 mg sodium (Nutrition information does not include the rice or pasta.)

Beef Curry with Minted Cucumber Yogurt Sauce

2 cups brown rice (to make 6 servings)
1 cup ½-inch diced onion
1 tablespoon butter
1 cup crushed tomato
1 cup beef broth, preferably natural
¼ cup mild Indian curry paste

1 cup peeled and diced tart apple
½ cup apple juice
1 cup ½-inch diced potato, preferably Yukon Gold
1 cup coarsely chopped green cabbage
1 cup cauliflower flowerets
1¼ pounds beef tenderloin, cut into 1-inch strips
½ teaspoon salt
½ cup frozen peas

Minted Cucumber Yogurt Sauce
½ cup whole-milk yogurt
1½ tablespoons chopped fresh mint
1 cup peeled and chopped cucumber
¼ teaspoon salt

Prepare brown rice according to package directions. Sauté onion in butter over medium-high heat until soft but not brown, 3 to 4 minutes. Add tomato, beef broth, curry paste, apple, and apple juice and bring to a simmer. Add potato and cabbage. Cover and simmer on medium heat, stirring occasionally for approximately 15 minutes, until potatoes are tender. Meanwhile, blanch cauliflower in boiling water for 2 minutes, drain, and cool in ice-water bath. Once cooled, drain thoroughly and set aside. Stir tenderloin and ½ teaspoon salt into simmering curry. Bring back to a simmer for 7 minutes. Add peas and cooked cauliflower. For Minted Cucumber Yogurt Sauce, mix yogurt, mint, cucumber, and salt. Serve curry warm over brown rice with a dollop of Minted Cucumber Yogurt Sauce.

Yield: 6 servings

Nutrition Information: 445 calories, 30 g fat, 23 g protein, 21 g carbohydrate, 4 g dietary fiber, 77 mg cholesterol, 724 mg sodium (Nutrition information does not include the rice.)

Vegetable Beef Soup

1 pound beef stew meat, cut into ½-inch pieces
1 cup ½-inch diced yellow onion
1 tablespoon butter
1 large clove garlic, minced
5 cups beef broth, preferably natural
1 cup ½-inch diced carrot
½ cup ½-inch diced rutabaga
1 cup ½-inch diced mushrooms
1 cup ½-inch diced green cabbage
½ cup grated new potato (large grate)
1 teaspoon dried thyme
1 teaspoon dried basil
½ teaspoon ground black pepper
¾ teaspoon salt
⅛ teaspoon cayenne (optional)
¼ teaspoon cinnamon
½ cup ½-inch pieces green beans
½ cup frozen peas
¼ cup chopped fresh parsley

Sauté beef and onion in butter in soup pot until onion is soft and beef is browned, approximately 4 to 5 minutes. Add garlic and sauté for 1 additional minute. Add beef broth, carrot, rutabaga, mushrooms, green cabbage, potato (which will act as a thickener), thyme, basil, pepper, salt, cayenne, and cinnamon. Simmer for 30 to 40 minutes or until beef is tender. Add green beans, peas, and parsley and continue to simmer for 5 additional minutes.

Yield: 4 servings

Nutrition Information: 365 calories, 13 g fat, 41 g protein, 21 g carbohydrate, 5 g dietary fiber, 70 mg cholesterol, 572 mg sodium

Grilled Lamb Chops with Purée of Rutabaga and Tart Apple

8 lamb chops

Marinade for Lamb
1 teaspoon finely chopped fresh rosemary
1 tablespoon extra-virgin olive oil
½ teaspoon salt
Ground black pepper
1 large clove garlic, minced

Purée of Rutabaga and Tart Apple
3 cups rutabaga, chopped
2 tart apples, peeled and chopped
2 cloves garlic, minced
3 teaspoons chopped fresh mint
1 tablespoon cream
2 tablespoons butter
¾ teaspoon salt

Cabbage with Sweet Onion
1 sweet yellow onion, thinly sliced
2 tablespoons pure olive oil
4 cups sliced green or red cabbage
Balsamic vinegar to taste
Salt to taste
Ground black pepper to taste
4 mint leaves for garnish (optional)

Mix marinade ingredients in a bowl and marinate lamb chops for 1 to 2 hours. Grill or broil lamb chops. To make Purée of Rutabaga and Tart Apple, boil rutabaga, apple, garlic, and 2 teaspoons mint in salted water for approximately 30 to 40 minutes until rutabaga is tender. Drain and purée in Cuisinart or blender with cream, butter, remaining mint, and salt. (The mixture can also be mashed instead of pureed.) To make Cabbage with Sweet Onion, sauté onion in olive oil over medium heat for 2 to 3 minutes. Add cabbage and continue to sauté until tender. While pan is still over the heat, add balsamic vinegar, salt, and pepper. Serve grilled chops on bed of Cabbage with Sweet Onion, accompanied by Rutabaga and Tart Apple Purée. Garnish with mint leaf.

Yield: 4 servings

Nutrition Information: 482 calories, 23 g fat, 50 g protein, 17 g carbohydrate, 4 g dietary fiber, 175 mg cholesterol, 612 mg sodium

Lamb and Black Bean Chili with Adobo

1½ pounds lamb leg or shoulder, cut into 1-inch pieces
1 tablespoon butter
1 cup diced yellow onion
1 cup chopped scallions
2 cloves garlic, minced
1½ tablespoons tomato paste
1 cup black beans, washed and soaked overnight in 3 cups water
½ cup diced red bell pepper
1 quart beef broth, preferably natural
½ cup red wine
1 teaspoon ground cumin
½ teaspoon cinnamon
½ teaspoon salt
¼ cup mild chili powder
1 teaspoon red wine vinegar

1 teaspoon adobo (Adobo is a Mexican condiment made
with chipotle peppers and chili paste.)
2 teaspoons cornstarch
Chopped fresh cilantro for topping (optional)
Sour cream for topping (optional)

In a large soup pot, sauté lamb in butter until browned. Add
yellow onion and scallions to pot and sauté until soft, about 3 to
4 minutes. Add garlic and sauté for an additional 30 seconds. Add
tomato paste and stir. Add beans, bell pepper, beef broth, red
wine, cumin, cinnamon, salt, chili powder, vinegar, and adobo.
Bring to a simmer. Simmer for 40 to 45 minutes or until lamb
and beans are tender. In a small bowl, mix cornstarch with 2 teaspoons water to make a smooth paste. Add cornstarch paste to
chili and stir. Simmer for an additional 5 minutes. Serve with
chopped cilantro and a dollop of sour cream.

Yield: 4 servings

Nutrition Information: 684 calories, 34 g fat, 46 g protein, 47 g
carbohydrate, 12 g dietary fiber, 105 mg cholesterol, 576 mg sodium

Lamb Stew

1½ pounds lamb leg or shoulder, cut into 1-inch pieces
2 tablespoons pure olive oil
1½ cups 1-inch diced yellow onion
2 cloves garlic, minced
1 15-ounce can crushed tomato with onion and garlic
1 quart beef broth, preferably natural
1 cup dry red wine
¼ teaspoon ground black pepper

1¼ teaspoons finely chopped fresh rosemary
1 tablespoon dry basil
1 teaspoon balsamic vinegar
2 cups 1-inch diced carrot
2 cups 1-inch diced rutabaga
1 cup grated potato, preferably Yukon Gold, grated at the
  last minute

Brown lamb with 1 tablespoon olive oil in a heavy soup pot over medium-high heat. Remove lamb from pot and set aside. In same pot, sauté onion in the remaining 1 tablespoon of olive oil until soft. Add garlic and sauté for an additional 30 seconds. Return lamb to pot with onion and garlic and add tomato, beef broth, wine, pepper, rosemary, basil, vinegar, carrot, and rutabaga. Bring to a simmer. Cover and simmer on low for 1 hour, or until lamb is tender. Once lamb is tender, grate potato and add to stew (potato will act as a thickener). Simmer for an additional 10 minutes.

Yield: 6 servings

Nutrition Information: 432 calories, 24 g fat, 26 g protein, 23 g carbohydrate, 4 g dietary fiber, 65 mg cholesterol, 380 mg sodium

Pork Tenderloin with Apple-Onion Compote

2 12- to 14-ounce pork tenderloins

Marinade for Pork
¼ cup dry white wine
1 tablespoon extra-virgin olive oil

¼ teaspoon salt
¼ teaspoon ground black pepper
¼ teaspoon chili pepper flakes
1 teaspoon chopped fresh thyme

Apple-Onion Compote
2 tart apples, peeled and ½-inch diced
1 tablespoon lemon juice
1 cup ½-inch diced sweet onion
1 tablespoon butter
1 tablespoon balsamic vinegar
1 teaspoon fresh chopped thyme
¼ cup chili pepper flakes
1 teaspoon honey
½ cup water
¼ teaspoon salt

Marinate pork tenderloins in wine, olive oil, salt, black pepper, chili pepper flakes, and thyme for 1 to 2 hours. Grill or roast tenderloin to desired doneness. For Apple-Onion Compote, toss apple in bowl with lemon juice. In a small saucepan, sauté onion in butter over medium-high heat until soft but not brown, approximately 4 to 5 minutes. Add balsamic vinegar and stir quickly. Immediately add apples, thyme, chili pepper, honey, water, and salt. Cook over medium heat, stirring occasionally, for 10 to 15 minutes until apples are tender. Compote may be served warm or cold and can be prepared up to a day or two in advance.

Yield: 4 servings

Nutrition Information: 259 calories, 10 g fat, 25 g protein, 15 g carbohydrate, 2 g dietary fiber, 81 mg cholesterol, 359 mg sodium

Mediterranean Lentil Stew

½ cup chopped yellow onion
1 tablespoon pure olive oil
2 cloves garlic, minced
1 cup finely diced celery
1 cup finely diced carrot
½ cup finely diced fennel bulb (optional)
½ cup finely diced red bell pepper
4 cups vegetable broth, preferably natural
½ cup dry white wine
¾ cup green lentils, preferably French, rinsed and drained
⅛ teaspoon crushed red pepper
½ teaspoon dried thyme
½ teaspoon dried basil
½ tablespoon dried oregano
Salt to taste

In medium sauce pot, sauté onion in olive oil until tender, about 5 minutes. Add garlic, sauté about 30 seconds. Add celery, carrot, fennel bulb, bell pepper, vegetable broth, wine, lentils, crushed red pepper, and herbs. Simmer until lentils are tender, approximately 45 to 50 minutes. Add salt.

Yield: 4 servings

Nutrition Information: 261 calories, 4 g fat, 22 g protein, 32 g carbohydrate, 17 g dietary fiber, 0 mg cholesterol, 567 mg sodium

Soups and Side Dishes

Golden Beet Soup

1¼ pounds beets, scrubbed and trimmed
6 cups water
1 cup apple juice
2 tablespoons apple cider vinegar
½ cup diced yellow onion
¾ teaspoon salt
1 tablespoon fresh chopped dill, plus extra for topping
¼ cup sour cream, plus extra for topping

Place beets in 6 cups of water and bring to simmer. Cook for approximately 20 to 25 minutes until beets are tender when poked with a knife. Drain beets, reserving cooking liquid. Peel and dice 1 cup beets and set aside. Chop the remaining beets into larger chunks. Over medium heat, simmer 3 cups of cooking liquid, larger beet chunks, apple juice, apple cider vinegar, onion, salt, and dill for approximately 25 minutes. Place soup in blender with sour cream. Blend until smooth. Remove from blender; add diced beets that have been set aside. Chill. Serve soup chilled with a dollop of sour cream and chopped fresh dill.

Yield: 4 servings

Nutrition Information: 111 calories, 3 g fat, 2 g protein, 20 g carbohydrate, 3 g dietary fiber, 6 mg cholesterol, 496 mg sodium

Potato Soup

2 medium-sized organic potatoes
3 medium-sized organic carrots
1 quarter small organic green cabbage
2 sprigs organic parsley

Slice vegetables, place in a pot, and cover with distilled or spring water. Bring to a boil, turn down heat, and let simmer for 10 minutes. Pour into a soup bowl. Eat both the broth and the vegetables. You can either eat it hot or cold after refrigeration.

Yield: 1 serving

Nutrition Information: 459 calories, 1.24 g fat, 13.1 g protein, 105 g carbohydrate, 19.4 g fiber, 0.0 mg cholesterol, 131 mg sodium

Creamy Polenta

6 cups water
1½ teaspoons salt
1¾ yellow cornmeal
3½ tablespoons unsalted butter

Bring water to boil in a large, heavy pan. Add salt and gradually stir in cornmeal, preferably with a whisk. Reduce heat to low and cook until the mixture thickens and the cornmeal is tender. This will take about 20 minutes. Remove pan from heat and stir in the butter.

Yield: 4 servings

Nutrition Information: 284 calories, 12.0 g fat, 4.48 g protein, 41.4 g carbohydrate, 3.93 g fiber, 27.2 mg cholesterol, 1143 mg sodium

Garlic Mashed Yams

4 yams
Garlic cloves to taste
Pure olive oil
Butter

Place yams and garlic cloves on separate pieces of foil, sprinkle with pure olive oil, and wrap. Bake at 400°F for 45 to 60 minutes or until done. Garlic should be creamy and yams soft when pricked with a fork. Remove yams and garlic from foil and mash together. Add a pat of butter to each serving.

Yield: 2 servings

Nutrition Information: 196 calories, 4.04 g fat, 2.26 g protein, 38.5 g carbohydrate, 5.37 g fiber, 10.4 mg cholesterol, 50.5 mg sodium

Roasted Vegetables

6 cups 1-inch chunks small red potatoes and/or other
   vegetables (Parsnips, carrots, and squash work especially
   well.)
¼ cup pure olive oil
Salt and pepper to taste

Preheat oven to 425°F. Line a baking sheet with parchment
paper (not necessary but helps stop burning and helps cleanup).
Put vegetable chucks on pan, sprinkle with olive oil, and toss.
Roast until tender; about 10 to 15 minutes. Insert fork or sharp
knife to test for doneness. Add salt and pepper.

Yield: 6 servings

Nutrition Information: 155 calories, 9.22 g fat, 1.52 g protein, 18.8 g
carbohydrate, 3.25 fiber, 0.0 mg cholesterol, 656 mg sodium

Organic Raw Egg Almond Milk Shake or
Organic Raw Egg Soy Milk Shake

1 cup soy milk or almond milk (Almond milk is made from
   almonds and contains no dairy or soy products.)‡
1 tablespoon honey, preferably unfiltered
1 organic whole raw egg
1 whole ripe banana or 3 to 5 ripe strawberries

‡Almond milk and soy milk can be found in health food stores and
   organic food supermarkets.

Blend all ingredients until liquefied. Add 1 tablespoon whey if it is in the menu plan you're using.

Yield: 1 serving

Nutrition Information: 330 calories, 10.2 g fat, 14.2 g protein, 50.8 g carbohydrate, 5.98 g fiber, 213 mg cholesterol, 102 mg sodium

Walnut-Basil Butter

¼ cup softened butter
1 tablespoon chopped basil
¼ cup chopped walnuts (can substitute hazelnuts)
Salt and pepper to taste

Blend all ingredients. Walnut-Basil Butter can be used as a topping for fish, meat, and vegetables.

Yield: 8 servings

Nutrition Information: 76 calories, 8.21 g fat, 0.64 g protein, 0.54 g carbohydrate, 0.27 fiber, 15.5 mg cholesterol, 178 mg sodium

Salads

Crunchy Coleslaw

1 medium yellow cabbage or ½ yellow and ½ red cabbage
1 medium onion, chopped
½ cup honey, to taste
1 cup extra-virgin olive oil or coconut oil
½ cup apple cider vinegar
½ cup low-fat yogurt
1 teaspoon salt
½ teaspoon celery seed
2 tablespoons lightly toasted sesame seeds

Slice cabbage into pieces about 1 inch long. Mix all other ingredients, add to cabbage, and toss together. Marinate for at least 1 hour. Can be made a day ahead.

Yield: 8 servings

Nutrition Information: 350 calories, 27.9 g fat, 2.46 g protein, 26.2 g carbohydrate, 2.39 g fiber, 0.92 mg cholesterol, 503 mg sodium

Sweet Potato and Green Bean Salad

½ cup ½-inch pieces diagonal-cut green beans
3 cups 1-inch cubes sweet potato
1 tablespoon pure olive oil
¼ teaspoon ground black pepper
¼ teaspoon salt

½ teaspoon fresh chopped thyme
¼ cup chopped raw almonds
1 tablespoon coarsely chopped chives

Dressing
2 teaspoons apple cider vinegar
1 tablespoon Dijon mustard
½ teaspoon honey
¼ teaspoon salt
2 teaspoons extra-virgin olive oil

Blanch green beans in boiling salted water until tender, approximately 4 minutes. When beans are done, drain immediately and place into ice water bath to preserve color and stop the cooking. After beans have cooled, drain and set aside. Preheat oven to 400°F. Toss sweet potatoes with olive oil, pepper, salt, and thyme. Place on cookie sheet that has been lined with foil or parchment paper. Roast sweet potatoes in 400°F oven for 17 to 20 minutes, until tender. Test with fork to see if they are done. Remove from oven and let cool at room temperature for 10 minutes. While sweet potatoes are roasting, mix dressing ingredients together. Set aside. Place almonds on a cookie sheet and heat in 400°F oven for 3 to 4 minutes, until lightly toasted. Remove from oven and set aside. Place green beans, almonds, sweet potato, and chives in a bowl and toss with dressing. Serve chilled or at room temperature.

Yield: 4 servings

Nutrition Information: 217 calories, 11 g fat, 4 g protein, 28 g carbohydrate, 5 g dietary fiber, 0 mg cholesterol, 328 mg sodium

White Bean and Kale Salad

1 cup great northern beans, soaked overnight in 1 quart
    water
½ medium sweet onion, cut into thin half-moon slices
¼ cup pure olive oil
2 tablespoons balsamic vinegar
6 cups coarsely chopped kale
2 tablespoons currants
2 teaspoons freshly squeezed lemon juice
¼ teaspoon salt
¼ teaspoon crushed red chili pepper
Ground black pepper to taste

Drain beans. Add 6 cups of water and cook over medium heat until tender, approximately 40 to 45 minutes. Sauté onion in large pan in 1 tablespoon olive oil until soft, approximately 5 to 7 minutes. Add 1 tablespoon balsamic vinegar and cook for an additional minute, stirring constantly to prevent scorching. Sauté kale in large pan over medium-high heat with 1 tablespoon olive oil until tender, about 3 to 4 minutes. Stir while cooking to avoid sticking. Just before removing kale from pan add the remaining 1 tablespoon balsamic vinegar. Set aside in a medium-sized bowl. When beans are tender, remove from heat, drain, and place in refrigerator to cool. Once beans have cooled for 10 minutes, toss them with kale, currants, lemon juice, salt, chili pepper, and sautéed onion. Add black pepper and additional salt to taste.

Yield: 4 servings

Nutrition Information: 345 calories, 15 g fat, 14 g protein, 44 g carbohydrate, 12 g dietary fiber, 0 mg cholesterol, 185 mg sodium

Salad Dressings

Apple Cider Vinaigrette

1 teaspoon Dijon mustard
1 teaspoon honey, preferably raw
2 tablespoons apple cider vinegar
1 tablespoon chopped fresh basil
1 teaspoon minced shallot
½ teaspoon salt
¼ cup extra-virgin olive oil

Place mustard, honey, vinegar, basil, shallot, and salt in bowl. Gradually add olive oil while continually whisking. Apple Cider Vinaigrette, like Balsamic Vinaigrette, can be used in simple green salads, grain and vegetable salads, or even chicken salads.

Yield: 2 servings

Nutrition Information: 127 calories, 14 g fat, trace protein, 2 g carbohydrate, trace dietary fiber, 0 mg cholesterol, 282 mg sodium

Balsamic Vinaigrette

1 teaspoon Dijon mustard
2 teaspoons balsamic vinegar
½ teaspoon salt
¼ cup extra-virgin olive oil
Ground black pepper to taste

Place mustard, vinegar, and salt in a small bowl. Gradually add olive oil while continually whisking. Add pepper. Balsamic

Vinaigrette is very versatile. It can be used in simple green salads, grain and vegetable salads, or even chicken salads.

Yield: 2 servings

Nutrition Information: 21 calories, 14 g fat, trace protein, trace carbohydrate, trace dietary fiber, 0 mg cholesterol, 282 mg sodium

Coconut Oil Dressing

¼ cup apple cider vinegar
¼ cup lemon juice
½ teaspoon ground mustard
½ teaspoon paprika
½ teaspoon salt
1 cup coconut oil

Blend vinegar, lemon juice, mustard, paprika, and salt in a bowl. Gradually add coconut oil while continually whisking. This dressing can be used in lettuce salads, chicken salads, and potato salad.

Yield: 8 servings

Nutrition Information: 238 calories, 27.2 g fat, trace protein, 1.20 g carbohydrate, trace fiber, 0.0 mg cholesterol, 243 mg sodium

Honey-Yogurt Dressing

1 cup yogurt
3 tablespoons honey
3 tablespoons lemon juice
1 tablespoon freshly grated lemon peel
¼ teaspoon salt

Blend all ingredients. This dressing can be used in lettuce salads, chicken salads, and potato salad.

Yield: 8 servings

Nutrition Information: 45 calories, 1.00 g fat, 1.12 g protein, 8.63 g carbohydrate, trace fiber, 4.00 mg cholesterol, 134 mg sodium

Appendix

Converting to Metrics

Volume Measurement Conversions

U.S.	Metric
1/4 teaspoon	1.25 ml
1/2 teaspoon	2.5 ml
3/4 teaspoon	3.75 ml
1 teaspoon	5 ml
1 tablespoon	15 ml
1/4 cup	62.5 ml
1/2 cup	125 ml
3/4 cup	187.5 ml
1 cup	250 ml

Weight Conversion Measurements

U.S.	Metric
1 ounce	28.4 g
8 ounces	226.8 g
16 ounces (1 pound)	455 g

Cooking Temperature Conversions	
Celsius/Centigrade	0°C and 100°C are defined as the melting and boiling points of water
Fahrenheit	0°F is defined as the stabilized temperature when equal amounts of ice, water, and salt are mixed

To convert temperatures in Fahrenheit to Celsius, use this formula:

$$C = (F - 32) \times 0.5555$$

So, for example, if recipe directions say to bake at 350°F, and you want to know that temperature in Celsius, use this calculation:

$$C = (350 - 32) \times 0.5555 = 176.66°C$$

Notes

Chapter 1

1. Mary Duenwald. "An Eat More Message for a Fattened America," *New York Times*, February 19, 2002.
2. Jane E. Brody. "For Unrefined Healthfulness: Whole Grains," *New York Times*, March 4, 2003.
3. Jocelyn Selim. "R & D News About Science, Medicine, and Technology," *Discover Magazine*, January 2003.
4. Paul Theroux. *Dark Star Safari*. New York: Houghton Mifflin, 2003.
5. Felicia Drury Kliment. "Landscape and Climate: Origins of Chinese Religious Beliefs," *International Journal of Comparative Religion and Philosophy* 1, No. 1 (January–June 1995).
6. A report by Dr. Marcus Feldman of Stanford University and Dr. Kenneth Kidd of Yale University titled "Gene Study Identifies Five Main Human Populations, Linking Them to Geography," as quoted by Nicholas Wade in article with the same title, *New York Times*, September 5, 2003.
7. Bruce Grierson. "What Your Genes Want You to Eat," *New York Times Magazine*, May 4, 2003.
8. Roger Thurow. "In Battling Hunger, A New Advance: Peanut-Butter Paste," *Wall Street Journal*, May 15, 2005.
9. Bruce Grierson. "What Your Genes Want You to Eat," *New York Times Magazine*, May 4, 2003.

10. Jane E. Brody. "Adding Cumin to the Curry: A Matter of Life and Death," *New York Times*, March 3, 1998.
11. Marshall Arisman, *New York Times Magazine*, December 22, 1991.
12. John Noble Wilford. "Don't Blame Columbus for All the Indians' Ills," *New York Times*, October 29, 2002.
13. Jared Diamond. *Germs, Guns, and Steel*. New York: W. W. Norton, 1999.
14. Ibid.
15. Kathy A. Svitil. "R&D News About Science, Medicine, and Technology," *Discover Magazine*, August 2004.
16. Norman Cantor. *In the Wake of the Plague: The Black Death and the World It Made*. New York: Perennial, 2001.
17. Jane E. Brody. "Cat Food for Aardvarks and Other Zoo Diets," *New York Times*, June 18, 2002.
18. Gay Talese. *Unto Thy Sons*. New York: Alfred Knopf, 1992.
19. Susie Post Rust. "The Garifuna," *National Geographic*, September 2001.
20. Mary Duenwald. "An Eat More Message for a Fattened America," *New York Times*, February 19, 2002.

Chapter 2

1. Sang Wang. *Reverse Aging*. Miami: JSP Publishing, 1996.
2. Dr. James H. O'Keefe, Jr. "The End of Stress as We Know It," *Mayo Clinic Proceedings*, (1970): 31–52.
3. Ibid.
4. Erica Goode. "The Heavy Cost of Chronic Stress," *New York Times*, December 17, 2002.
5. Benedict Carey. "Stress and Distress May Give Your Genes Gray Hair," *New York Times*, November 20, 2004.
6. Daniel D. Chiras. *Human Biology, Health, Homeostasis, and the Environment*. Sudbury, MA: Jones and Bartlett Publishers, Inc., 2002.
7. James I. Robertson, Jr. *The Man, the Soldier, the Legend*. New York: MacMillian Reference Books, 1997.

Chapter 3

1. "Interview with Dr. William Donald Kelley." *Healthview Newsletter* 1, No. 12 (1977): 1–8.
2. Joe Sharkey. "Aggressive Precaution in the Food You Eat," *New York Times*, October 12, 2004.
3. Dr. Jonathan V. Wright. WrightNewsletter.com, Volume II, Issue 5, May 2004, accessed June 2004.
4. "Interview with Dr. William Donald Kelley." *Healthview Newsletter* 1, No. 12 (1977): 1–8.
5. Edwin O. Reischauer. *The Japanese*. Cambridge, MA: Harvard University Press, 1978.
6. Gary Bullock. "Opinion-Fitness," *University Club News Bulletin*, May 2004.
7. J. Schwartz. "Caffeine Intake and Asthma Symptoms," *Annals of Epidemiology*, (1992), 127–35.
8. P. Vergauwen. "Adenosine Receptors Mediate Synergistic Stimulation of Glucose Uptake," *Journal of Clinical Investigation*, (March 1994): 974–81.
9. Dr. Jack F. Bukowski, et al. "Study Concludes Tea Helps Fight Infection," *New York Times*, April 22, 2003.
10. Ibid.
11. Jean Carper. *Food: Your Miracle Medicine*. New York: HarperCollins, 1993.
12. Jane E. Brody. "Drink Your Milk: A Refrain for All Ages, Now More Than Ever," *New York Times*, January 21, 2003.
13. Ibid.
14. C. J. Metlin. "Patterns of Milk Consumption and Risk of Cancer," *Journal of American Medical Association* 13, No. 1–2 (2004): 89–99.
15. "Pancreatic Cancer-Reducing the Risk," *Saturday Evening Post*, Jan./Feb. 2003.
16. Marian Burros. "U.S. Introducing a Revised Pyramid," *New York Times*, April 20, 2005.
17. Jane E. Brody. "Drink Your Milk: A Refrain for All Ages, Now More Than Ever," *New York Times*, January 21, 2003.

Chapter 4

1. Raymond Peat. *Generative Energy*. Eugene, OR: self-published, 1994.
2. T. L. Cleave. *The Saccharine Disease*. Bristol, England: John Wright & Sons, Ltd., 1974.
3. Janice M. Horowitz. "10 Foods That Pack a Wallop," *Time*, December 9, 2002.
4. Sally W. Fallon. "Human Diet," *Price Pottenger Nutrition Foundation Journal* 21, No. 1 (Spring 1997).
5. Michael Schmidt. *Smart Fats*. Berkeley, CA: Frog Ltd., 1997.
6. R. T. Homan. "Deficiency of Essential Fatty Acids and Membranes Fluidity During Pregnancy and Lactation," *National Academy of Science* 88 (1991): 4835–9.
7. Dr. Weston A. Price. *Nutrition and Physical Degeneration*. New Canaan, CT.: Keats, 2003.
8. John Nobel Wilford. "The Backbone of History: Health and Nutrition in the Western Hemisphere," *New York Times*, October, 29, 2002.
9. Jane E. Brody. "Drink Your Milk: A Refrain for All Ages, Now More Than Ever," *New York Times*, January 21, 2003.
10. Mary G. Enig. "Fats and Oils," *Federation Proceedings*. 37, no. 9 (July 1987): 2215–2220.
11. Patricia Gadsby. "The Inuit Paradox," *Discover Magazine*, October 2004.
12. P. J. D. Bouic. *International Journal of Sports Medicine* 20 (1999): 258–262.
13. Jane E. Brody. "Dr. Ancel Keyes, 100, Promoter of Mediter-ranean Diet, Dies," *New York Times*, November, 23, 2004.
14. Wolfgang Saxon. "Phil Sokolof, 82: A Crusader Against Cholesterol, Is Dead," *New York Times*, April 17, 2004.
15. Dr. Michael Miller, Director of the Center of Preventative Cardiology at the University of Maryland Medical Center.

16. C. Anderson. "Cholesterol and Morality: Thirty Years Follow-up," *Circulation*, 106 (2002): 3143–3421.
17. "Randomised trial of cholesterol lowering in 4444 patients with coronary heart disease: the Scandinavian Simvastatin Survival Study," *Lancet*, 344, No. 8934 1994 November 19): 1383–9.
18. Mary Enig. *Know Your Fats: The Complete Primer for Understanding the Nutrition of Fats, Oils, and Cholesterol.* Bethesda, MD: Bethesda Press, 2000.
19. "Low-Carb Craze Has Rustlers Riding Range," *Seattle Times*, April 5, 2004.
20. Jane E. Brody. "Preserving a Delicate Balance of Potassium," *New York Times*, June 22, 2004.
21. Narayan deVera. "Seven Secrets of Metabolism," *Health Freedom News*, October/December 2004.
22. Kenneth Kamler. *Surviving Extremes*. New York: St. Martin's Press, 2004.
23. Robert Atkins. *The New Diet Revolution*. New York: Avon Books, 1997.
24. Arthur Agatson. *The South Beach Diet*. Emmaus, PA: Rodale Press, 2003.
25. Abby Goodnough. "New Doctor, New Diet, But Still No Cookies," *New York Times*, October 7, 2003.
26. Rita Elkins. *Miracle Sugars*. Orem, UT: Woodlands Publishing, 2003.
27. Anahad O'Conner. "Study Details, 30-Year Increase in Calorie Consumption," *New York Times*, February 6, 2004.
28. Sherri Day. "They Come to Praise the Carb, Not Bury It," *New York Times*, February 4, 2004.
29. Donald G. McNeil. "A Beer Company Responds to the Low-Carb Crowd, Saying Its Product Isn't at Fault," *New York Times*, April 24, 2004.
30. Melanie Warner. "Sugar Is Latest Supermarket Demon," *New York Times*, May 15, 2005.

31. Ibid.
32. Gina Kolata. "Vegetarians vs. Atkins: Diet Wars Are Almost Religious," *New York Times*, February 22, 2004.
33. Ibid.
34. David Heber. *What Color Is Your Diet?* New York: Harper-Collins, 2002.

Chapter 5

1. Claudia Dreifus. "New Rockefeller Chief Discovered Lessons of Life in a Cell of Yeast," *New York Times*, May 13, 2003.
2. Ibid.
3. Dr. Cornelia M. Ulrich. *Full on Fewer Calories*. New York: HarperCollins, 2000.
4. Barbara Rolls with Robert A. Barnett. *The Volumetrics Weight-Control Plan: Feel Full on Fewer Calories*. New York: Harper Collins, 2000.
5. John O'Neil. "Vital Signs," *New York Times*, June 5, 2004.
6. Susan Clotfelter. "Good Eggs," *Natural Home*, March/April 2002.
7. Sandra Blakeslee. "Comfort Foods Switch Off Stress, Scientists Find," *New York Times*, September 16, 2003.
8. Annemarie Colbin. *Food and Healing*. New York: Ballantine Books, 1996.
9. Simmone Gabbay. *Nourishing the Body Temple: Edgar Cayce's Approach to Nutrition*. Virginia Beach, VA: A. R. E. Press, 2000.

Index